# One the Risen

## LIVING THE PASCHAL MYSTERY AS DISCIPLES OF CHRIST

**COURSE III**

The Mission of **Jesus Christ** *(The Paschal Mystery)*

**Our Sunday Visitor**

Curriculum Division

hs.osvcurriculum.com

The Subcommittee on the Catechism, United States Conference of Catholic Bishops, has found that this catechetical high school text *The Risen One*, copyright 2012, is in conformity with the *Catechism of the Catholic Church* and that it fulfills the requirements of Course III of the *Doctrinal Elements of a Curriculum Framework for the Development of Catechetical Materials for Young People of High School Age.*

**Nihil Obstat**
Rev. Fr. Jeremiah L. Payne, S.Th.L.
Censor Librorum, Diocese of Orlando

**Imprimatur**
✠ Most Rev. John Noonan
Bishop of Orlando
August 20, 2012

For permission to reprint copyrighted material, grateful acknowledgement is made to the following sources:

Unless otherwise noted, all quotations from papal and other Vatican documents are © *Libreria Editrice Vaticana*. Used with permission. All rights reserved.

The Scripture quotations contained herein are from the *New Revised Standard Version Bible: Catholic Edition* copyright © 1993 and 1989 by the Division of Christian Education of the National Council of the Churches of Christ in the United States of America. Used by permission. All rights reserved.

*Catechism of the Catholic Church* Second Edition. English translation of the *Catechism of the Catholic Church* for the United States of America copyright © 1994, United States Catholic Conference, Inc.—Libreria Editrice Vaticana. English translation of the *Catechism of the Catholic Church*: Modifications from the Editio Typica copyright © 1997, United States Catholic Conference, Inc. Used by permission. All rights reserved.

Excerpts from the *United States Catholic Catechism for Adults*, copyright © 2006, United States Catholic Conference, Inc.—Libreria Editrice Vaticana. Used by permission. All rights reserved.

Excerpts from the English translation of *The Roman Missal* © 2010, International Commission on English in the Liturgy Corporation (ICEL); excerpts from the English translation of *Rite of Baptism for Children* © 1969, ICEL; excerpts from the English translation of *Rite of Marriage* © 1969, ICEL. All rights reserved.

Reprinted by permission of *National Catholic Reporter*, 115 E. Armour Blvd., Kansas City, MO 64111 www.ncronline.org

The Risen One Student Edition
ISBN: 978-0-15-902420-1
Item Number: CU1515

1 2 3 4 5 6 7 8   015016   16 15 14 13 12
Webcrafters, Inc., Madison, WI, USA; October 2012; Job# 101783

# CONTENTS

# SCRIPTURE & OTHER PRIMARY SOURCES

## PRIMARY SOURCES

### CHAPTER 1

## My Faith

*A private reflection space that allows you to track your spiritual journey, discoveries, aspirations, truths, and goals.*

## GO TO THE SOURCE

*We send you directly to the Bible to listen to God's Word, analyze the passage, break it open, discuss it, and apply it to your life.*

## PRIMARY SOURCES

This feature takes you to a source that is not the Bible, such as Church documents, the Catechism, or historical writings, to help you process the core doctrines presented.

## Catholic LIFE

Here you will consider stories of Saints who have modeled virtues, prayer, and the life of discipleship.

## A *Spiritual Practice* for the life of DISCIPLESHIP

Specific behaviors that, when done over time, help us open up to God's grace and make us instruments of his grace.

## JUSTICE AND DISCIPLESHIP

Serves as a reminder that discipleship involves praying to the Father, studying Jesus' teachings and example, participating in the Eucharist, living the virtues, and acting for justice.

## Faith & Culture

Historical, geographical, and cultural snapshots designed to give you a better appreciation for a time, place, or culture you have read about.

## GLOBAL PERSPECTIVES

Includes statistics, connections, and other information to bring global awareness to a subject such as the spread of Christianity and the roles of Catholics in the world.

## EXPRESSIONS OF FAITH

Focuses on Catholic practices, symbols, and seasons, that introduces or reacquaints you with the rich fabric, layers, and expressions of Catholicism.

## Going Moral

Designed to involve you in the process of making moral decisions, this feature presents real-life moral dilemmas connected to teachings presented in the chapter.

○ What does this photo say about the way of life and God?

○ How would you depict your way of life with God?

# A Way of **Life** and **Love**

Go to the student site at
**hs.osvcurriculum.com**

## YOU WILL

- Identify how the Paschal Mystery is our way to eternal life.

- Learn more about the call to holiness.

- Know that faith is a response to the mystery of God.

- Examine what it means to be a member of the Church.

- Describe how Catholic spirituality is rooted in a relationship with Jesus.

- Explore how the interior life is a key element of spirituality.

## DEFINE

| | |
|---|---|
| Paschal Mystery | agape |
| triptych | philia |
| Passion Narratives | eros |
| Resurrection Narratives | conviction |
| | spiritual poverty |
| holiness | Spiritual Exercises |

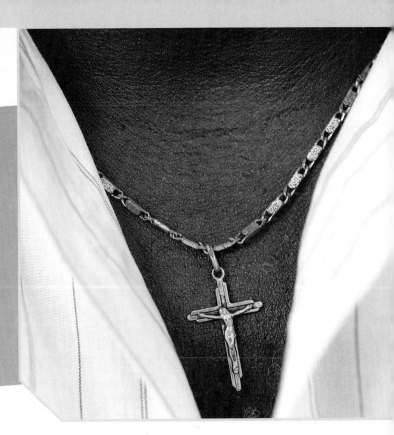

## "What Catholic symbol means the most to you, and why?"

**On a sophomore retreat,** everyone in the class is asked "What Catholic symbol means the most to you, and why?" Everyone mentions different things: nativity sets, candles on the altar, holy water, statues, stained glass windows, the Stations of the Cross, Advent wreath, religious medals, and so on. Then three students name the exact same symbol, but for three different reasons.

**"The crucifix,"** someone says quietly, "because it reminds me of what Jesus did for me. And that's why he's so important in my life."

"The crucifix," says another. "When you're going through a hard time, you look up and see what Jesus went through and you realize that you can get through it, too."

"Yeah, the crucifix," says a third person. "When I see what Jesus did for us, it reminds me to love others the way Jesus loves me."

*How can the crucifix mean three different things?*

## WHERE ARE YOU?

**Check the answer that best matches where you are today.**

*I understand what we mean by Paschal Mystery.*
☐ Quite a bit  ☐ Somewhat  ☐ A little  ☐ Not at all

*I have heard of the Passover Lamb.*
☐ Quite a bit  ☐ Somewhat  ☐ A little  ☐ Not at all

*I know what holiness really means.*
☐ Quite a bit  ☐ Somewhat  ☐ A little  ☐ Not at all

*I want to learn more about the mystery of God.*
☐ Quite a bit  ☐ Somewhat  ☐ A little  ☐ Not at all

*I'm interested in deepening my spirituality.*
☐ Quite a bit  ☐ Somewhat  ☐ A little  ☐ Not at all

# A Portrait of Love

*What images would you choose to describe Jesus?*
*How would you choose?*

*Which part of his life would be most important for you to show?*

Imagine you had to choose three—and only three—images from the Gospels to describe who Jesus is. What would you choose, and why? Chances are, at least one of those images would be from the Paschal Mystery.

The **Paschal Mystery** is Christ's work of saving us from our sins—accomplished through his Passion, Death, Resurrection, and Ascension.

The term *mystery* in religious language refers to truths revealed to us by God.

> 'Great is the mystery of the faith!' The Church professes this mystery in the Apostles' Creed (*Part One*) and celebrates it in the sacramental liturgy (*Part Two*), so that the life of the faithful may be conformed to Christ in the Holy Spirit to the glory of God the Father (*Part Three*).
>
> —*Catechism of the Catholic Church*, 2558

The mystery of faith requires a response from us. Our response is to believe in the mystery of faith, celebrate it, and live from it in our relationship with the one true God. The *Catechism* calls this relationship prayer (see CCC, 2558).

The mysteries of faith increase our knowledge of God. Faith in the mysteries of God's Revelation gives us greater access to their meaning. Saint Anselm liked to put it this way: Believe so you can understand.

We call Christ's Death, burial, Resurrection, and Ascension a mystery because we can never fully understand it. The Paschal Mystery gives us an unending revelation of who God is, who we are, and the goodness of Creation. It is like a pitcher that never runs out of water, no matter how many times you pour from it. It's life-giving and never ending.

The *Catechism* teaches that the Paschal Mystery is Jesus Christ's Passion, Death, Resurrection, and Ascension. It also lists Jesus' Crucifixion, burial, and descent into Hell in the definition (see CCC, 512). The *Catechism* also refers to Christ's Passion, his life and Death, and Resurrection as fulfilling Isaiah's prophecy of the suffering servant (see CCC, 601). It explains that the various aspects of the Paschal Mystery are celebrated throughout our liturgical year (see CCC, 1171).

The idea of choosing three images as we did above is an actual method of artistic presentation that became popular in Christian art beginning in the Middle Ages. This presentation is called a **triptych** and simply contains a set of three paintings or sculptures. The three images are usually connected side by side, and the center panel is often wider than the others.

**Paschal Mystery** the work of Redemption brought about by Christ's Passion, Death, Resurrection, and glorious Ascension; We celebrate the Paschal Mystery in the liturgy of the Church, during which Christ's saving work is made present and communicated, most especially in the Sacrament of the Eucharist

**triptych** picture or carving on three panels often connected side by side with the middle panel often larger than the other two

## RECALL

Remember a movie scene of Jesus' Passion, Death, or Resurrection, perhaps from *Jesus of Nazareth*.

○ What thoughts and feelings came to mind as you watched the movie clip?

If we were to create our own triptych of Jesus' life, each of us would have our own ideas about which images to choose. Even if we agreed that the first image would center on the birth of Jesus, the second his Crucifixion or Resurrection, and the third on his Ascension, we would still have to make more specific decisions.

For example, which picture from the Infancy Narratives would work for the first panel? Would it come from the accounts of the first Christmas in the Gospels according to Matthew or Luke? Maybe it could depict the Magi bringing gifts to Jesus of gold, frankincense, and myrrh? Perhaps it would be a picture of angels speaking to shepherds in a field, or of shepherds visiting the baby Jesus, with his parents Mary and Joseph. Other possibilities might be a painting of the bright star over Bethlehem or one of Jesus in a manger, surrounded by barn animals and his parents.

The Paschal Mystery refers to the events of Jesus' life that prompt us to confess that he is the Christ. It is the reason for our faith in him as the Messiah. It is why we call him Son of God, and it is why we aren't satisfied focusing only on Jesus as a great moral teacher. Even if you were limited to three images, it would be hard to offer an artistic description of who Jesus is without touching on the Paschal Mystery.

All four Gospels—Matthew, Mark, Luke, and John—contain the **Passion Narratives**, about the suffering and Death of Jesus, as well as the **Resurrection Narratives**. Two of the Gospels—Mark and Luke—and the Acts of the Apostles mention the Ascension of Jesus. "So then the Lord Jesus, after he had spoken to them, was taken up into heaven and sat down at the right hand of God" (Mark 16:19).

As the Gospels tell the story of the Passion, Death, Resurrection, and Ascension of Jesus, we are presented with many images. Yet, no one image or even a set of three in a triptych can capture the Paschal Mystery of Jesus.

**Resurrection Narratives** the scriptural accounts of Jesus' bodily rising from the dead on the third day after his Crucifixion and burial

**Passion Narratives** the scriptural accounts of the suffering and Death of Jesus

### GO TO THE SOURCE

**We can find many images in the Passion and Resurrection Narratives.** Read the following passages and offer a one-sentence description of each image:

Passion Narratives
*Matthew 26:23-25; Luke 39-46; Mark 14:43-52; John 19:1-5; John 19:16-20; Luke 23:44-49; Matthew 27:57-60*

Resurrection Narratives
*Matthew 28:1-10; Mark 16:1-8; Luke 24:13-35; John 20:19-29*

○ If you could only choose one image from each category for your triptych, which of these would you want? Why?

### RELATE

Find photos or draw a set of three images to capture the Paschal Mystery in your own triptych. Include the Gospel, chapter, and verse that each picture describes.
○ Why did you choose the pictures that make up your triptych?
○ What did you learn about the Paschal Mystery from this exercise?

# PRIMARY SOURCES

Saint Teresa of Ávila (1515–1582), a Spanish Carmelite sister, would understand why young people often have trouble developing a real spiritual life. It's sometimes easy to be distracted by other things in every day life. Even Saint Teresa knew a time when she spent little energy in building her relationship with God. As a young and witty nun, Dōna (Sister) Teresa really enjoyed fine things, delicious food, and lots of visitors at her convent.

Then one day in 1553, something new happened. Teresa saw an unfamiliar "statue" in the chapel. The bleeding, battered Jesus was there, lit by a flickering candle. At first, she turned away in disgust. Then, she was touched by a sudden and overwhelming realization. The sufferings and love of Jesus were real. Jesus was real! She dropped to her knees and burst into tears. Remorse and love flooded into her heart.

From that day, Jesus was always real for Teresa. She spent time in prayer and got to know him more and more. She taught others to do the same. Teresa wrote three books on spirituality: *The Way of Perfection, Autobiography,* and *The Interior Castle.* She was named a saint in 1622, forty years after her death. She gained the title of doctor of the Church in 1970. All people, Saint Teresa said, have a call to holiness—to be connected so closely with Jesus that he lives in them. This passage by Saint Teresa reminds us of the relationship we *can* have with Jesus.

*However softly we speak, he is near enough to hear us. Neither is there any need for wings to go to find him. All one need do is go into solitude and look at him within oneself. . . . Since he does not force our will, he takes what we give him; but he does not give himself completely unless we give ourselves completely.*

> ❝ **However softly we speak, he is near enough to hear us.** ❞
>
> —*Saint Teresa of Ávila*

**When have you felt very close to Jesus?**

**What are the biggest blocks to a real relationship with Jesus?**

➤ Go to the student site at **hs.osvcurriculum.com**

**The Ascension accounts focus on Jesus' being taken up into Heaven.** Compare the passages from Mark, Luke, and Acts that describe the Ascension.

Read *Mark 16:19-20, Luke 24:50-53,* and *Acts 1:6-12.*

○ What did Jesus say or do with his disciples before he was taken into Heaven?

○ How did Jesus' followers respond after he ascended into Heaven?

### The Origins of the Word 'Paschal'

The Greek and Latin word *Pascha* and the Hebrew word *Pesach* both mean "Passover." What is the link between the Passover and the Paschal Mystery? The Book of Exodus tells the Passover story (see Exodus 11:1-12:50). You may recall it concerns the tenth plague, in which the first born of the Egyptians was to die. The Israelites were told to mark their doorposts and lintel with the blood of a lamb. The angel of death "passed over" the homes of the Israelites, "saving" them from death. Christians can easily see many parallels between the tenth plague from Exodus and the Passover of Jesus.

The Passover of Jesus occurred when he died as the "Lamb of God" (John 1:29). Whereas the lamb's blood saved the Israelites from political slavery, Jesus' blood shed on the Cross saved all of humanity from sin and death. Through the saving action of his

Death and Resurrection, death, in a sense, now "passes over" all of humanity. At funerals, for example, we say that when someone dies, life is not over; it is changed. Then seven weeks after Easter Sunday, Christ's Passover was fulfilled when the Holy Spirit poured out his grace on Pentecost (see CCC, 731). Jesus instituted the Eucharist at a Jewish Passover meal. Every time we gather at Mass to celebrate Jesus' Paschal Mystery, we remember the Last Supper and how Jesus died for us so that we might have eternal life. We celebrate that his saving work is made present in the liturgy.

**Define** The words *Pascha* and *Pesach* share what meaning?

**Infer** What do we mean by "death now passes over all of humanity"?

### Meaning of the Paschal Mystery

Knowing what the Paschal Mystery refers to is not the same thing as knowing what the Paschal Mystery *means.* It is faith that helps us understand its meaning. Faith, like reason, is a way of knowing. You can memorize the definition, but the meaning of the Paschal Mystery involves our Redemption, which is celebrated and made present in the Eucharist. This has meaning for your life, the life of the Church, and the life of all humanity.

Understanding and believing in the Passion, Death, Resurrection, and Ascension of Jesus is a foundation of our faith. Saying Jesus saves basically means that, through God's action, from death comes new life. Our salvation through Christ is from both sin and death. It is a mystery to us because as finite, or limited, beings, we cannot fully understand the infinite meaning of what Jesus has done for us. In faith, however, we are certain that this "from death to life" Redemption comes from Christ. For Christ's Resurrection is a promise of our resurrection.

While the Paschal Mystery specifically refers to Christ's Passion, Death, Resurrection, and Ascension, we see God's saving work all around us.

The film *The Ten Commandments* (1956) depicts the Passover story from the Book of Exodus.

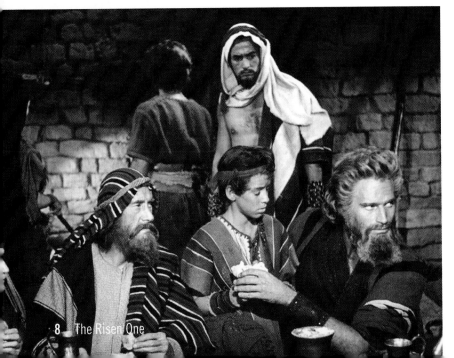

What about when you've gone through a difficult time? Think of that darkness, pain, or sadness that we all feel when we are in crisis as a "death." Perhaps the difficult time was actually due to the death of a loved one or when a family goes through a painful divorce, a discovery of abuse, a financial crisis, or a serious illness.

The pain and suffering one feels in the midst of a crisis is real. Yet, the Good News of our faith assures us that suffering and pain are not the end of the story. The reality of the Paschal Mystery gives us hope. As the Son of God overcame death, God is able to transform our pain and suffering into new life. Although the painful situation itself may not have been a good thing, God's grace can make something good come from something painful.

## REFLECT

**The Paschal Mystery is a foundation of our faith.**

○ What do you think Jesus' first followers saw in him that they had never seen before?

Christ, who suffered the Passion and crucifixion, strengthens us in our own suffering. When we turn to him, in prayer and the Sacraments, and unite our suffering to his, it can become a means of purification and salvation.

**Recall** What is the meaning of the Paschal Mystery?

**Elaborate** What does it mean to say we experience the Paschal Mystery in our lives?

## SECTION 1 REVIEW

### QUICK REVIEW

**1a. Identify** What are the elements of the Paschal Mystery?

**b. Select** Which aspect of the Paschal Mystery is most important to you? Explain your answer.

**2a. Tell** Who has been saved by the Paschal Mystery?

**b. Explain** What is the meaning of the Paschal Mystery?

**c. Reflect** Would it be easy or difficult to make an artistic representation of the Paschal Mystery? Explain your answer.

**3. Summarize** How did the term "Passover" become associated with Jesus' Death?

### ACT

Examine your parish's Paschal candle. Explain its symbols and their significance.

○ Would you add any additional symbols to it?

**Pray** Compose a short prayer asking for God's guidance in understanding the Paschal Mystery.

### SELF-ASSESS

Which statement best reflects where you are now?

☐ I'm confident enough about the material in this section to be able to explain it to someone else.

☐ I have a good grasp of the material in this section, but I could use more review.

☐ I'm lost. I need help catching up before moving on.

# Universal Call to Holiness

**holiness** "A state of goodness in which a person—with the help of God's grace, the action of the Holy Spirit, and a life of prayer—is freed from sin and evil" (*United States Catholic Catechism for Adults*, Glossary p. 514)

The Paschal Mystery has gained for us our Redemption. Through it we receive new life, new possibilities, and new hope. In our day-to-day lives through the Church and by the grace of God (see CCC, 824), we are called to **holiness**. But what does it mean to be holy? What comes to mind when you hear the word holiness?

Most of us use the adjective *holy* when we are referring to something sacred or divine. This definition suggests that something holy is worthy of devotion. While this definition is accurate, we miss the full meaning of *holy* if we don't realize how it could apply to ourselves. Holiness is from God, but it does not apply only to God and the saints. As Catholics, we know that holiness comes to us through the grace of our Baptism. Our Baptism calls us to holiness in each area of our lives, and we grow in holiness of life in and through the Church.

"The Dogmatic Constitution of the Church," the Vatican II document with the Latin title *Lumen Gentium*, makes clear that every member of the Church is called to holiness because it is God's desire. As Saint Paul says: "For this is the will of God, your sanctification" (1 Thessalonians 4:3).

Our holiness comes from the work of the Holy Spirit. "It is expressed in many ways in individuals, who in their walk of life, tend toward the perfection of charity, thus causing the edification of others," (*Lumen Gentium*, 39). We maintain our holiness through a life of prayer, through taking part in the Church's liturgies, and responding to the Holy Spirit's work in our lives.

Our call to holiness through our Baptism is a high calling. It is one that requires us to trust in Christ's wisdom and to live up to his divine expectations:

- "Be perfect, therefore, as your heavenly Father is perfect" (Matthew 5:48).

- "Be merciful, just as your Father is merciful" (Luke 6:36).

- "This is my commandment, that you love one another as I have loved you" (John 15:12).

The sanctification we received at Baptism is something we have to hold onto in our lives and Saint Paul offers a plan.

> As God's chosen ones, holy and beloved, clothe yourselves with compassion, kindness, humility, meekness, and patience. Bear with one another and, if anyone has a complaint against another, forgive each other . . . Above all, clothe yourselves with love, which binds everything together in perfect harmony.
>
> —Colossians 3:12-14

As we become more united with Christ and his Paschal Mystery, we grow in holiness. This is a lifelong process. Growing in holiness is not something we could do on our own. We can only do this with a strong connection with God.

To be holy is not the same as being literally perfect. Holiness applies to our physical and spiritual well-being. To be holy is to be connected with God. We are only complete—we are only holy—with a healthy spiritual connection to God. We need to take care of ourselves physically, mentally, emotionally, and spiritually. This requires proper rest, a good diet, intellectual stimulation, healthy habits, and the feeding and nourishing of our souls.

The reason we are called to be holy is because Christ, with the Father and the Holy Spirit, is holy: "You shall be holy, for I am holy" (Leviticus 11:45). God calls us to holiness because he wants us to live out our Catholic life wholeheartedly with enthusiasm, will, and commitment. This may sometimes seem impossible because our whole heart is divided by many distractions. God can sometimes be the last thing on our minds as we live out our daily lives.

As Catholics, we recognize our struggle to be perfect and holy is actually the struggle to stay focused on living the way God intended. Every Ash Wednesday we read the words of the Prophet Joel, who calls all believers to a life of holiness by repentance or conversion. "Yet even now, says the Lord, return to me with all your heart, with fasting, with weeping, and with mourning" (Joel 2:12). The season of Lent is a special time to examine our lives. It is a time to ask ourselves: are we giving our whole heart to God? Are we living in ways that are holy as God is holy?

The ashes placed on our foreheads remind us of our limited time on Earth and call us to reflect on how we are living out our Catholic faith. Mary, the Mother of God, through God's grace and her openness to it, was granted the perfection of holiness that we are working toward. We strive to avoid sin and increase our holiness, and we have Mary as a model (see CCC, 829).

The Ninevites acknowledged their sins and welcomed holiness. This reflects the

## GO TO THE SOURCE

**The Scriptures speak of people putting on ashes and sackcloth** as symbols of repentance and sorrow for the sins they have committed. The Book of Jonah, though short, offers an example of repentance and conversion.

Read the Book of *Jonah*.

○ What was the message Jonah was to deliver, and to whom was he to deliver it?

○ What do you find most surprising: the people's response or Jonah's reaction to God's response? Why?

○ Which of these can you most relate to? Explain.

Paschal Mystery, which we are called to embrace. Like the people of Nineveh in the story of Jonah, we must examine our lives, recognize our sins, express sorrow, and repent. Our conversion is met with God's loving forgiveness. The Holy Spirit first turns our hearts toward him. He gives us the strength to try again (see CCC, 1432). With God's grace, then, we turn away from sin and become faithful to the Gospel and once again we see the Paschal Mystery active in our lives. As our sinfulness dies and we follow our call to holiness, we encounter new life in Christ.

- Which of these is harder for you to do—stay fully focused on your relationship with God, acknowledge your mistakes and repent?
- Write a short paragraph explaining your answer.

The season of Lent ends before the Mass of the Lord's Supper on Holy Thursday, the beginning of the Easter Triduum. These celebrations in the Church are about what Jesus did for us and invite us to see the Paschal Mystery—the dying and rising—in our own lives.

**Restate** What do the ashes on Ash Wednesday symbolize?

**Elaborate** Why should we be like the Ninevites in the story of Jonah?

### Called to the Body of Christ

The call to be holy and the call to love are not simply individual matters. There is a universal call to holiness of life. We are called to be part of the Church, and it is through faith and our Baptism that we become members of the one Body. The Church, though made up of many individuals, is one Body, and that one Body, with Christ as the Head, is known as the "Body of Christ" alive in the world today. "The Church increases, grows, and develops through the holiness of her faithful" (CCC, 2045).

The Church is described as "light" in a world of darkness, doubt, and despair. Jesus said, "Let your light shine before others, so that they may see your good works and give glory to your Father in heaven" (Matthew 5:16). The Church is also described as "salt," since it is meant to preserve a good example for the people of the world, just as salt preserves food. Jesus said, "You are the salt of the earth" (Matthew 5:13).

When someone is living our Catholic faith fully, they live as a disciple of Jesus. They serve as an example to others and a witness to Christ's life and teaching, representing well our Church (see CCC, 2044). Food without salt can go bad, and it is very difficult to get around in a dark room without light. Jesus said: "I give you a new commandment, that you love one another. Just as I have loved you, you also should love one another. By this everyone will know that you are my disciples, if you have love for one another" (John 13:34-35).

### CONNECT

Think of someone in your life or broader community who has served as an example of holiness and love, or someone who serves others by the life that they live—someone who has a faith that can be seen not just by their words but by their actions.

- Write a paragraph describing this person.

### The Call to Love

The Bible is full of expressions of this love that is at the root of holiness. For example, 1 John 4:16 reads, "God is love, and those who abide in love abide in God, and God abides in them." So not only are we called to be holy because God is holy, we are called to love because God is love.

Our English language is limited when it comes to the word love. We can say we love pizza, but what happens after we eat three slices? We usually have had enough of what we love. The love we have for our parents, our friends, or simply someone who needs our help, are all different kinds of love.

### GO TO THE SOURCE

**Saint Paul describes what love is** and what it is not.

Read *1 Corinthians 13:1-13.*
- Which of the qualities of love have the strongest meaning for you?
- Use your own code words, phrases, or someone's initials to represent how you have experienced any of these qualities of love in your life.

Think about someone with whom you have had an experience of reconciliation or forgiveness. Maybe it was with someone you had considered an enemy or rival.

○ What brought about the reconciliation, and who initiated it?

○ What situation caused this person to be an enemy or at least to be a conflict in your life?

○ Was there prayer involved? If so, did it help? If not, do you believe it would it have helped? If so, how?

The New Testament was originally written in the Greek language, which uses three different words for love. **Agape** (ah•GAH•pay) is considered divine love, a self-giving love. Saint Paul wrote about this kind of love: "God's love has been poured into our hearts through the Holy Spirit that has been given to us" (Romans 5:5). The great hymn to love that we just read from First Corinthians is about this kind of love. It is an unconditional gift of oneself that is offered out of care and concern for another's well-being. Agape involves serving others or making a sacrifice for others. Jesus expressed this type of love when he said, "This is my commandment, that you love one another as I have loved you. No one has greater love than this, to lay down one's life for one's friends" (John 15:12-13).

Another word, **philia**, (FILL•e•ah) describes friendship and can refer to love between friends. **Eros** (air•ohs) refers to the passion of romantic love.

When Jesus calls us to *love one another*, it is significant to note that he uses agape and not philia. Jesus knows that we may not be able to be friends with everyone, but we can have agape for everyone to the extent that we are concerned for the well-being of our friends and family, as well as that of strangers and even our enemies. To love in this way means to will the good of another.

Another significant dimension of agape is that it is *unconditional*. We can be concerned for the well-being of another regardless of how we may feel about the person. In order to have philia for a person, you need to be friends with him or her. In order to have eros for a person, you need to be in a relationship with him or her. Eros—passionate, romantic love—is not the same thing as a one-sided infatuation.

Unfortunately, eros is tremendously misunderstood. It is the source of the word *erotic*, which has taken on a negative meaning often connected to adult entertainment or pornography rather than a healthy romantic love. Romantic and sexual love in its proper place and context, fully expressed within the marriage relationship, are sacred gifts that can lead to new life.

The three different words for love help us clarify what we mean when we speak of love. However, they are not exclusive categories. A married couple should have the romantic love of eros in addition to philia.

Holiness calls us to appreciate the meaning of the three forms of love and to live them out in a way that gives glory to God while serving our neighbor (see CCC, 2013), including the poor and marginalized. When we pray

**agape** describes selfless love that is concerned for the well-being of another, an unconditional gift of oneself, serving others, or making a sacrifice for others

**philia** describes love between friends

**eros** describes romantic, passionate love

**We can find some powerful stories** of reconciliation in the Old Testament.

Read these accounts of reconciliation between brothers Jacob and Esau in *Genesis 27:1-29* and *32:1-33:17*; among Joseph and his brothers in *Genesis 37:1-36* and *45:1-28, 50:15-26*; and between leaders David and Saul in *1 Samuel 19:1-17* and *24:1-23*.

○ Compare and contrast the three stories of reconciliation.

○ How does each account address love of one's enemies?

○ Which of these stories do you identify with the most, and why?

"Thy will be done" in the Lord's Prayer, we are praying to wholeheartedly devote ourselves to giving glory to God and serving our neighbors by loving them. Saint Gregory of Nyssa said: "Christian perfection has but one limit, that of having none" (St. Gregory of Nyssa, *De vita Mos.*: PG 44, 300D) (CCC, 2028).

**Select** Which kind of love—agape, philia or eros—describes love for your best friend?

**Elaborate** What does it mean to say that we are called to love?

## Love of Enemies?

Part of Jesus' new commandment of love, and one of the most difficult things he gave us to do, is to love our enemies.

In 1983, Blessed Pope John Paul II met with, and forgave, Mehmet Ali Agca—the man who had tried to assassinate him two years earlier.

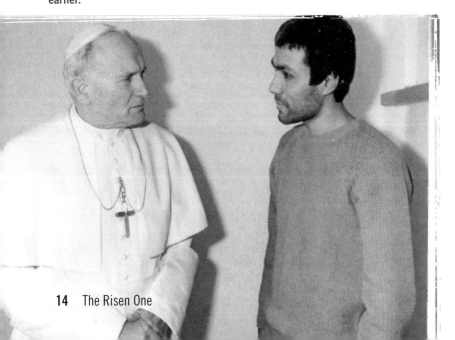

You have heard that it was said, "You shall love your neighbor and hate your enemy." But I say to you, Love your enemies and pray for those who persecute you.

—Matthew 5:43-44

What does this teaching mean? What does it mean to love our enemies? First, remember that Jesus is calling us to practice agape, which is concern for the well-being of others, regardless of how we may feel about them.

Wishing an adversary well, even when that person has been hurtful, can actually help the one who has been offended. Revenge and resentment can lead people to harmful, and sinful, actions. Instead, call upon God's forgiveness. When Jesus prayed from the cross: "Father, forgive them; for they do not know what they are doing" (Luke 23:34), he was showing that forgiveness and reconciliation are also parts of the Paschal Mystery.

It is truly a moment of hope when two enemies can forgive one another and become friends, or at least respect one another in a new way. An enemy does not have to be someone's best friend, but it is important to pray for one's adversaries so they may no longer be enemies.

**After calling followers to "love your enemies,"** Jesus offers a series of questions. List the questions, and in your own words describe what Jesus' message was to his followers.

Read *Matthew 5:43–6:14*.

○ Right after this passage on love of enemies, what prayer does Jesus teach his disciples?

○ Comment on your own ability to forgive your enemies.

**At thirteen, author C. S. Lewis (1898–1963) shocked his family by becoming an atheist.** As a small boy, he'd endured a terrifying time at a boarding school. Then, when he was ten, his mother died. Many years later, as an English professor at Oxford in England, a need and love for God came gloriously back to life in him. He became one of the best-known modern Christian writers.

- In 1949, Lewis began writing seven books to create a Christian fantasy for children.

- *The Chronicles of Narnia* have sold more than 100 million copies in forty-seven languages and have been adapted as feature films.

- They explore great Christian themes: sin, repentance, death, and resurrection. In the stories, a noble king (Aslan) lovingly dies for others and breathes life back into a frozen, lifeless kingdom. Aslan is always present when the characters need him.

- Lewis' love for God grew over time. How have you experienced something similar in your relationship with God?

- If you've read or watched *The Chronicles of Narnia*, how does Aslan remind us of God?

King Aslan takes the form of a lion. The word "aslan" is Turkish for lion.

# Faith & Culture

Go to the student site at **hs.osvcurriculum.com**

---

## SECTION 2 REVIEW

### QUICK REVIEW

**1a. Connect** How is holiness connected to the Paschal Mystery?

**b. Relate** How do most of us use the term "holy"?

**c. Explain** Why and how are we called to be holy?

**2a. Summarize** Retell the message of the Prophet Joel and explain why we need to hear it at the beginning of Lent.

**b. Interpret** Explain the origin of ashes as a symbol of Lent, and tell their meaning today.

**3a. List** Name and define the kinds of love that the Greeks differentiated.

**b. Explain** Why is it important to pray for our enemies?

**Pray** Compose a prayer asking for the intercession of Mary to help us lead holier lives.

### SELF-ASSESS

Which statement best reflects where you are now?

☐ I'm confident enough about the material in this section to be able to explain it to someone else.

☐ I have a good grasp of the material in this section, but I could use more review.

☐ I'm lost. I need help catching up before moving on.

# Made In the Image and Likeness of God

One of the most famous Scripture passages in the New Testament can be found in the Gospel of John: "For God so loved the world that he gave his only Son, so that everyone who believes in him may not perish but may have eternal life" (John 3:16).

God loved us so much that he sent his Son to us. Jesus taught us about who God the Father is and what he wants of us. Through the Paschal Mystery, Jesus showed us God's love for us. Christ continually shared his teachings during his whole life, especially through his willing acceptance of the total sacrifice he made on the Cross for the Redemption of us all (see CCC, 561). God loved us enough to let us see the consequences of our actions. Human pride, arrogance, and sinfulness led to the Crucifixion of Jesus. Yet, despite human sinfulness, in the Paschal Mystery, Christ triumphed over death.

In sending his Son, and in the Paschal Mystery, God the Father reveals the deep and unique love he has for humanity. Think about it: God did not send his Son to any other of his Creation, but to us, because we are the ones who are made in God's image and likeness.

**RECALL**

○ Read and memorize the verse from John 3:16.

○ What does this verse tell you about the meaning of the Paschal Mystery?

To be made in the image and likeness of God is to possess four abilities unique to humans: intelligence, love, freedom, and conscience.

- *Intelligence:* As beings created in God's image and likeness, we first have the capacity to know and love him. We also are able to know truth about God and to affirm that the truth exists.

- *Love:* We are able to be loved and to give love.

- *Freedom:* We have freedom to choose what is good. This means choosing not necessarily what we want, but what we should. We could also choose evil, but that reduces our freedom.

- *Conscience:* When properly formed, our conscience helps us discern good from evil and truth from falsehood.

The Book of Genesis reveals that God created man and woman in his own divine image. This Scripture passage prompts our understanding of human dignity, the sacredness of all life, and the equality of each and every person that comes from being made in God's image.

Human Dignity is the foundation for Catholic Social Teaching. Every person is to be treated with respect and dignity. Respect for human dignity means that every person is to have the basic necessities and right to life, food, shelter, clothing, clean water, work, and freedom.

**Read** *Genesis 1:26-27*, the passage that is the foundation of the concept of human dignity.

○ Which words or phrases are repeated? How many times? What do you think is the significance of this repetition?

○ Comment on your ability to detect and respect the image of God in yourself. How about in others

Every society and government is to look out for the welfare of the poor, the orphan, and the widow. If the poor are not taken care of, there is something morally wrong with the society and government. A society or culture is not fulfilling its responsibilities when people suffer due to hunger, lack of health care, lack of work, and lack of love.

We were created in the image and likeness of God, yet we sin. Recall that our first parents, Adam and Eve, transmitted to their descendants a human nature wounded by their own first sin and so deprived us of the original holiness and justice of Creation. We call this deprivation Original Sin. In discussing Original Sin, Saint Thomas Aquinas speaks of its four wounds:

• *ignorance*, meaning our difficulty in knowing the truth and a loss of confidence that truth can be known;

• *malice*, in our minds that inclines us to think the worst about others;

• *weakness*, in our will that makes it hard to choose the good;

• *disorder*, in the passions and emotions causing us to lose control of ourselves.

God's response to the reality of Original Sin is ultimately the gift of the Paschal Mystery. Christ's Passion, Death, Resurrection, and Ascension redeem us, save us, and restore us to life in God's grace. And as members of his Body, the Church, we are asked to use our lives to be his image in the world. We are to be his feet, eyes, hands, ears, and voice so that people can know God's love, learn Jesus' message of Good News, and see the importance of the Catholic faith in our lives and our world. Our personal response to God's call is shown in our way of life, our contributions to better help in society, and our active involvement in the Church.

We are the summit of God's Creation, and we possess the gift of chastity through the saving grace of Christ and the work of the Holy Spirit. When we act out of love we become models of God's faithfulness and kindness. The virtue of chastity grows from these relationships. In doing so, we act as Jesus who called us his friends because he fully revealed everything the Father wanted us to know (see John 15:15). Friendship is good for all of us because it creates a "spiritual communion" (CCC, 2347).

Human dignity comes from God as we are made in his image and likeness. From the moment of our creation to the moment of our death, we must respect that dignity. From the moment of conception we are endowed with "a spiritual and immortal" soul.[1] We are "destined for eternal beatitude," a state of utter bliss (CCC, 1703). Equal in God's eyes, we are called to treat each other equally and respect the dignity of life, from the moment of conception until death. No matter age or ability, we provide for and protect human life, thus upholding the Fifth Commandment.

**Psalm 139 describes our conception and how God created us.**

Read *Psalm 139:13-16*.
○ What words from the psalm reflect God's creative activity in our conception?

○ Too often we are overly self-critical about some dimension of our physical appearance. Instead of criticizing, how does the psalmist assess God's creative activity?

○ Comment on your ability to prayerfully speak this passage from the Psalms to God about yourself.

# Blessed Miguel Pro, S.J.

## (1891–1927)

Over the centuries, thousands of Christian martyrs have borne witness to these words. Even today, in places like China, men and women offer their very lives in service to the Gospel. In the early twentieth century, some Catholics in Mexico were killed because of their faith.

Those who find their life will lose it, and those who lose their life for my sake will find it"

—Matthew 10:39

Blessed Miguel Agustín Pro was one such martyr. He was born in Guadalupe, Mexico, in 1891. As a child, he loved practical jokes and pranks. His call to become a priest did not change his playful nature. During his time in the seminary one of his friends said that he knew two Miguels—the playful one and the prayerful one.

In the first few decades of the twentieth century, the Mexican government closed churches and anti-Catholic sentiment increased. Miguel and other seminarians had to flee the country. He finished his studies at a seminary in Spain and then chose to return to Mexico. During the years he had been away, the government had passed strict anti-Catholic laws. In many areas, priests were outlawed. To continue their ministry, they were forced into hiding. Father Miguel became one of these clandestine priests.

Assuming a variety of disguises, such as a beggar or a policeman, he would secretly conduct Baptisms and marriages and perform the Last Rites for the sick. Once, when a suspicious official was eyeing him, Miguel took the arm of a young woman, pretending to be her boyfriend. This threw the official off track since he assumed a priest would never be so friendly with a woman.

Miguel managed to evade detection for nearly seven years, but then he and his brother were discovered and falsely accused of an

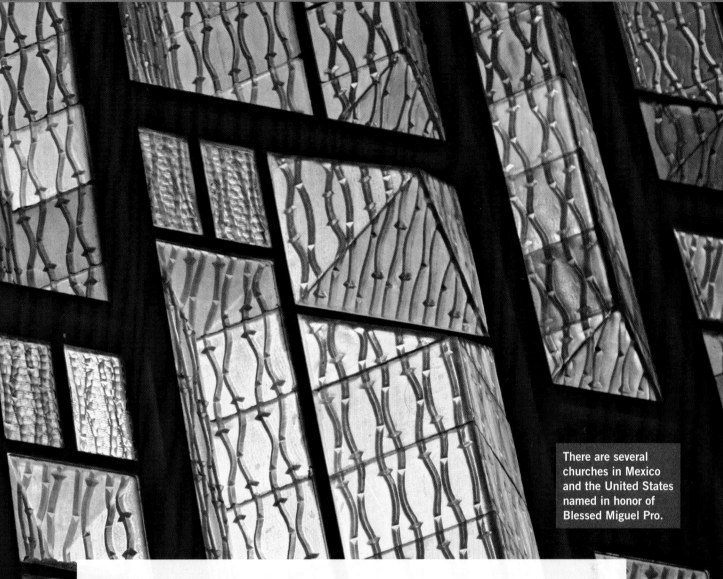

There are several churches in Mexico and the United States named in honor of Blessed Miguel Pro.

assassination attempt on a public official. The government wanted to make an example of a priest, so they sentenced Miguel to death by firing squad.

Government leaders believed that pictures of the execution would serve to silence Catholics, so they had his death photographed and recorded. At his execution on November 23, 1927, Miguel blessed the soldiers and then prayed briefly. He refused the final offer of a blindfold, and holding his crucifix in one hand and a rosary in the other, he extended his arms in the shape of the Cross. As the order to shoot rang out, he cried "Viva Cristo Rey!" "Long live Christ the King."

Later, the government released the photos. Instead of silencing dissenters, they actually bolstered the desire for freedom of worship and encouraged rebellion.

At Miguel's beatification in 1988, Blessed Pope John Paul II said, "Neither suffering nor . . . the exhausting ministerial activity, frequently carried out in difficult and dangerous circumstances, could stifle the radiating and contagious joy which he brought to his life for Christ and which nothing could take away."

**Think About It** If you were being arrested for being a Catholic, what evidence would an investigation find? How would people know you were a Catholic by the way you live? At times, we are called to defend our beliefs. What do you do when someone ridicules your faith? Blessed Miguel died holding a rosary and a crucifix. What symbols of your faith do you have with you at all times?

Go to the student site at
**hs.osvcurriculum.com**

# Making a PILGRIMAGE

> The very word *practice* brings with it the idea of learning. . . .
> And any practice is awkward and difficult. But it is necessary to
> attain any kind of proficiency in the spiritual life.
>
> —Dorothy Day

The spiritual practice of making a pilgrimage means journeying to a particular holy site or shrine. Making the pilgrimage reminds us that Jesus calls us to follow him just as he once called his first Apostles.

"And he said to them, 'Follow me, and I will make you fish for people.' Immediately, they left their nets and followed him. As he went from there, he saw two other brothers, James son of Zebedee and his brother John, in the boat with their father Zebedee, mending their nets, and he called them. Immediately they left the boat and their father, and followed him." (Matthew 4:19-22).

In Catholic history, the practice of making pilgrimages reached a high point during the Middle Ages. Medieval Catholics often walked—in groups—from their homes in Europe to the Holy Land. The pilgrims knew their journeys would take years. They also knew that they might die on the way because of diseases, bandits, injuries and unpredictable

weather. Nonetheless, they wanted to walk where Jesus had walked. They traveled simply and prayerfully and wore their entire pilgrim wardrobe: a broad-brimmed hat to protect against sun and rain, a long belted tunic like Jesus wore, simple shoes, and a pilgrim's pouch slung across the shoulder.

Today, Catholics of all ages and from all over the world still journey to holy places. Many of the most popular shrines are dedicated to Mary, the Blessed Mother of Jesus. Ten million people travel to the Our Lady of Guadalupe Shrine in Mexico City each year, for example. Six million go annually to the Our Lady of Lourdes Shrine in France, and five million pilgrims trek to Czestochowa in Poland to view the Black Madonna Shrine.

However, there are many ways to make a pilgrimage, which is simply a journey of prayer and faith. A pilgrimage doesn't have to take you thousands of miles away. It doesn't have to be expensive. A pilgrimage could mean a twenty-minute trip to a church or shrine across town. Being a pilgrim just means making your way to a change in heart or growth in faith.

Pilgrimages are part of the sacramental life of the Church. The Catechism describes the Church, the Body of Christ, as on a pilgrimage to God's Kingdom. In that sense, we are all pilgrims as we grow in faith to someday be with God in Heaven.

The Basilica of the National Shrine of the Immaculate Conception is located in Washington, D.C.

When have you made a pilgrimage—a journey of faith?

What holy place or shrine would you want to visit as a pilgrim and why?

What do you think pilgrims can learn about prayer, about themselves, and about God on a pilgrimage?

For he created all things so that they might
exist;
the generative forces of the world are
wholesome,
and there is no destructive poison in them.

—Wisdom 1:14

You know God gave humans gifts of intellect and free will. God did not create us so that we had no choice but to respond to him. Humans can and, at times, do reject God. In fact, because of our wounded nature through Original Sin, we are prone to error and "inclined to evil" in exercising our freedom (see CCC, 1714). But human reason also gives us the natural curiosity, freedom, and desire to recognize the voice of God deep within our conscience "to do what is good and avoid what is evil"[2] (CCC, 1706). We are made with the natural ability to recognize the voice of God.

Earlier, we discussed the invitation to "Be perfect, therefore, as your heavenly Father is perfect" (Matthew 5:48). Simply put, we find our perfection "in seeking and loving what is true and good"[3] (CCC, 1704, 1711). The Holy Spirit and grace enable us to live out our holiness through how we love and treat one another. This is called the moral life. "Living a moral life bears witness to the dignity of the person" (CCC, 1706).

The Body of Christ—the Church—relies on the baptized to continue her mission of bringing the Kingdom of God to Earth. "Christians contribute to *building up the Church* by the constancy of their convictions and their moral lives" (CCC, 2045). A **conviction** is a belief in something that we believe to be true and worth doing or believing. "Because our message of the gospel came to you not in word only, but also in power and in the Holy Spirit and with full conviction" (1 Thessalonians 1:5).

The Paschal Mystery enables us to be convinced that Jesus is the Savior of the world, and that we are created in God's image and likeness, called to be members of the Church as the living Body of Christ. We are able to believe that living a moral life, with the help of God's grace, will result in eternal life.

**Explain** How does Psalm 139 describe God's Creation of each of us?

**Restate** Why are we called to make a difference in the world?

**conviction** a firmly held belief in something that we are sure is real and worth doing or believing

## SECTION 3 REVIEW

> ### QUICK REVIEW

**1a. Interpret** What does it mean to be made in the image and likeness of God?

  **b. Link** How is Catholic Social Teaching connected to holiness?

**2a. Summarize** Why did God create the world and humankind?

  **b. Elaborate** Having an intellect and free will obligates us to respond to God. Given what you have learned about human intellect and free will, what do you think it means to say we are "obligated"? How is being "obligated" different from being "forced"?

**3. Recall** How did Blessed Miguel Pro continue his ministry during the government oppression in Mexico?

**Listen and Discuss** In a small group, read aloud your favorite Bible or *Catechism* quotation from this section of the chapter.

○ Talk with group members about why you chose the quotation.

○ Rephrase the quotations in your own words if you have difficulty interpreting them.

**Pray** Compose a prayer asking for the intercession of Blessed Miguel Pro for the oppressed people in our world and the priests who minister to them.

> ### SELF-ASSESS

Which statement best reflects where you are now?

☐ I'm confident enough about the material in this section to be able to explain it to someone else.

☐ I have a good grasp of the material in this section, but I could use more review.

☐ I'm lost. I need help catching up before moving on.

# Essentials of Catholic Spirituality

There can be no understanding of Catholic spirituality without a perception and experience of the Holy Spirit who has been present in the world from the very beginning and has remained with God's People and his Church. The Holy Spirit guides us, strengthens us, and teaches us to pray for example. Scripture, liturgy, personal prayer, and theology are the main supports for a sound spirituality.

> A distinct spirituality can also arise at the point of convergence of liturgical and theological currents, bearing witness to the integration of the faith into a particular human environment and its history. The different schools of Christian spirituality share in the living tradition of prayer and are essential guides for the faithful. In their rich diversity they are refractions of the one pure light of the Holy Spirit.
>
> —CCC, 2684

The Holy Spirit helps us understand and apply God's Word proclaimed in the celebration of the Eucharist and the other Sacraments. How much this helps us depends on how open our hearts are to the Holy Spirit's gift. Through the words, actions, and the symbols used in liturgical celebrations, the Holy Spirit puts the ministers and all those gathered "into a living relationship with Christ" (CCC, 1101). We encounter Christ and are strengthened to live out what we hear, what we celebrate, and what we do at Mass.

> In the celebration of the liturgy, Sacred Scripture is extremely important. From it come the lessons that are read and explained in the homily and the psalms that are sung. It is from the Scriptures that the prayers, collects, and hymns draw their inspiration and their force, and that actions and signs derive their meaning.[4]
>
> —CCC, 1100

Catholic spirituality involves trying to love Jesus, accepting his teaching, and living as his disciple. This is possible through the Cross of Christ, his sacrifice as the one mediator between God and man. Through the Cross, Jesus united himself to all of us. The possibility of entering into Christ's Paschal Mystery is offered to each one of us. Christ suffered for and with us, giving us an example of what we should do. We make a commitment to Jesus to follow him.

## Two Directions of Spirituality

Spirituality for Catholics is not a vague concept. Our spirituality is the practice of the faith, when we put our faith and talents at the service of God and his Kingdom.

| Dimensions of Faith | |
| --- | --- |
| Vertical Direction | Our relationship with God begins at the moment of existence. From the very beginning of our lives, God calls us to himself. We respond to God's desire to know us. We are open to God's presence and revelation, and we seek God's grace in the Sacraments. This dimension of spirituality grows when a person invests in his or her prayer life, seeks to know God, recognizes God's presence in daily life, or tries to figure out God's will for her or his life. |
| Horizontal Direction | A person's faith guides the way she or he treats others. People with a strong horizontal spirituality live out their faith by treating others with love and compassion. They keep God's Commandments, grow in the virtues, and model Christ to others. |

## DISCUSS

- How is a person's spirituality expressed, developed, and strengthened?

One way to understand spirituality is to describe the practice of our faith as having two directions.

For some people, one of these directions might be stronger than another. But both are critical for us. A noble goal would be to evaluate both directions and try to grow the less developed one.

Two mysteries shape our spirituality as Catholics and our relationship with God.

- Our belief and relationship with the Triune God, as expressed in our creeds. We believe in God as three divine Persons in one God; they are inseparable in what they are and what they do. Each divine Person, however, proclaims what is proper to him as a member of the Trinity. This is especially true in the Son's taking on human nature and in the gift of the Holy Spirit (see CCC, 267). When it comes to Creation, the work is attributed to God the Father, but it is also true that the Father, Son, and Holy Spirit "are the one, indivisible principle of creation" (CCC, 316).

> The mystery of the Most Holy Trinity is the central mystery of Christian faith and life. It is the mystery of God in himself. It is therefore the source of all the other mysteries of faith, the light that enlightens them. It is the most fundamental and essential teaching in the "hierarchy of the truths of faith."[5] The whole history of salvation is identical with the history of the way and the means by which the one true God, Father, Son, and Holy Spirit, reveals himself to men "and reconciles and unites with himself those who turn away from sin."[6]
>
> —CCC, 234

- The Paschal Mystery of Christ's Passion, Death, Resurrection, and Ascension forms a Catholic faith that helps us deal with life's pain and losses with an assurance that the Son of God endured suffering, our God knows what we experience, and he will help us get through it.

Paschal Mystery spirituality accepts that hardships will come, but that through faithfulness and trust in God, hardships can become opportunities for the joy of new life, and ultimately the eternal happiness for which God made us.

**Recall** At Mass, how and why does the Holy Spirit put us into a living relationship with Christ?

**Explain** What do we mean when we describe spirituality as having two "directions"?

## Obstacles to Spirituality

No material item can compete with the gift of wisdom and the other gifts of the Holy Spirit. It should come as no surprise that what often takes wisdom away from people, or distracts people from the wisdom of God, is a focus on material riches. This misguided focus is one of the reasons Jesus said it is so hard for the rich to get into the Kingdom of Heaven.

Why is it that riches and material things can keep a person from the Kingdom of God? It's not that money and material things are bad in and of themselves; rather, the problem arises when our focus on material wealth takes precedence over our relationship with God. At that point we not only struggle with spiritual poverty, but we've also broken the First Commandment: "I am the Lord your God, . . . you shall have no other gods before me" (Deuteronomy 5:7).

## GO TO THE SOURCE

**Just as Jesus was heading out on a trip,** a man ran up to him, knelt in front of him, and asked: "Good Teacher, what must I do to inherit eternal life?" (Mark 10:17).

Read Jesus' answer to the enthusiastic man in *Mark 10:18-28*.

○ Why do you think it wasn't enough that the man knew and had lived the Commandments since he was a child?

○ Put yourself in the man's shoes. What would you do if Jesus had told you the same thing?

○ What is your reaction to Jesus saying "For God all things are possible"? (Mark 10:27)

## DISCUSS

○ Why would someone feel depressed and unhappy when they have all kinds of material things?

○ What material items bring more stress and worry than peace of mind?

○ How can the desire for more material goods and success affect our relationship with God and our spirituality?

○ What are some of the other obstacles to spiritual health?

○ When have you experienced "spiritual poverty" in your life? How did you find God again?

**spiritual poverty** refers to an absence of God in our lives

On the other hand, asking for and being open to the wisdom and spirit of God can bring someone great wealth, be it material or spiritual. King Solomon asked for wisdom and God also gave him great wealth. Later, Solomon became distracted by his many wives and suffered God's disfavor (see 1 Kings 11:1-13).

God created us with a natural sense of longing. Our yearning and longing is a hunger and thirst for something more in life that can only be properly fulfilled by God. When we try to fulfill this longing with material things, products or procedures, athletic achievements, or substance abuse, we end up suffering from **spiritual poverty**, which refers to an absence of God in our lives.

The vice and evil of spiritual poverty is a direct result of failing to achieve the virtue and goodness of "poverty of spirit." Though these concepts sound similar, they are direct opposites. To have poverty of spirit means to empty ourselves and to get rid of sins such as materialism, greed, lust, addiction, indifference, and self-pity. When we allow God's grace to banish these things from our lives, we realize that it is God we are really longing for. It's then that the Holy Spirit can fill us with abundant love, joy, peace, healing, gratitude, and eternal life.

## GLOBAL PERSPECTIVES

Many people love and remember Blessed Mother Teresa for her work among the poor in Calcutta, India. The Missionaries of Charity order she founded reaches around the world. Mother Teresa often told the story of the train ride on which she describes her call to establish an order of religious sisters. On October 7, 1950, four years after she felt that call, the Missionaries of Charity were founded as a religious institute for the Archdiocese of Calcutta. Mother Teresa also founded a branch of religious brothers in Calcutta in 1963, a contemplative branch of sisters in New York in 1976, and a group of contemplative brothers in Rome in 1979. Lay people also joined Mother Teresa in serving the poor, and in 1969 the Co-Workers of Mother Teresa were officially established. Then in 1984, the Lay Missionaries of Charity were established. Today, there are more than 4,000 Sisters of Charity working in more than 130 countries.

➚ Go to the student site at **hs.osvcurriculum.com**

For what will it profit them if they gain the whole world but forfeit their life?

—Matthew 16:26

Blessed Mother Teresa of Calcutta took care of the poorest people in India but often spoke of the great spiritual poverty found in the richest countries of the world. Anyone can succumb to spiritual poverty, but it is often found in those who seem to have everything. People can still feel depressed even when have all the material comforts they want: a credit card with no limits, a sports car, the latest phone or computer, or other technological gadgets.

The horizontal dimension of spirituality affirms the goodness of our relationships with friends and family. God is pleased with our relationships when our friends and family help us become better people, strengthen and affirm our moral decision making, and encourage us to grow—and when we do the same for them. However, a problem can arise when a person chooses one of these relationships over his or her relationship with God. This is evident when what seems cool or more fun conflicts with the will of God, or when one's family encourages practices that are degrading to human dignity.

One important way to gauge how well we live out the fullness of the Christian life is how we love one another, especially family members. Unfortunately, many families experience division and disagreements, and need reconciliation and forgiveness. Death, separation, and divorce sometimes play roles in dividing families. Under such conditions one needs to possess spirituality strengthened by God the Father, Jesus, and the Holy Spirit. One

## NAME

- Make a list of concrete examples of things you can do to demonstrate your love for God and neighbor, family, friends, the poor, the marginalized, and the stranger.

## GO TO THE SOURCE

**Jesus cautioned about placing our happiness on material things:** the treasures of Heaven are much more durable and everlasting.

Read *Matthew 6:19-24*.

- Which of these sayings do you like best? Is that because it's advice you need to hear or advice you deeply agree with, or both? Explain.
- Which of these sayings do you struggle with understanding?

should never take his or her family and friends for granted.

Jesus explains the conditions for discipleship: "Whoever loves father or mother more than me is not worthy of me; and whoever loves son or daughter more than me is not worthy of me; and whoever does not take up the cross and follow me is not worthy of me. Those who find their life will lose it, and those who lose their life for my sake will find it" (Matthew 10:37-39).

**Name** What did Solomon prefer over the power of being a king?

**Conclude** Why does Jesus tell us not to place our happiness on material things?

## Essential Elements of Spirituality

We have been given direction from God and the Church on how to be holy and spiritual. We have guidance on how to be holy, namely the Beatitudes and teachings from the Sermon on the Mount, the Ten Commandments as well as the Great Commandment to love one another. These direct and build our holiness; our spirituality. We also grow in holiness by practicing the theological virtues of faith, hope, and charity as well as the cardinal virtues of prudence, justice, fortitude, and temperance. These all come from God to help us lead holy and spiritual lives.

**Spiritual Exercises** Saint Ignatius' month-long program of prayers, meditations, and practices that help Catholics live their everyday life

Reflection, self-examination, and introspection are all essential elements of our spirituality. It is about taking time to really think about our lives and being honest with ourselves before God. When we do so, we have the opportunity to encounter our conscience in daily decisions. A fully formed conscience, guided by the Holy Spirit, can be like a messenger of Christ's will into our lives (see CCC, 1778).

> Return to your conscience, question it. . . . Turn inward, brethren, and in everything you do, see God as your witness.[7]
>
> —Saint Augustine, CCC, 1779

We must accept and live the grace of Redemption. As we grow spiritually, we help build up the Church with our firmly held faith and good, upstanding lives. "The Church increases, grows, and develops through the holiness of her faithful" (CCC, 2045). All of us work to build our spirituality so we can reach a unity of faith and eventually to attain the fullness of Christ.

The greatest figures in Christian theology affirm these essential elements of spirituality. Saint Augustine's book *The Confessions* deliberately recalls events in his life when he recognized the mysterious actions of God's grace. Our lives become conversations with God when we work on spirituality and holiness.

Another example of Catholic spirituality includes the **Spiritual Exercises** of Saint Ignatius of Loyola are based on reflection and meditation on Sacred Scripture. The exercises encourage self-examination at three different times of each day: upon rising, after the noon meal, and after the evening meal. The exercises are usually performed in one of these ways: extended over thirty days in a silent retreat away from home; as a weekend or eight-day retreat; or as part of daily life at home, over several months.

Our spirituality can be strengthened by learning from our parents, family, and the "text" or context of our daily lives. Our families, no matter how imperfect, have a strong influence on the formation of our spirituality. The Paschal Mystery reminds us that the power of Christ will show us the way to truth. He will teach us, keep us, and help us through family pain, disagreements, and all the other experiences that come along with the messiness of life.

# My Faith

**SPIRITUALITY HAS BEEN** discussed a lot in this chapter. Describe your Catholic spirituality. What aspect of spirituality would you like to develop most this year? Take this informal survey and score it to see for yourself.

____ 1. My relationship with God is the biggest part of my faith.

____ 2. My faith is what motivates me to treat others kindly.

____ 3. I think about God a lot.

____ 4. My faith helps me stay hopeful.

____ 5. Going to Mass is an important way for me to stay close to God.

____ 6. My faith helps me determine what's right and wrong.

____ 7. I pay attention to the needs of others.

____ 8. When I look at the crucifix, it reminds me of what Jesus did for me.

____ 9. When I look at the crucifix, it challenges me to be more giving.

____ 10. My relationship with Jesus brings me inner peace.

____ 11. When I pray, I pray for others a lot.

____ 12. Doing the right thing is an important part of my faith.

On a scale of 1 to 5, rate each of these statements according to how true it is about you.

　　　　1 = Not True　　　　5 = Very True

Some of these statements will be more true for you than others. To create an accurate portrait of your spirituality, be as honest as you can, and take your time with each statement.

Scoring: Add up the total for 1, 3, 4, 5, 8, 10. _____

　　　　　Add up the total for 2, 6, 7, 9, 11, 12. _____

## Strengthening Your Spirituality:

After your teacher explains what each score means, write down which dimension of your spirituality you want to develop for yourself this year and what your first steps might be. Remember that you may decide to include something from this exercise as part of the report you give at the end of this course.

*Discipleship ... within the Body of Christ ... for the glory of God and the good of the world.*

We can increase our spirituality more formally through organized religious education and worship. Religious education teaches someone about a particular religion, be it Christian, Jewish, and/or Muslim, and it also teaches how to live out the practices of the religion. Formal religious education for Catholics takes place in parish catechetical programs for children, families, and adults of all ages as well as in Catholic school religion classes.

Our spirituality gives us strength to face everyday life. The liturgy and especially the Sacraments are keys to our spirituality as Christians. In his 1995 encyclical, *Evangelium Vitae* (The Gospel of Life),

Blessed Pope John Paul II made the connection between our spiritual lives and the Paschal Mystery.

The Sacraments make us sharers in divine life, and provide the spiritual strength necessary to experience life, suffering and death in their fullest meaning. Thanks to a genuine rediscovery and a better appreciation of the significance of these rites, our liturgical celebrations, especially celebrations of the Sacraments, will be ever more capable of expressing the full truth about birth, life, suffering and death, and will help us to live these moments as a participation in the Paschal Mystery of the Crucified and Risen Christ.

—Pope John Paul II, *Evangelium Vitae*, paragraph 84

**List** Name three essential elements of our spirituality.

**Elaborate** Why is self-examination important to spirituality?

## SECTION 4 REVIEW

### QUICK REVIEW

1. **Define** What is spirituality?

2. **Explain** Define the two directions of spirituality.

3. **Tell** Describe who helps us develop our spirituality.

4. **Name** What are the essential elements of spirituality?

### SELF-ASSESS

Which statement best reflects where you are now?

☐ I'm confident enough about the material in this section to be able to explain it to someone else.

☐ I have a good grasp of the material in this section, but I could use more review.

☐ I'm lost. I need help catching up before moving on.

# PRAYER

**Prayer for Families**

**Opening Prayer**
We bless your name, O Lord,
for sending your own incarnate Son,
to become part of a family,
so that, as he lived its life,
he would experience its worries and its joys.

We ask you, Lord,
to protect and watch over this family,
so that in the strength of your grace
its members may enjoy prosperity,
possess the priceless gift of your peace,
and, as the Church alive in the home,
bear witness in this world to your glory.

We ask this through Christ our Lord.

Amen

## TERMS

Use each of the following terms in a sentence that shows you know what the term means. You may include more than one term in a sentence.

Paschal Mystery

triptych

Passion Narratives

Resurrection Narratives

holiness

agape

philia

eros

conviction

spiritual poverty

Spiritual Exercises

## PEOPLE

Write a description of each person's significance in this chapter.

1. Joel

2. Blessed Miguel Pro

3. Jonah

4. Saint Teresa of Ávila

5. Saint Ignatius of Loyola

6. Solomon

7. Ezekiel

## UNDERSTANDING

Answer each question and complete each exercise.

### SECTION 1

1. **Analyze** Are there any aspects of the Paschal Mystery that you can especially relate to? Explain your answer.

2. **Conclude** What is the result of the Paschal Mystery, and why is it important?

3. **Connect** How are Old Testament and New Testament events connected by the Paschal Mystery?

4. **Analyze** How does the Paschal Mystery affect all people?

### SECTION 2

5. **Explain** What does it mean to be called to be holy?

6. **Relate** How is the call to holiness a call to love?

7. **Name** Which word meaning love describes friendship and can refer to the love between friends?

### SECTION 3

8. **Analyze** What image does Saint Paul use to describe the many parts of the Church?

9. **Interpret** What comes from being made in God's image and likeness? How is this idea linked to Catholic Social Teaching?

10. **Explain** The Paschal Mystery enables us to be convinced of what?

11. **Infer** What does Christian spirituality involve and recognize?
12. **Relate** Tell how the two dimensions of spirituality are part of your life.
13. **Discuss** Explain the role of the Holy Spirit in forming the spirituality of individuals.
14. **Infer** What is the ultimate obstacle that keeps people from developing spiritually?

## CONNECTING

**Visual** This photo was taken at World Youth Day.

What does this photo show about the spirituality of these people?

**Challenge** A friend from religion class says he just isn't getting the connection between the Paschal Mystery and how it matters in his life.

○ What do you tell your friend to help him understand?

○ Write out three things you could say or do.

**Imagine** You have been given the task to lessen spiritual poverty in your community.

○ How would you begin to do this?

○ Which groups of people would you expect to help you the most? Which would be most hesitant?

○ How would you rely on God's direction during the program?

○ How would you tell if your program was successful?

## SELF-ASSESS

**On Your Own** Make a list of the most important things you learned from this chapter. Select three things that represent your growth in understanding as you worked through this chapter. Write a paragraph explaining your choices.

**With a Partner** List what you found most helpful or interesting in this chapter as well as any other questions that have surfaced.

○ How does this photo show the goodness of creation?

○ Where do you find goodness in God's creation?

# The Goodness of
# Creation
## and the
## Fall From
# Grace

➚ Go to the student site at
**hs.osvcurriculum.com**

## YOU WILL

○ Survey the primeval stories of Israel.

○ Explore the two accounts of the Creation.

○ Identify the truths of God's Creation.

○ Explain that we call Jesus the "New Adam," and Mary the "New Eve."

○ Learn about the consequences of the Fall and Original Sin.

○ Recognize the problem of evil in the world.

## DEFINE

| | |
|---|---|
| theology | polytheistic |
| religious truth | monotheistic |
| Sheol | protoevangelium |
| theophany | covenant |
| anthropomorphic | |

# WHAT DOES IT MEAN?

## We are made in God's image.

My grandmother prays daily and she is the one who leads the prayer at big family meals like Thanksgiving. She is the image of God I have in my mind. She is always the last one to eat. She doesn't seem to be able to do enough for people. When we visit she always wants to know how she can make you more comfortable. She'll have sandwiches or a bag of leftovers when we leave. She serves others and that's what God wants.

I think of the homeless man we often see at a nearby intersection. He's stooped over when he stands, but is usually sitting. I don't think he has much energy. The cardboard sign he holds simply says, "Need food." When people give him something, he always tells them, "Thank you," and "God bless you." I see Jesus in the poor.

Whenever we need someone to sing in our class, we turn to this one student. She sings hymns, but she sings a lot of other music, too. She's the one we get to lead songs during weekly Masses. Recently, I found out she also sings opera. She doesn't share that with everyone because people usually don't like that kind of music. Still, she had several friends over to hear her sing opera. When she finished we were amazed at how beautiful it was. She sings with the voice of God.

## WHERE ARE YOU?

**Check the answer that best matches where you are today.**

*I understand the story of Creation.*
☐ Quite a bit   ☐ Somewhat   ☐ A little   ☐ Not at all

*I know that humans brought sin into the world.*
☐ Quite a bit   ☐ Somewhat   ☐ A little   ☐ Not at all

*I know the Catholic approach to Interpreting the Bible.*
☐ Quite a bit   ☐ Somewhat   ☐ A little   ☐ Not at all

*I believe in angels.*
☐ Quite a bit   ☐ Somewhat   ☐ A little   ☐ Not at all

*I think Biblical stories apply to modern life.*
☐ Quite a bit   ☐ Somewhat   ☐ A little   ☐ Not at all

# The Creation of the World

*How were the very first humans created?*

*Why is there so much evil in the world?*

*Does the Paschal Mystery hold any of these answers?*

It might seem easier to focus on the scientific answer: we were conceived by our mother and father and born from our mother's womb. It might be more difficult to see how we fit into God's Creation. It's no accident that we are here. We are part of God's plan. Let's take a look at what God has told us in the Bible about the beginning of Creation and our origin in the world.

The Book of Genesis, like all the books in the Bible, is God's revelation to us and addresses these questions. The word "genesis" *means* original or beginning. The first three chapters of Genesis, for example, tell about the beginning, or origin, of everything. These chapters were written by human authors who, inspired by the Holy Spirit, wrote according to the style of early peoples. These chapters do not describe things as historical records would today. They use symbolic or figurative literary tools that teach truths of faith. These accounts are very important ways for God, who inspired the writers of the Old Testament, to reveal himself and his relationship with the People of Israel.

The first three chapters of Genesis hold a unique place at the beginning of Scripture. From a literary point of view, they may have been written by diverse sources. These authors, however, were inspired by the Holy Spirit, and these three chapters at the start of Scripture convey these specific truths:

• Creation's origin and end in God

• Creation's order and goodness

• the vocation of mankind

• the drama of sin

• the hope of salvation

"Read in the light of Christ, within the unity of Sacred Scripture and in the living Tradition of the Church, these texts remain the principal source for catechesis on the mysteries of the 'beginning': creation, fall and promise of salvation" (CCC, 289).

While many literary forms are found in Scripture, we must always keep in mind that Sacred Scripture is inspired by the Holy Spirit. Interpreting and understanding Scripture then must be done through the same Holy "Spirit by whom it was written" (CCC, 111). The Second Vatican Council lists three points for the Church to properly interpret Scripture: the interpretation must consider the unity of the Old and New Testaments as the whole of Scripture; the interpretation must take into account the living Tradition of the entire Church; and the interpretation must be consistent with the truths of faith revealed by God (see CCC, 112-114; see Reference Section, p. 248).

Studying these texts from Genesis is an integral part of **theology**—studying and seeking to gain understanding of who God is. As a Church, we understand and celebrate certain things about God, especially as he is revealed in the Person of Jesus Christ. However, God is still, in fact, a mystery.

**theology** the study of God or of religious faith and practice based on Divine Revelation to help better understand who God is

# PRIMARY SOURCES

The human person is created in the image of God in the sense that he or she is capable to know and love the Creator in freedom. The capacity for knowledge, love, and freedom are keys to being an image of God. Precisely because they are images of God, all human beings have the dignity of a person. A person is not a something but a someone, capable of self-knowledge. Such a person is able to enter into deep relationships with God and other persons. God has given humans the capacity of sharing in his divine life. Therefore, I am more than what I do. I am someone who can freely know and love God and other people. What I do is meant to help me fulfill that calling.

Father Alfred McBride, O.Praem., *Truth for Your Mind, Love for Your Heart: Satisfying Your Hunger for God*, pp. 60–61.

> "The capacity for **knowledge, love,** and **freedom** are keys to being an image of God."
>
> —Father Alfred McBride

Who in your life reminds you that we are more than what we do?

How can this teaching help you focus your time and priorities?

What in culture makes it difficult to accept that we are more than what we do, or what we have?

Go to the student site at **hs.osvcurriculum.com**

As we mentioned in Chapter 1, this mystery requires a response from us: that we believe in it, celebrate the mystery, and, through living it, build a relationship with God. The theology found in Sacred Scripture then give us a richer, wider, and deeper understanding of the mystery of God. That continues through Tradition, as the Church helps us to understand God in our lives.

We cannot overstate the importance of learning about the stories of Creation. This primeval history helps us find answers to the questions that every human who ever lived has pondered: "'Where do we come from?' 'Where are we going?' 'What is our origin?' 'What is our end?' 'Where does everything that exists come from and where is it going?'" (CCC, 282)

We might get confused if we try to read the Creation accounts in the Book of Genesis in a historical or scientific way. It is not meant to provide a historical or scientific account of how the world was created. The Creation accounts reveal truths about which science and history can only speculate.

The human writers of Genesis expressed an important understanding of God. Guided by the Holy Spirit, they wrote what God wanted us to know about himself. Truth comes from God. Genesis is not necessarily scientific; it is about a deeper reality called **religious truth**. We are all obligated to seek truth, especially religious truth (see CCC, 2467).

These human writers used their own style and skills to write, but they wrote under the inspiration of the Holy Spirit to communicate God's Word. This divine inspiration makes God the true author of Scripture as he revealed what he wanted us to know about himself, all that he created, and, in particular, his plan for all people.

The Creation accounts focus on who God is and who we are in relation to God. The origin and end of Creation, like our origin and end, is in God. He is "the cause and the end of everything" (CCC, 46). We came from God and we will return to God. Already this truth implies an understanding of eternal life with God.

Genesis also shows us that the Spirit of God was present even in the midst of chaos and confusion. The Spirit of God, like a "mighty wind" covers the formless wasteland and chaos before the Creation of the world. When have we experienced God's Holy Spirit take the chaos and confusion in our lives and restore it to order and goodness?

"And God saw that it was good. And there was evening and there was morning . . . " (Genesis 1:12-13). This statement is repeated throughout the six days of Creation. It reveals the goodness and order of Creation. When do we see the goodness of God around us and within each person? How do we care for the goodness of Creation? The dominion given to humankind by God over the resources of the world carries the moral obligation of respect, especially toward future generations.

How does Creation reveal God's goodness? "The one true God, our Creator and Lord, can be known with certainty from his works by the natural light of human reason," (cf. Vatican Council I, can. § # 1: DS 3026) the *Catechism* tells us (CCC, 47). In the Book of Psalms, we read that "The Lord is good to all, and his compassion is over all that he has made" (Psalm 145:9).

The goodness and order of Creation culminates with the creation of man and woman made in God's image and likeness. This means we can use reason, and love (and hurt), and choose, and be responsible for our actions. No other earthly creature possesses these abilities. Being made in God's image gives us our human dignity.

God created everything for mankind. "God attached so much importance to his salvation that he did not spare his own Son for the sake of man" (CCC, 358). God never

**religious truth** the truth that comes from what God has revealed in divine and natural ways

## Key Truths of Creation

**1** The origin and end of Creation, like our origin and end, is God—the Father, Son, and Holy Spirit. God the Father made the universe and keeps all things in existence by his Word, the Son, and by the Holy Spirit, the giver of life.

**2** God did not need help to create; he alone created the universe. God created freely; nothing outside of him forced or prompted him. He created directly; he did not delegate the task to anyone. He made the universe and all that's in it to share and make his glory known.

**3** The Spirit of God, the source of everything that is good, is with us even in the midst of chaos and confusion.

**4** Creation reveals an order and goodness—God's first and universal sign of his almighty love and wisdom, an announcement of the "plan of his loving goodness" (CCC, 315).

**5** The goodness and order of Creation culminates with the creation of man and woman made in God's image and likeness. God made his creatures, most especially humans, for glory—to know and share in his truth, goodness, and beauty.

**6** The vocation or calling of man and woman is found in the call to holiness, to be whole and good, to love and serve God and neighbor as we love ourselves.

**7** The drama of sin and the hope of salvation can be found in the Original Sin of Adam and Eve and the salvation experienced through the New Adam, found in the Person of Jesus and his Paschal Mystery. The goal of God's plan is our new life in Christ.

when we love others. When we treat each other with dignity, we are treating the image and likeness of God with dignity. That's a big part of our call to holiness.

The vocation or calling of man and woman is found in the call to holiness, to be whole and good. This call to holiness is understood to be the Great Commandment to love God: "You shall love the Lord your God with all your heart, and with all your soul, and with all your mind" (Matthew 22:36). It also includes loving our neighbor as we love ourselves. We were created to love by a God who is love. "God's very being is Truth and Love" (CCC, 231). How do we specifically respond to this call to holiness on a daily basis? The *Catechism* calls charity, or love, the "soul of holiness" (CCC, 826). We are all called to love.

> Love, in fact, is the vocation which includes all others; it's a universe of its own, comprising all time and space—it's eternal![9]
>
> —CCC, 826

stops working until we are united with him in Heaven. This is a mystery revealed in the life of Christ, who now sits at the right hand of the Father, and who unites all humans to God.

We are truly united through Christ as human and spiritual beings with a body and soul. We are human bodies because we have souls (see CCC, 364). "The unity of soul and body is so profound that one has to consider the soul to be the 'form' of the body"[8] (CCC, 365). God creates every soul immediately. The soul is immortal, meaning it doesn't end when the body dies. The Church teaches that the body and soul will reunite at the final Resurrection (see CCC, 366).

We show our love to God by prioritizing our lives based on his will for us, by praying and being part of the Church, by learning more about him through Scripture and Tradition, and by trying to live like Jesus did. And we are showing our love to God

The Genesis story doesn't stop there. After the first people disobey God, we read of the *offspring of the woman* that will *crush* the head of the serpent. This refers to the hope of salvation that we know to be the salvation experienced through the New Adam, in the Person of Jesus and the Paschal Mystery—his Passion, Death, Resurrection, and Ascension.

Later in this chapter, we'll learn more about Original Sin and the promise of salvation. "Our salvation flows from God's initiative of love for us, because 'he loved us and sent his Son to be the expiation for our sins.'

### DISCUSS

○ How do we as individuals, and members of the Church, as the "Body of Christ," pattern our lives after Jesus in our world and communities today?

(*I Jn* 4:10). Jesus freely offered himself for our salvation" (CCC, 620-621). We are meant to pattern our lives after the image of God's Son made man, the "image of the invisible God" (Colossians 1:15).

We often talk about the Father's role in the work of Creation, but it is equally true that the Trinity—Father, Son, and Holy Spirit—is the principle of Creation. The Apostle's Creed begins with belief in God, "the Father Almighty, Creator of heaven and earth," and the Nicene Creed adds "of all things visible and invisible" (*Roman Missal*).

**Identify** What kind of truth is found in the first chapters of Genesis?

**Elaborate** How should we look at the early chapters in Genesis?

## Two Creation Accounts

The Book of Genesis begins with two Creation accounts that were written under the inspiration and guidance of the Holy Spirit. The first Creation account, Genesis 1:1–2:23 contains the fixed order of the world created in six days and God resting on the seventh day. It emphasizes the order and goodness of God the Creator.

In the second verse of Genesis, we recognize the "mighty wind" of God's Spirit present. Just as the Book of Genesis begins with "In the beginning . . ." so does the Gospel according to John. "In the beginning was the Word, and the Word was with God, and the Word was God. He was in the beginning with God. All things came into being through him, and without him not one thing came into being. What has come into being in him was life, and the life was the light of all people. The light shines in the darkness, and the darkness did not overcome it." (John 1:1-5). These verses help us to understand how all of Creation was the common work of the Trinity, through Christ and the Holy Spirit, one in being with the Father.

Saint Irenaeus also speaks of the work of the Trinity in the Creation of the world.

"'There exists but one God . . . he is the Father, God, the Creator, the author, the giver of order. He made all things by himself, that is, by his Word and by his Wisdom', 'by the Son and the Spirit' who, so to speak, are 'his hands'.[10] Creation is the common work of the Holy Trinity" (CCC, 292).

In ancient Hebrew cosmology, snow, hail, and rain were considered above the dome or sky. Cosmology is the understanding of the origin and structure of the universe. The first account describes how elements fall to Earth through floodgates in the sky. Ancient Hebrew cosmology described the ground as sitting on pillars that were sunk into the sea, and deep below the ground was **Sheol**, the abode of the dead entered through the grave.

God rested after finishing with the work of Creation and blessed the seventh day making it holy (see Genesis 2:1-3). This is why the Jewish Sabbath is regarded as a day of rest and prayer. Within the Jewish tradition, the Sabbath lasts from sundown on Friday evening until sundown on Saturday. While Friday night begins the Sabbath, Saturday is the day of the Sabbath.

**Name** Who created the world?

**Explain** What is the Sabbath?

**Sheol** in ancient Hebrew cosmology this was the underworld, the dwelling place of the dead

## The Sabbath Day

In addition to God resting on the seventh-day of Creation, the Book of Exodus adds more details to the Sabbath day when the Third Commandment is given to Moses. "Remember the sabbath day, and keep it holy. Six days you shall labor and do all your work. But the seventh day is a sabbath to the Lord your God; you shall not do any work—you, your son or your daughter, your male or female slave, your livestock, or the alien resident in your towns. For in six days the Lord made heaven and earth, the sea, and all that is in them, but rested the seventh day; therefore the Lord blessed the sabbath day and consecrated it" (Exodus 20:8-11).

Jewish law in the Old Testament emphasized the seriousness and importance of the Sabbath as a day of rest and holiness ordained by God. The Book of Deuteronomy adds a reminder of when the people of Israel were slaves in Egypt, before God rescued them, when the Sabbath calls for the rest of male and female slaves. "Remember that you were a slave in the land of Egypt, and the Lord your God brought you out from there with a mighty hand and an outstretched arm; therefore the Lord your God commanded you to keep the sabbath day" (Deuteronomy 5:15).

Today we find examples of how care is taken outside the religious community to respect the practices of the Jewish Sabbath. In some hospitals, for example, a special Shabbat elevator automatically stops on every floor to prevent Jewish family members and patients from having to push the elevator buttons on the Sabbath.

From the time of the Apostles, our Christian tradition replaced the Sabbath with Sunday as the Lord's Day. It was the day of Christ's Resurrection, which is the first day of the week and the memorial of the first day of Creation. It is the eighth day, on which Jesus declares after the Sabbath that this is the day the Lord has made. It is the day we celebrate the Lord's Supper, the banquet at which all faithful encounter Christ (see CCC, 1166).

## The Power of God's Spoken Word

God's Word in the first Creation account causes the universe to be created out of nothing. It is an active, dynamic, and creative Word. "Let there be light; and there was light" (Genesis 1:3). The opening Creation story describes God creating with his Word, his Son, the Second Person of the Trinity.

We see in the first Creation account that the diversity of creatures—each with their own unique goodness—were part of God's plan. Each has an order in role and purpose, interdependent, needing one another and the functions each serve. All of this Creation was made to benefit humans, for people, and through us all, Creation is intended for the glory of God.

Man and woman are not created to be alone, solitary beings living in isolation, to get by or make do without needing each other. Not only do Adam and Eve need each other, they need all that God has created to live and thrive. We find in this partnership of man and woman the first type of community and relationship between people, a communion.

# JUSTICE AND DISCIPLESHIP

Jesus tells us that discipleship involves praying to the Father, studying his teachings and following his example, participating in the Eucharist, and living the virtues. He also calls us to act for justice.

**MOST PEOPLE KNOW** that the Catholic Church is opposed to abortion. However, not everyone understands *why.*

Love and human dignity are the foundations of all social justice teaching in the Church. "The equality of men concerns their dignity as persons and the rights that flow from it" (CCC, 1945). We are called to respect others as if they were ourselves.

> *Human life must be respected and protected absolutely from the moment of conception. From the first moment of existence, a human being must be recognized as having the rights of a person—among which is the inviolable right of every innocent being to life.*[11]
>
> —CCC, 2270

The reason the Church teaches what she does about abortion has to do with the question of when life begins. Does life begin at the moment of conception, when the sperm fertilizes the egg? Does life begin sometime during the pregnancy, between conception and birth? Or does life begin at the moment of birth?

*Life begins at the moment of conception.* Life comes from God, and therein, a person's human dignity is present from the very moment of conception. Direct abortion is actively and intentionally ending a life created by God, and thus disrespects the human dignity of that unborn child.

As discussions about abortion tend toward the woman's body, personal choice, or the circumstances surrounding the conception, the Church consistently reminds us that in all cases, we are still talking about a human life—a creation of God endowed with dignity which must be respected.

Many women with unplanned pregnancies may worry about being judged by society if they do, in fact, choose life. But abortion is always an immoral choice and a grave sin. This does not mean we should ever judge a person who faces an unplanned pregnancy or a woman who has had an abortion. Abortion is always an injustice, but we must trust in God's mercy and love the sinner. In fact, the Church offers Project Gabriel to assist those who are pregnant and don't know what to do, and Project Rachel to counsel those who have had an abortion. We are called to love and offer compassion and support. Only God knows the condition of someone's heart and mind. Only God can perform this kind of judgment.

### As a matter of justice:

**Learn** more about pro-life issues from the United States Conference of Catholic Bishops Pro-Life Activities office.

**Volunteer** to assist with Project Gabriel or Project Rachel in your parish, or contact a local crisis pregnancy center. Hold a baby-items drive to help those who choose life.

**Advocate** by learning what your local diocese does to promote the importance of respecting human dignity, and figure out some way to participate in getting this message out.

↗ Go to the student site at
**hs.osvcurriculum.com**

**Life comes from God.**

You can be for justice without being a disciple, but you cannot be a disciple without being for justice.

We are truly "in communion" with another when we give of ourselves to someone, and when we allow ourselves to receive from the other. This is why Jesus gives us his New Commandment: "Just as I have loved you, you also should love one another" (John 13:34). This gift of one's self to another is clear in the Sacrament of Marriage as well as in the priesthood and religious life. These vocations exist for the perfection of charity and to permit people to answer Christ's call as individuals.

○ Discuss examples of how someone can give of himself or herself to another in accordance with their vocation and state of life.

○ How does this gift of self allow them to be in *communion* with one another?

The Second Book of Maccabees contains a heartbreaking story of a mother who is about to see her seven sons killed before her. Instead of turning against God, she speaks to her sons and gives them hope about the power of God to make them live again.

> I do not know how you came into being in my womb. It was not I who gave you life and breath, nor I who set in order the elements within each of you. Therefore the Creator of the world, who shaped the beginning of humankind and devised the origin of all things, will in his mercy give life and breath back to you again. . . . Look at the heaven and the earth and see everything that is in them, and recognize that God did not make them out of things that existed.
>
> —2 Maccabees 7:22-23, 28

The New Testament affirms the hope we have in our knowledge of the Trinity. As God creates out of nothing, "for God all things are possible" (Mark 10:27). Since all things are possible for God, then the Holy Spirit can heal any of us truly contrite sinners and create in us a pure heart no matter what we've done. Hope for us should be unwavering. Since all things are possible for God, then we can stay hopeful during difficult times. And all things are possible for God, then even those who hate each other may someday come to peace. Not only that, but through the Resurrection, we know God gives eternal life to those who have died. And there is hope for those who do not know God. Through his Word, God gives the light of faith to those who do not know him (see CCC, 298).

The Prophet Isaiah also speaks of the creative power of God's Word. The rain and snow makes the Earth fertile, and God's Word produces good things according to his will (see Isaiah 55:10-11). We know that the will of God is spoken in a unique and definitive way through the life and teachings of Jesus, the Son of God. His will is achieved by how we love and serve God and one another, following Christ's example. It is how we answer the call to holiness.

> By the word of the Lord the heavens were made, and all their host by the breath of his mouth. . . .
> Let all the earth fear the Lord; let all the inhabitants of the world stand in awe of him.
> For he spoke, and it came to be;
> he commanded, and it stood firm.
>
> —Psalm 33:6, 8-9

The Book of Wisdom expresses a prayer of Solomon about the world being created through God's wisdom. "With you is wisdom, she who knows your works and was present when you made the world" (Wisdom 9:9).

**Recall** How does a mother in the Second Book of Maccabees give witness to God who can create things out of nothing?

**Relate** What are some implications for us that God created things out of nothing?

## GO TO THE SOURCE

**Psalm 104 echoes the thought of the writer of Wisdom.** It speaks of God [as] the Creator.

Read *Psalm 104*.

○ Make a list of at least ten things that God made and mention the purpose as written in the Psalm for which God created it.

○ Now list five things you are glad God created and why you are happy about that.

### QUICK REVIEW

**1a. Infer** Why are stories of Creation called "primeval"?

**b. Define** What is theology?

**2a. Summarize** Briefly tell the first Creation story.

**b. Tell** What is the origin of resting on the Sabbath day?

**3a. Explain** What is the role of God's Word in the Creation stories?

**b. Tell** How does God's Word affect us today?

**Pray** Compose a short prayer thanking God for the variety of Creation.

### SELF-ASSESS

Which statement best reflects where you are now?

☐ I'm confident enough about the material in this section to be able to explain it to someone else.

☐ I have a good grasp of the material in this section, but I could use more review.

☐ I'm lost. I need help catching up before moving on.

# Creation Provides Evidence of God

**N**ature provides constant evidence of God. He has made himself known from the earliest times to point the way to heavenly salvation (see CCC, 54).

An account from Exodus reveals God, along with his holy name, in the burning bush to Moses (see Exodus 3:1-2). Mountains were also places to encounter God. Mount Horeb/Mount Sinai, for example, is called the mountain of God. The desert was seen as a place of being tested by God or of finding him. This is indicated in the story of the Israelites in the desert for forty years, and the temptations of Jesus in the desert (see Matthew 4:1-11).

In the Old Testament, we hear about how God saves Israel by the parting of the Red Sea (see Exodus 14:20-22). He feeds the Israelites in the desert by providing quail and manna (see Exodus 16:4-35), and draws water from a rock (see Exodus 17:1-7).

**theophany** God revealing himself to humans through nature, or a visible appearance of God.

Each of these stories is a **theophany**, or a manifestation of God's presence experienced through nature. God can appear in a human form, a burning bush, or a gentle breeze.

In the Book of Leviticus the glory of the Lord is a fire that "came out from the Lord and consumed the burnt offering and the fat on the altar; and when all the people

## GO TO THE SOURCE

**In these two passages** God reveals himself to humans through nature.

Read *Exodus 19:16-25* and *24:12-18*.
○ What forms of nature manifest God in each theophany?

○ Why do you think these theophanies took place when they did?

○ How did people, especially Moses, react to the presence of God?

saw it, they shouted and fell on their faces" (Leviticus 9:24).

The Book of Deuteronomy also speaks of the image of God revealed through fire. Mount Horeb blazed "up to the very heavens, shrouded in dark clouds. Then the Lord spoke to you out of the fire" (Deuteronomy 4:11-12). "For the Lord your God is a devouring fire, a jealous God" (Deuteronomy 4:24).

> Praise the Lord from the earth,
>  you sea monsters and all deeps,
> fire and hail, snow and frost,
>  stormy wind fulfilling his command!
> Mountains and all hills,
>  fruit trees and all cedars!
> Wild animals and all cattle,
>  creeping things and flying birds!
>
> —Psalm 148:7-10

Another well-known theophany that reveals God's existence in nature and Creation is found in Psalm 8:3: "When I look at your heavens, the work of your fingers, the moon and the stars that you have established. . . ." And in the New Testament, we read this evidence of God

Saint Catherine's Monastery (Greek Orthodox) sits at the base of Mount Sinai.

**The Book of Genesis mentions four rivers that meet in the Garden of Eden. Two of the rivers—the Tigris and the Euphrates—still exist.**

- The locations of the other two rivers—the Pishon and the Gihon—are not known. Some have speculated that the Pishon once flowed from Kuwaiti highlands, but it is now a dry riverbed. Others have made guesses about the Gihon, and have claimed that all four rivers fed into the Persian Gulf. Some have even suggested that the Garden of Eden could have existed in the Gulf.

- The Tigris and Euphrates both begin about fifty miles apart in eastern Turkey. They wind through northern Syria and Iraq almost meeting each other in Bahgdad. They finally converge near Basrah, Iraq, seventy-five miles from the Persian Gulf.

- In world history class, you may have learned that the lower region between the rivers was the ancient cradle of civilization known as Mesopotamia.

The Tigris-Euphrates region is an environmentally endangered ecosystem.

# Faith & Culture

➚ Go to the student site at **hs.osvcurriculum.com**

in nature: "Ever since the creation of the world his eternal power and divine nature, invisible though they are, have been understood and seen through the things he has made" (Romans 1:20).

> If you will only heed his every commandment that I am commanding you today—loving the Lord your God, and serving him with all your heart and with all your soul—then he will give the rain for your land in its season, the early rain and the later rain, and you will gather in your grain, your wine, and your oil; and he will give grass in your fields for your livestock, and you will eat your fill. Take care, or you will be seduced into turning away, serving other gods and worshiping them, for the anger of the Lord will be kindled against you and he will shut up the heavens.
>
> —Deuteronomy 11:13-17

The first Creation account does not contain the story of the Fall or Original Sin. It continues the prayerful pattern of a refrain one would hear at a Temple prayer service. One can understand the power of the story in the telling and reading of it and why it is read at every Easter Vigil when the newly baptized become new creations. Our creation story defines who we are and whose we are. God blesses his creation with the words, "Be fruitful and multiply" (Genesis 1:28). When all of Creation is given to humanity, humanity now has the responsibility to take care of Creation.

**Name** Give an example of a theophany.

**Infer** Tell one way in which we can experience God through nature.

## Second Creation Account

The second Creation account is covered in Genesis 2:4–3:24. This text begins with the creation of man and how the world is built up around him. Two key characteristics can be found in the Creation account: (1) A sacred name is given for God—a Hebrew name that translates to "I am that I am." (2) God seems to be characterized as **anthropomorphic**, or having human characteristics. The Church teaches that God creates using his hands and breath (see

**anthropomorphic** described as attributing human characteristics to an object or a being who is not human

**The second Creation account** attributes human characteristics to God.

Read *Genesis 2:4-25*

○ Identify specific anthropomorphic features and actions that the writer gives God.

○ Why does God create woman? How does he create her?

○ What Sacrament is implied in this story?

CCC, 703-704). "The Word of God and his Breath are at the origin of being and life of every creature"[12] (CCC, 703).

This second Creation account emphasizes that the one God begins with the creation of man, and the rest of the world and all living things. Together, man and woman are to be responsible for God's Creation as stewards of God (see CCC, 373). Man and woman possess an inalienable dignity, which comes to them because they are created "in the image of God" (CCC, 369).

God created man and woman "to be a communion of persons, in which each can be 'helpmate' to the other, for they

are equal as persons . . . and complementary as masculine and feminine" (CCC, 372). Both genders reflect the power and tenderness of God, but in different ways that come together in the Sacrament of Marriage. Jesus emphasized the purity of the marriage union when he addressed the Commandment not to commit adultery. He said every man who even looks at a woman with lust has already committed adultery in his heart. "Therefore what God has joined together, let no one separate" (Matthew 19:6).

Both Creation accounts, though different, complement one another and are the foundation of the Israelite's understanding of God and his relationship with the created world and human beings. This is different from Babylonian and Mesopotamian **polytheistic** belief in many gods. The truth as revealed to the writers of the Old Testament is that there is one, true God. The **monotheistic** Israelite theology meant believing in one God.

**polytheistic** believing in many gods

**monotheistic** believing in one God

## SECTION 2 REVIEW

### QUICK REVIEW

**1a. Infer** Why would the Bible include songs of praise to God?

**b. Define** What is a theophany? Given an example of one.

**2a. Explain** What is anthropomorphism and how is it shown in Creation accounts?

**3. Summarize** Retell the second Creation account.

**Listen and Discuss** With a few classmates, discuss the following statements.

○ How are the meanings of *make* and *create* similar and different?

○ Look up the dictionary definitions of "create." Which one is closest to the Biblical meaning? Why do you think that the meaning has changed over time?

○ How can people join in God's creative work?

**Pray** Compose a short prayer thanking God for the variety of Creation.

### SELF-ASSESS

Which statement best reflects where you are now?

☐ I'm confident enough about the material in this section to be able to explain it to someone else.

☐ I have a good grasp of the material in this section, but I could use more review.

☐ I'm lost. I need help catching up before moving on.

# The Fall and the Promise

The Book of Genesis speaks of the origin and presence of sin and evil in the world through the Original Sin and the Fall of Adam and Eve.

The simple rule that God gave to Adam, before Eve was created, involved recognizing and respecting limits and trusting in the reason for the limits. Humans were created with freedom, but freedom does not mean having the license to do whatever you want to do (see CCC, 396). Freedom allows for our choices to be our own. Yet, this very freedom to be genuine allows for the possibility to abuse our freedom. You may have experienced this in your friendships over the years. When a friend freely chooses to do something helpful for you, it strengthens the relationship. However, when a friend is unreliable or lets you down, it can weaken your friendship (see CCC, 1731).

> Man is obliged to follow the moral law, which urges him "to do what is good and avoid what is evil" (cf. GS 16). This law makes itself heard in his conscience.
>
> —CCC, 1713

Adam and Eve's choice is a sin of disobedience toward God and a rejecting of a God-centered life for a self-centered life.

All sin after this event will be of disobedience toward God and lack of trust in God's goodness.

Saint Maximus the Confessor explained that man and woman wanted to "be like God," but "without God, before God, and not in accordance with God"[13] (CCC, 398). Tempted by the devil, they were seduced by the power of becoming like God.

The story of the Fall shows man and woman abusing the freedom God gave them at the very start of human history. Man "lofted himself up against God and

## GO TO THE SOURCE

**Most of us know the story of how Eve** was enticed by the serpent to eat the forbidden fruit.

Read *Genesis Chapter 3*.

○ Where was Adam when the exchange between Eve and the serpent occurred? Why do you think Adam didn't say anything to stop Eve? Why do you think Adam didn't refuse to eat the fruit?

○ Think about the last time you got in trouble for doing something you were explicitly told not to do. What are the similarities and differences between the dialogue in the Garden and the dialogue of reckoning which you have had in your own life?

**What happened after Adam and Eve ate the forbidden fruit?**

Read *Genesis 3:7-22*.

○ What anthropomorphic images do you notice the author attributes to God in Genesis 3:8?

○ What religious truths do you notice regarding human tendencies?

○ When do you take responsibility for your actions? When might you be tempted do you hide, or to blame others?

sought to attain his goal apart from him" (CCC, 415). The more good that a person does, the freer that person becomes. The only true freedom, the *Catechism* says, is in doing what is good and just (see CCC, 1731-1742). "The choice to disobey and do evil is an abuse of freedom and leads to 'the slavery of sin'"[14] (CCC, 1733).

The original holiness and original justice that Adam had received from God was lost, "not only for himself but for all human beings" (CCC, 416). This deprivation, or lacking, and its consequences passed down for all future generations, is Original Sin. It is transferred through a wounded human nature, but not by imitation (see CCC, 419).

### SUMMARIZE

○ Prepare a one-page summary for a discussion on free will and the limits that God asks humans to face on a daily basis.

### After the Fall: The Consequences

We read that after the Fall, our first parents covered themselves with fig leaves and loincloths. This illustrates their sense of shame in knowing they disobeyed God. They both show the human tendency not to accept responsibility for their actions.

The consequences of the Fall speak to the origin of many things. Our pain and struggles in life were not part of life with God in the Garden. The sin of our first parents shows the human tendency to do what we

want, when we want it, how we want it, and then to deflect any and all personal responsibility. The consequences of this assertion of independence involve more work and more pain than what God had originally intended.

Adam and Eve commit three sins that, like all sin, were not present prior to the Fall. These include an inclination to sin due to "the pleasure of the senses [lust, gluttony], covetousness for earthly goods [greed and selfishness], and self-assertion [pride], contrary to the dictates of reason" (CCC, 377). These are the same sins that the devil later uses to tempt Jesus in the desert.

In the second Creation story of Genesis, we are told that the serpent will strike at the heel of the offspring of the woman. Often, we are tempted at our weakest moments and in the most vulnerable places. Typical weak moments are when we are *hungry, angry, lonely,* and *tired.* Each of these words begins with a letter that spells the acronym "H.A.L.T." When we are feeling these four things we need to stop and take care of ourselves. That will help us facing any temptation or difficulty in life. Eat something if you are hungry. Talk to a friend or family member if you are angry or lonely. And, most importantly, get a good night's sleep, or take a nap if you are tired or frustrated. It's amazing the difference a good night's sleep makes.

### The First Gospel

We read in Genesis 3:14-15 that the serpent will be banned from all the other animals, crawling on its belly all the

### DEVELOP

○ Memorize H.A.L.T. and ask others in class if they remember it, or come up with another acronym that can remind you of the most important way to handle difficulties and temptations in life.

○ Tell friends outside of class or family members about H.A.L.T. Share their reactions with the class.

## GLOBAL PERSPECTIVES

God not only created the Earth and the physical world, but also the spiritual or angelic. Scripture contains many accounts of angels including the angel who guards the tree of life when Adam and Eve are expelled from the Garden of Eden. Angels are servants and messengers of God. "As purely spiritual creatures angels have intelligence and will: they are personal and immortal creatures, surpassing in perfection all the visible creatures, as the splendor of their glory bears witness"[15] (CCC, 330).

Angels give glory to God at all times, and work together for the good of all. They are an important part of God's plans to save us. There are also fallen angels who became evil through their own actions. They rejected God and one in particular, Satan, "has sinned from the beginning" (CCC, 392). "'The reason the Son of God appeared was to destroy the works of the devil'"[16] (CCC, 394). It was after being tempted by Satan in the desert that good angels served Jesus.

Later angels were with Jesus in the Garden of Gethsemane as he prayed. They also proclaimed the Good News of Christ's birth and

Resurrection. The Feast Day of the Archangels—Michael, Gabriel, and Raphael—is celebrated September 29. The Feast Day of the Guardian Angels is October 2.

○ Read and summarize two of these biblical accounts involving angels: Genesis 19:1-28; Genesis 22:1-19; Exodus 23:20-26; Judges 13:6-8, 10-24; Matthew 1:18-24; Matthew 28:1-10; Luke 1:5-38.

↗ Go to the student site at hs.osvcurriculum.com

days of its life. God places mutual distrust between the serpent and the woman and her offspring. The offspring of the woman will strike at the head of the serpent while the offspring of the serpent will strike at the heel of the offspring of the woman.

The Church sees the woman as Mary, the Mother of Christ and the "new Eve." The serpent is interpreted to be the devil and representative of all that is evil. It prefigures the battle between light and darkness, between good and evil. The Church views this passage as the "first announcement of the Messiah and Redeemer, of a battle between the serpent and the Woman, and of the final victory of a descendent of hers" (CCC, 410). If you closely examine many statues of Mary, you may notice that she is depicted standing atop a serpent, representing this final victory.

The account of the fall in Genesis 3 uses figurative language, but affirms a primeval event, a deed that took place at the beginning of the history of man.[17] Revelation gives us the certainty of faith that the whole of human history is marked by the original fault freely committed by our first parents.[18]

—CCC, 390

After this passage in Genesis, known as the **protoevangelium** (Greek: Proto=First; Evangelium=Good News or Gospel), other consequences of the Fall are given. God causes women to experience the pain of childbirth, "in pain you shall bring forth children" (Genesis 3:16). Humans face the consequences of having to work, sweat, and toil in the fields. Suffering, pain, death, and human mortality now become part of human life. We also know that the inclination to sin is now part of human reality. This wounded human nature means we can make errors in judgment and decisions. Concupiscence—this inclination to sin—is a tendency toward what is evil or morally wrong when using our free will. We are weak, but we are not evil.

This verse is a familiar one: "You are dust, and to dust you shall return." These words from Genesis 3:19 are heard at funerals, and also are one of the statements that can be said when ashes are placed on the foreheads of people on Ash Wednesday. Although death was to be a consequence of eating the fruit from the tree of knowledge of good and evil, it is not an immediate death. It is the death that occurs at the end of each person's life, which again, was not part of God's original plan for us.

**protoevangelium** refers to the passage in Genesis describing God's words to the serpent and woman and literally means first Gospel

The story of the Fall ends with the woman being named Eve, meaning the "mother of all living" (Genesis 3:20). Despite their blatant disobedience, God still displays care and concern, making garments for Adam and Eve and clothing them before banishing them from the Garden. The reasons for the existence of sin, suffering, and death come from the disobedience of Adam and Eve, our first parents, who represent all of humanity.

> After his fall, man was not abandoned by God. On the contrary, God calls him and in a mysterious way heralds the coming victory over evil and his restoration from his fall.[19]
>
> —CCC, 410

In his Letters, Saint Paul repeatedly makes reference to Jesus as the "New Adam," and points out that the Paschal Mystery responds to the consequence of death. "For

## APPLY

- Do you recognize and respect limits or do you push limits?
- What are the consequences?
- Do you trust in the reason for the limits or do you question everything?
- What are the implications?

since death came through a human being, the resurrection of the dead has also come through a human being; for as all die in Adam, so all will be made alive in Christ." (1 Corinthians 15:21-22). This new life is found in the Church through Baptism.

**Name** What resulted from Adam and Eve's disobedience and the resulting consequences?

**Explain** How is the protoevangelium seen as the first Gospel?

## SECTION 3 REVIEW

### QUICK REVIEW

**1a. Summarize** Tell the story of the Fall.

**b. Explain** Which order from God did Adam and Eve break?

**c. Tell** Which truths are contained in the story of the Fall?

**2a. Contrast** According to the second Creation account, how did Adam and Eve's lives change because of the Fall?

**b. List** Which sins do we inherit because of the Fall?

**3a. Define** What is the Protoevangelium, and why is it important?

**b. Connect** What event is affirmed in Genesis 3?

**4a. Interpret** Why do we call Jesus the "New Adam"?

**b. Analyze** How is Original Sin similar and different from other sins?

**Listen and Discuss** In a small group, discuss situations you have seen or heard about where good things came from hardships.

- What lessons could be learned from the situations and their outcomes?
- Talk about how your view of the situation changed from the beginning to the end of the events.

**Pray** Write a short prayer thanking God for strength to endure hardships and the lessons that you have learned through them.

### SELF-ASSESS

Which statement best reflects where you are now?

☐ I'm confident enough about the material in this section to be able to explain it to someone else.

☐ I have a good grasp of the material in this section, but I could use more review.

☐ I'm lost. I need help catching up before moving on.

# Stories after the Fall

Many people point to evil and sin as a problem with God. If God is so powerful and loving why does he allow sin and suffering? Why does evil flourish? These questions are not easy to answer.

Ultimately, to understand and have hope, we need to have faith in a God who allows evil to exist and does not prevent it. God created us in love, to be free. The consequence of this certainly allows for humans to abuse our freedom with choosing sin and evil. However, if God prevented the consequences of human actions, then we wouldn't truly be free. Rather than expecting God to prevent evil, we need to look at each human being as having the responsibility and ability to do good and avoid evil.

God can and does bring good out of evil through his power and mercy. Saint Thomas Aquinas said nothing stops us from doing great things, even after we have sinned. "God permits evil in order to draw forth some greater good. Thus St. Paul says, 'Where sin increased, grace abounded all the more'; and the Exultet sings, 'O happy fault, . . . which gained for us so great a Redeemer'"[20] (CCC, 412).

## Evil in the Scriptures

We find in the Old Testament several examples of suffering. One is the story of Job. Job is a good and honest man whose faith is tested. The story of Job challenged the thinking that people who suffer must have done something to deserve it.

First, everything is taken away from Job. Once considered wealthy by the standards of the day, he loses his livestock, children,

> ## DISCUSS
>
> Here are three quotations from the *Catechism* that adress the topic of evil in the world:
>
> 1. *"There is not a single aspect of the Christian message that is not in part an answer to the question of evil"* (CCC, 309).
> 2. "We must therefore approach the question of the origin of evil by fixing the eyes of our faith on him who alone is its conqueror"[21] (CCC, 385).
> 3. "Sin is present in human history; any attempt to ignore it or to give this dark reality other names would be futile" (CCC, 386).
> ○ Choose one of the above quotations and explain how it helps you best understand the problem of evil in the world.

and house. His response to this great evil and calamity is simply, "Naked I came from my mother's womb, and naked shall I return there; the Lord gave, and the Lord has taken away; blessed be the name of the Lord" (Job 1:21).

Many people regard famine as an evil that exists because of unequal distribution of resources.

In the second trial, Job suffers great bodily affliction, but his life is spared. Job was struck with boils from the bottom of his feet to the top of his head. Job's wife confronts him in his plight and says, "Do you still persist in your integrity? Curse God, and die." But Job responds to her, "Shall we receive the good at the hand of God, and not receive the bad?" (Job 2:9-10). Through all this Job said nothing sinful.

Job is then visited by friends who suspect him of being a sinner and deserving his affliction as punishment from God. Job holds to his innocence. At one point Job says, "I will say to God, Do not condemn me; let me know why you contend against me. Does it seem good to you to oppress, to despise the work of your hands and favor the schemes of the wicked? Your hands fashioned and made me; and now you turn and destroy me. Remember that you fashioned me like clay; and will you turn me to dust again?" (Job 10:2-3, 8-9). Job is referring to the second Creation story.

The story concludes with God, in the voice of a storm, responding to Job's questions. God asks Job questions that only God can answer. Job, in humility, admits he does not understand the mysteries of life and suffering. He repents for questioning God. God criticizes the friends of Job who tried to explain Job's suffering by blaming him. Because of Job's perseverance and faithfulness, God gives him back everything he lost, including twice as much as he had before. God blesses Job who lives to be 140 years old.

If someone says a person has "the patience of Job," it usually refers to the ability to withstand suffering or great hardships. The suffering of the innocent is still a very difficult problem to understand. When we see bad things happen to innocent people, we should not become disillusioned or remain idle. In those cases where we can actively help others, we should do all that we can.

And in those cases when we cannot actively help others, we should pray for them.

The ultimate evil of the Crucifixion and Death of Jesus led to his Resurrection and our salvation through his Paschal Mystery (see CCC, 312). An ultimate goodness for us as Catholics is to remain faithful to God and choose to do acts of goodness even when faced with evil and suffering. Just as Jesus shared in the pain and suffering of our humanity, we can share in his divinity through the grace of Baptism and the other

## IDENTIFY

Think of a time in your own life when you witnessed good coming out of an evil situation.
○ Summarize what happened.

Sacraments. Every experience of evil and suffering holds within it the opportunity to enter into the Paschal Mystery by putting aside our momentary situation and choosing an eternal vision of love and life. We can share in the Resurrection of Christ by embracing his life and Death. When we embrace the Paschal Mystery, and enter into it through the Sacraments and in our daily lives, we experience new life and hope in our own lives.

**Recall** What does Job lose in the beginning of his story?

**Explain** What does God do when Job's friends say he has himself to blame for his suffering?

# My Faith

**IN THIS CHAPTER** you see that the primeval stories of the Book of Genesis point to many truths of faith. One deeper truth is that God is present in the midst of everything. These accounts show the earliest belief of the human race. No matter how much the world changes, shifts, or breaks, God is always present.

Reflect back on the different ways God was present in the different "breaks" of your life:

"lucky break"

"tough break"                    "rest break"

"break through"                    "break up"

"break down"

Pick three of these "breaks" in your life and write a paragraph describing each one.

○ What happened? What kind of "break" was it and why?

○ What did you learn from it?

○ How did you experience *God in the midst of it?* How did it affect your spirituality?

Remember that you may choose to include some of this as part of the final report you give at the end of the of course.

**↗** Go to the student site at **hs.osvcurriculum.com**

*Discipleship ... within the Body of Christ ...*
*for the glory of God and the good of the world.*

# Saint Thomas Aquinas (1225–1274)

Saint Thomas Aquinas stands as one of the greatest minds of Western civilization as a theologian, philosopher, and Saint. His thoughts helped shape modern philosophy and continue to influence religious and secular writers.

Aquinas' understanding of angels—what they are, what they can do, and how they fit into God's overall plan of Creation—are among his many contributions to Catholic teaching.

He wrote that angels are pure spirit, having no body and no material form. They are separate and unique creations of God, not the souls of dead humans. He theorized that sometimes angels assume human appearance, as when Gabriel appeared to Mary, but this is just the look of a physical form, not an actual body. Aquinas taught that the main role of angels was to lead people to God. Angels were God's messengers, not divine in and of themselves.

Aquinas also classified angels according to hierarchies and orders. The highest are the Seraphim, Cherubim and Thrones. Next come Dominations, Virtues and Powers. Finally, the lowest ranks include Principalities, Archangels and Angels.

Saint Thomas's insights about angels are especially relevant today, when a quick Internet search turns up more than 340 million references to angels. However, many people might have misguided ideas about the beings who Saint Thomas described as "pure intellects." This isn't to say that Thomas believed that the angels were somehow distant or apart from us. On the contrary, he wrote that, "Each human being, without exception, has a guardian angel as long as he is a wayfarer, that is, during his whole earthly life."

In addition to Aquinas' twenty books on spiritual matters, he was a sought-after preacher and close friend of King Saint Louis of France. Despite being offered several chances to become a bishop, Thomas refused any higher appointment, preferring to remain a priest. Near the end of his life, while saying Mass, he received a vision, after which he never returned to his writing. When a friend begged him to work again, Thomas replied, "I cannot, because all that I have written seems like straw to me." He died at age 49, while traveling to the Second Council of Lyon.

> **Think About It** What times in your life have you asked your Guardian Angel for guidance and protection? How would you explain angels to someone who thinks that we become angels after death? Besides the Angel Gabriel appearing to Mary, what other examples of angels can you recall from stories in the Bible?

Go to the student site at
**hs.osvcurriculum.com**

## GO TO THE SOURCE 📖

**When God favors the sacrifice of Abel over Cain's,** evil comes to the brothers.

Read *Genesis 4:1-16*.

○ How does God respond to Cain's resentfulness in Genesis 4:6-7?

○ Do you take personal ownership of your actions or are your reactions dependent upon what others say and do?

○ When God asks Cain where Abel is, Cain responds with an often-quoted question. Identify the question and indicate your own answer to it.

### Cain and Abel

Other primeval stories have shaped our faith. After Adam and Eve were banished from Eden, we learn about their two sons, Cain and Abel. Abel is a shepherd and Cain is a farmer. When each makes an offering to God, he looks with favor on Abel's offering but not Cain's.

Sin takes hold quickly after the Fall. The Cain and Abel story indicates that murder is one of the earliest evils that is a consequence of the Fall and disobedience of Adam and Eve. God, however, shows mercy on the murderer. Cain fears for his life because he believes someone will kill him on sight. Cain is protected from retaliation and revenge when God places a special mark on Cain. "Whoever kills Cain will suffer a sevenfold vengeance" (Genesis 4:15). Cain leaves the presence of the Lord and settles east of Eden in Nod.

### Noah and the Flood

As we read in Genesis, evil continues to spread after the Fall. The world becomes so evil that God regrets having created humans and decides to destroy all the people and animals on Earth. However, Noah and his family find favor with God. Noah is a good man in an evil world.

One of the key insights we gain from the Noah story is its emphasis on God's mercy. Not only does God show mercy to Noah and the animals, but God also offers the promise of a **covenant** blessing and a sign to honor his promise. The covenant promise

**covenant** a sacred agreement or treaty between two parties before God, or between God and persons or a people, such as Israel, that involves agreed-upon commitments and guarantees on both parties

God makes with Noah is to never destroy the world again by flood, and the sign of this covenant is the rainbow. God renews his blessing for all people and living things that he made at Creation (see CCC, 1080).

Applied to the situation of the time, each son of Noah represents a different race or group of people. Shem represents the Arameans, Assyrians, and Arabs or the Semitic na-tions. Ham represents the Semitic people of color among the Canaanites, and people of North Africa (Egyptians, Libyans, Sudanese). Japheth represents the non-Semitic people including the Greeks, Hittites, and people of Cypress (Boadt, Lawrence. *Reading the Old Testament, An Introduction.* N.Y. N.Y: Paulist Press, 1984. Page 128).

This division into nations is designed to keep humankind humble and focused on God until Christ gathers us all into one

## GO TO THE SOURCE 📖

**In Genesis, we find that wickedness had taken hold in the world** except for one righteous man named Noah.

Read *Genesis Chapters 6 through 9*.

○ What instructions (one set in Chapter 6 and one in Chapter 7) did Noah receive regarding the animals?

○ Describe Noah and the other humans on the ark with him.

○ After the rain stops and the floodwaters begin to lessen, how does Noah determine whether or not they can find land?

○ What does God promise Noah after they leave the ark?

○ God establishes a covenant with Noah and his family and blesses them with the same words said in the first Creation story. Write out the words to this blessing, found in Genesis 9:1.

○ What religious truths do you find in this account?

with God—the children of God—at the end times. This covenant between God and Noah remains in effect until Christ comes again (see CCC, 58).

There is a notable positive contribution of this group of ancestors. The descendants of Ham, listed in Genesis 10:6-20, and the continents of Africa and Asia play a significant role throughout the Bible. Nimrod, the son of Cush, is considered the first potentate or ruler on Earth and is a mighty hunter by the grace of the Lord. The great nations of Babylon, Assyria, and Egypt are part of the Hamitic heritage. Egypt is, of course, the setting for many major Biblical events, particularly the accounts of Joseph and Moses.

**Recall** How does God react after Cain kills his brother Abel?

**Explain** Why does God spare Noah?

## DISCUSS

After the terrorist attacks on September 11, 2001, a news editorial asked the question, "Are we better or bitter?" Perhaps the answer to the question is how we understand the suffering of the innocent.
- Talk about natural and man-made disasters and discuss ways that good came out of them or could come out of them.
- Share any negative experiences you have had that turned out to be good.

### The Tower of Babel

The final primeval story in the Book of Genesis 1:11, is the Tower of Babel.

The Babylonians were known to build temple towers or ziggurat step pyramids to honor their gods. God punishes the tower builders by confusing their language. In Hebrew, the term "Balal" refers to confusion of languages. Today, we use the word "babbling" to refer to speech that is not understood.

## GO TO THE SOURCE

**The Book of Genesis contains the story of the Tower of Babel.**

Read *Genesis 11:1-9*.
- Why do you think the Lord decided to stop their plans?
- Describe a time when you had great plans that never quite came to fruition. What lesson did you learn?
- How would you describe modern communication and what impact it has on our relationship with God?

The lesson in the Tower of Babel focuses on the sin of pride. The story points to a deeper truth: Our human pride can cause us to go so far as to think we don't need God. He punishes the tower builders because of their pride. This story is reversed in the Acts of the Apostles in the story of Pentecost. Instead of confusion, everyone understands the languages that are being spoken. The words spoken are of the "mighty acts of God" (Acts 2:1-13).

**Identify** What sin drives the actions of the people building the Tower of Babel?

**Connect** How are the Tower of Babel passage and the account of Pentecost related?

## QUICK REVIEW

**1a.** **Explain** What common idea does the story of Job challenge?

  **b.** **Summarize** Retell the story of Cain and Abel.

  **c.** **Tell** How is the story of Noah a story of rebirth?

**2a.** **Recall** What is a covenant?

  **b.** **Explain** Why was pride the sin at the root of the Tower of Babel?

## ACT

Find some fine art depicting the Tower of Babel.

○ In a small group, note the details that the artist has used.

○ Are the details consistent with the lessons that should be learned from the story?

○ Present your findings to the entire group.

## SELF-ASSESS

Which statement best reflects where you are now?

☐ I'm confident enough about the material in this section to be able to explain it to someone else.

☐ I have a good grasp of the material in this section, but I could use more review.

☐ I'm lost. I need help catching up before moving on.

# PRAYER

**St. Francis' Canticle of the Sun**

O most High, almighty, good Lord God,
to you belong praise, glory, honor, and all blessing!

Praised be my Lord God with all creatures;
and especially our brother the sun,
which brings us the day, and the light;
fair is he, and shining with a very great splendor:
O Lord, he signifies you to us!

Praised be my Lord for our sister the moon,
and for the stars,
which God has set clear and lovely in Heaven.

Praised be my Lord for our brother the wind,
and for air and cloud, calms and all weather,
by which you uphold in life all creatures.

Praised be my Lord for our sister water,
which is very serviceable to us,
and humble, and precious, and clean.

Praised be my Lord for brother fire,
through which you give us light in the darkness:
and he is bright, and pleasant, and very mighty,
and strong.

Praised be my Lord for our mother the Earth,
which sustains us and keeps us,
and yields divers fruits, and flowers of
many colors, and grass.

Praised be my Lord for all those who pardon
one another for God's love's sake,
and who endure weakness and tribulation;
blessed are they who peaceably shall endure,
for you, O most High, shall give them a crown!
Praised be my Lord for our sister,
the death of the body, from which no one escapes.
Woe to him who dies in mortal sin!
Blessed are they who are found walking by your
most holy will,
for the second death shall have no power to do
them harm.

Praise you, and bless you the Lord,
and give thanks to God, and serve God
with great humility.

## TERMS

Use each of the following terms in a sentence that shows you know what the term means. You may include more than one term in a sentence.

theology

religious truth

Sheol

theophany

anthropomorphic

polytheistic

monotheistic

protoevangelium

covenant

## PEOPLE

Use information from the chapter to tell why each person or term is significant.

1. Saint Irenaeus

2. New Adam

3. New Eve

4. Job

5. Saint Thomas Aquinas

6. Cain

7. Abel

8. Noah

## UNDERSTANDING

Answer each question and complete each exercise.

### SECTION **1**

1. **List** What are some truths about God and humans that the Creation accounts reveal?
2. **Clarify** What is the role of humans in God's Creation?
3. **Infer** What benefits came from observing the Sabbath?

### SECTION **2**

4. **Interpret** What are the implications of God creating everything from nothing?
5. **Specify** Give an example of a theophany in the Pentateuch.
6. **Recap** How does the Old Testament illustrate God's rewards and punishments?
7. **Infer** What does the Creation story imply about community?

### SECTION **3**

8. **Infer** What led to the Fall?
9. **List** What changes did the Fall cause in human lives?
10. **Interpret** Why did God permit sin to enter the world?
11. **Explain** How do the stories from the "beginning" of Genesis reflect the Paschal Mystery of God?

### SECTION **4**

12. **Explain** Tell what the story of Job teaches about evil.
13. **Examine** How do the Cain and Abel story and the Tower of Babel story continue the lessons of the Creation stories?
14. **Elaborate** Why is God's mercy one of the key insights of the Noah story?
15. **Conclude** What truth does the story of the Tower of Babel point to?

**Visual** This painting shows Jesus freeing souls after the Resurrection.

What can be inferred about Jesus? What can you tell about the souls that are being freed? What sign of Satan can you see in the painting?

**Challenge** A friend sees a Bible in your house, sees that Genesis is flagged, and starts a conversation.

**Friend:** I believe the world was created in seven days. Do you?

**You:** Not exactly. Sure God created the world, but not in seven days.

**Friend:** If you believe God made the world, the Bible says it was created in seven days.

**You:** The Catholic Church teaches that the two Creation accounts in Genesis and some other stories in the Bible aren't historical or scientific facts. They reveal religious truth that God wants us to know.

**Friend:** Why would a church tell people that not everything in the Bible is true?

○ What is your next reply?

○ Then continue the conversation with at least two more questions from your friend and how you would answer. Use information from the chapter in the conversation.

**Imagine** You are a web developer who has received an assignment to design a series of web pages telling the Creation story.

○ Which Creation account from Genesis would you use or how would you blend the stories? Explain your choice.

○ What sort of images would you use to depict the story? Would you use still images or animation?

○ What songs would you use as background music?

○ What overriding impression would you want your viewers to get from the pages?

## SELF-ASSESS

**On Your Own** Make a list of the most important things you learned from this chapter. Select three things that represent your growth in understanding as you worked through this chapter. Write a paragraph explaining your choices.

**With a Partner** List what you found most helpful in this chapter as well as any other questions that have surfaced.

# The Promise of a Messiah

- Explore the meaning of covenant.

- Identify the continuity between the Old and New Testaments.

- Explain the covenant promises God made with Adam and Eve, Noah, Abraham, Moses, and David.

- Discover the pattern of the Call Narrative in the Old Testament.

- Compare the different expectations of the Messiah in the Old Testament and of Jesus the Messiah in the New Testament.

- Learn about the Messianic prophecies from the prophets.

- Understand the different stages of Royal Davidic Messiah.

New Covenant

Magisterium

typology

prefiguration

genealogy

patriarch

Ten Commandments

shalom

Messiah

consecrated

**A high school sophomore** downloads new software to a laptop. During the install, the program asks the user to read an agreement with the software company. The student quickly scrolls to the end of the agreement and clicks on the Agree button. An older sibling is watching and asks: "Did you even read the agreement?" The student answers, "No, I never do, they always say the same thing."

**A teenager asks** his friend to drive him to the mall for a job interview on Saturday morning. The friend says sure, but the teenager is eager to make sure he's going to get there. "You have to be on time because I can't be late." The friend assures him that it is no problem. On Saturday, the friend shows up thirty minutes late. The teenager misses his interview and loses the job opportunity.

**A junior wants** to stay out late after going to the movies Friday night. She has a midnight curfew, but she begs her dad to extend it. He trusts his daughter and says, "OK, we'll make an agreement, you can be home by 1 A.M., but no later or your curfew will move up to 10 P.M." About 1:15 A.M., she receives a text from her dad, "Where are you?" She replies: "We're almost home." She doesn't walk in the door until nearly 2 A.M. and is greeted by an anxious and angry father.

# WHERE ARE YOU?

**Check the answer that best matches where you are today.**

I know what a covenant relationship is.
☐ Quite a bit  ☐ Somewhat  ☐ A little  ☐ Not at all

I understand the covenant God made with humanity.
☐ Quite a bit  ☐ Somewhat  ☐ A little  ☐ Not at all

I know who the Children of Abraham are today.
☐ Quite a bit  ☐ Somewhat  ☐ A little  ☐ Not at all

I actively oppose religious and racial discrimination.
☐ Quite a bit  ☐ Somewhat  ☐ A little  ☐ Not at all

I know the Old Testament figures whose stories parallel Christ's.
☐ Quite a bit  ☐ Somewhat  ☐ A little  ☐ Not at all

# God's Covenant with Israel

*What characteristics describe our relationship with God?*

*How did Jesus fulfill the concept of a Messiah?*

*What do the covenant stories tell us about this relationship?*

God has communicated himself to us in a gradual way leading up Christ. The Letter to the Hebrews begins by talking about how God spoke to the ancient Israelites in many different ways, including through the prophets. But now God speaks to us through his Son. "He is the reflection of God's glory and the exact imprint of God's very being" (Hebrews 1:3). It is out of love for us that God has done this: "See what love the Father has given us, that we should be called children of God" (1 John 3:1).

> God has revealed himself fully by sending his own Son, in whom he has established his covenant for ever.
>
> —*Catechism of the Catholic Church, 73*

Jesus is the Messiah, and through his Paschal Mystery, God's promises—the promises of both the Old Testament and Jesus himself—are fulfilled. The New Covenant has been sealed by the blood of Christ. We hear these terms and phrases in Mass and throughout religious education, but what do they really mean?

God cares so much about us that he makes sacred promises to us; he enters into a covenant with us. As noted earlier, a covenant is a sacred agreement that places permanent obligations on both parties.

There is a code of conduct and respect between best friends. The two usually form a strong bond over a long term, sharing the good and bad times in life. Best friends know each other's strengths and weaknesses, and exploit neither of them. True friends don't turn on or betray each other. Some of the greatest pain we experience in life can come when someone we love hurts us by betrayal or through a broken trust.

Now think about the relationship between a parent and child. A parent is meant to be a child's first experience of God and Church with the responsibility to raise the child in a loving way. The parent is also the first teacher. As the child grows up, rules need to be established and consequences identified. A criterion of reward and punishment develops along with praise and correction. The parent has the authority to set rules, and it is up to the child to follow them or face the consequences. However, the rules, consequences, and authority are not the point of the relationship. A loving parent asserts authority with responsibility, aiming to teach the child how to *be* in the world. There is meant to be an unbreakable bond of love, trust, and mercy between them.

In the case of the relationship between a husband and wife a man and a woman choose to enter into a covenant relationship through the Sacrament of Marriage.

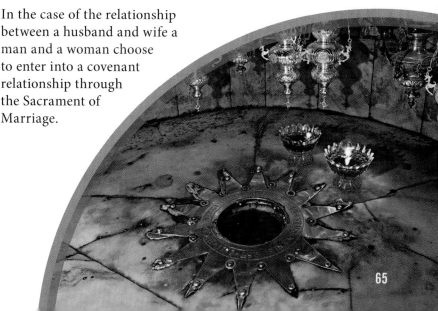

**The site of the Nativity in Bethlehem, Israel.**

According to *The Official Catholic Directory,* more than 170,000 Catholic marriages took place in 2011, meaning that thousands of people received the Nuptial Blessing. The Old and New Testaments are represented in the blessing. One form of the nuptial blessing includes the following elements:

○ "In the beginning you created the universe and made mankind in your own likeness."

○ "Married life has been established as the one blessing that was not forfeited by original sin."

○ (To the bride) "May she always follow the examples of the holy women whose praises are sung in the Scriptures."

○ (To the groom) "May he always honor her and love her as Christ loves his bride, the Church." (Rite of Marriage)

With the strength that comes from the Gospel, may they bear true witness to Christ before all; (may they be blessed with children, and prove themselves virtuous parents, who live to see their children's children). And grant that, reaching at last together the fullness of years for which they hope, they may come to the life of the blessed in the Kingdom of Heaven. Through Christ our Lord. Amen.

—Nuptial Blessing For the Celebration of Marriage, *Roman Missal*

➚ Go to the student site at **hs.osvcurriculum.com**

The marriage vows speak of the commitment the husband and wife promise to each other.

"I, Adam, take you, Eve, to be my wife. I promise to be true to you in good times and in bad, in sickness and in health. I will love you and honor you all the days of my life" (*Rite of Marriage*, 25). The essential sign of this covenant relationship is the public expression of marriage vows.

> Since marriage establishes the couple in a public state of life in the Church, it is fitting that its celebration be public, in the framework of a liturgical celebration, before the priest (or a witness authorized by the Church), the witnesses, and the assembly of the faithful.
>
> —CCC, 1663

The Nuptial Blessing prayed by the priest during the ceremony recalls many images from the Old Testament: the creation of the world, the Creation of man and woman, Original Sin, and the flood. Marriage in the New Covenant models Christ's love for his bride, the Church. A baptized man and a baptized woman "signify and share in the mystery of the unity and fruitful love that exists between Christ and his Church" (*Rite of Marriage*, 1).

A covenant binds people to their word. In the honesty and sincerity of this mutual promise, we find the reliability and trustworthiness of commitment. This is the basis of unconditional love. When people in a healthy relationship form ties with each other, there is tremendous freedom. In each of the above examples, people freely share themselves with another.

The same thing is true for our covenant relationship with God. We see this in the Old Testament covenant relationship between God and the people of Israel; it involves deep, binding relationships. The Bible reveals the story about an unbreakable bond or relationship between God and his Chosen People. Promises and signs are found in the covenant stories, similar to the promises and signs of the wedding vows, the promises between best friends, and the dedication of a parent toward children.

At times throughout history, the covenant promise between God and humanity is threatened or appears broken through sin, disobedience, war, and death. Not all covenants are romantic, but all covenants are stories of love. Even when sin enters in, God never washes his hands of us and ends the relationship. His covenant remains in effect. God always seeks reconciliation and to reestablish the right relationship.

- Think about one relationship that you have that involves a covenant.
- Reflect on the good times and bad times that strengthened or tested the relationship.
- What does it take to maintain a covenant relationship?

This chapter explores the covenant relationship between God and the people of Israel. It also considers how God established a **New Covenant** between himself and all of humanity through the Paschal Mystery of Jesus' life, Passion, Death, Resurrection, and Ascension.

**Name** In marriage, what is the sign of the couple's love and fidelity?

**Explain** In what ways do you see freedom as important to any relationship?

## Covenant Promises with Israel

A promise, a blessing, and a sign seal the covenant relationships that God makes with the People of Israel. God establishes a covenant relationship in the following stories:

**New Covenant** "the new 'dispensation,' order or covenant, established by God in Jesus Christ, to succeed and perfect the Old Covenant" (CCC, Glossary p.893)

| God's Covenant Relationships | | | |
|---|---|---|---|
| **WHO the covenant is made with.** | **HOW the covenant appears in the context of Scripture.** | **WHAT the covenant promise is.** | **WHERE to find the Scripture reference** |
| Adam and Eve | Our first parents are made in God's image and likeness | He blesses them to be fruitful and multiply. | (Genesis 1:26-27; 2:7, 20-22) |
| Noah | After the flood, God repeats the blessing first made to Adam and Eve, to Noah and his family and says "be fertile and multiply." | God promises never to destroy the Earth by flood again. The sign of this promise is the rainbow. This promise will last forever. (see CCC, 71) | (Genesis 9:1-17) |
| Abraham | God promises Abraham a homeland. | His descendants will become a great nation, and be a blessing for all nations. The sign of the covenant is circumcision, the physical marking of the male anatomy. | (Genesis 12:1-3; 15:1-21; 17:1-14 and CCC, 59-60, 72) |
| Moses | The Exodus: the Israelites are freed from slavery and journey to the Promised Land. | The covenant gave them God's Law to recognize and serve him. | (Exodus 19:1-20:17 and CCC, 62) |
| David | Israel becomes a nation with a king and a temple, and Jerusalem is the capital city. | The promise is that David's rule will last forever, and the signs of the promise are the throne, the city of Jerusalem, and the Temple. | (1 Samuel 16:1-13; 2 Samuel 5:1-5; 7:1-29) |

In each instance, the one true God made a covenant through an individual but with all People of Israel. God's covenant relationships and story of love continue with us up to our present day.

God made a covenant with the People of Israel: *I will be your God and you will be my People.* Time after time, the covenant was tested. God has always cared for the human race, and again and again he affirms and reaffirms his covenant with his people. "For he wishes to give eternal life to all those who seek salvation by patience in well-doing"[22] (CCC, 55).

In Christ, we understand that God makes a new and definitive Covenant with all people for all time. This New Covenant will never end (see CCC, 66). Jesus Christ, the Son of God, is God's final Word—the Father's definitive promise to humanity, and that promise is one of salvation and Redemption from sin and death. In Jesus, God has fully revealed himself and "has established his covenant for ever" (CCC, 73). But even though Revelation is complete, it is still not completely understandable. "It remains for Christian faith gradually to grasp its full significance over the course of the centuries" (CCC, 66).

These points are extremely important in understanding the covenant stories of the Old Testament and the New Covenant of the New Testament. The *Catechism* teaches that the unity of the Old and New Testaments form one Sacred Revelation of God. Their unity is apparent in God's plan, which Jesus revealed in the Paschal Mystery. All of Sacred Scripture is one because it speaks of Christ and it is fulfilled by him (see CCC, 134).

The Church—especially the **Magisterium**, the living, teaching office of the Church—continues to probe the full significance of the New Covenant and its relationship with the Old Testament covenants. Understanding our past can help us better understand how God is present with us and acting in our world today.

Christ gave to the Magisterium the charism of infallibility on matters of faith and morals. Infallibility is a gift of the Holy Spirit in which the Pope and the bishops in union with him "can definitively proclaim a doctrine of faith or morals for belief of the faithful" (CCC, Glossary, p. 883; see CCC, 891).

> The New Testament has to be read in the light of the Old. Early Christian catechesis made constant use of the Old Testament. As an old saying put it, the New Testament lies hidden in the Old and the Old Testament is unveiled in the New.
>
> —*Dei Verbum* 16

Understanding our Jewish roots helps us better understand the significance of the New Covenant. The New Covenant with Jesus Christ fulfills the promises of the first Covenant made between God and the Israelites. When God makes a covenant, it lasts forever. The New Covenant expands our understanding with the fullest Revelation of God. Through the Paschal Mystery, the New Covenant shows us the depth and transforming power of God's love in the Resurrection, in salvation, and in Redemption.

**List** What three things seal the covenant relationships between God and the People of Israel?

**Summarize** What do the covenant relationships between God and Abraham and God and Moses represent, and how long do they last?

**Magisterium** the official teaching office of the Church, entrusted to the bishops in communion with the Pope, whose task it is to interpret Sacred Scripture and Sacred Tradition and ensure faithfulness to the teachings of the Apostles, and who Christ gave the charism of infallibility when it comes to faith and morals

## The Old and New Covenants

It is very important that we have a proper understanding of the Old (or first) Covenant in light of the revelation of the New Covenant through Christ. The Old and New Testaments are united. We can better understand God's revelation in Jesus through studying the messages, signs, and symbols in the Old Testament. The Old Covenant offers us early indications of what is to come in Jesus Christ as the Messiah.

Biblical scholars interpret and study different symbols and types to develop what is called **typology**. The Protoevangelium (after the Fall) is an example of typology. Christians find in this passage a **prefiguration**, or foreshadowing, of what will be accomplished by Jesus, God's incarnate Son. Ultimately, through Mary, Jesus would "strike [the] head" of the devil (Genesis 3:15). Typology gives us information about things that move us "toward the fulfillment of the divine plan when 'God [will] be everything to everyone'"[23] (CCC, 130).

The New Testament is filled with allegorical passages, including references and images from the Old Testament that help us understand Jesus as the "New Adam," "Messiah" and "Christ" (both of which mean Anointed One), "Son of Man," and "Son of David. An acknowledgment of this is expressed in the Letter to the Hebrews.

> Long ago God spoke to our ancestors in many and various ways by the prophets, but in these last days he has spoken to us by a Son, whom he appointed heir of all things, through whom he also created the worlds.
>
> —Hebrews 1:1-2

The Old Covenant has never been revoked (see CCC, 121). The Old Testament writings declare the coming of Jesus, and "are a storehouse of sublime teaching on God and of sound wisdom on human life, as well as a wonderful treasury of prayers; in them, too, the mystery of our salvation is present in a hidden way"[24] (CCC, 122). Catholics venerate the Old Testament as God's inspired Revelation. The New Testament does not void, invalidate, or replace the Old (see CCC, 123).

> I ask, then, has God rejected his people? By no means! I myself am an Israelite, a descendant of Abraham, a member of the tribe of Benjamin. God has not rejected his people whom he foreknew.
>
> —Romans 11:1-2

**Recall** Why is the Old Testament indispensable?

**Connect** Why is the Old Covenant of the Old Testament still relevant?

## Anti-Semitism

"It is, in fact, a practical impossibility to present Christianity while abstracting from the Jews and Judaism, unless one were to suppress the Old Testament (Hebrew Scriptures), forget about the Jewishness of Jesus and the Apostles, and dismiss the vital cultural and religious context of the primitive Church (*L'Osservatore Romano*, June 24, 1985)." (*Within Context: Guidelines for the Catechetical Presentation of Jews and Judaism in the New Testament.* United States Catholic Conference. Washington, D.C., 1987, p. 10)

The *Catechism* states that neither all Jews during Jesus' life on Earth, nor any Jews today, can be blamed for Christ's Death. Jews should not be referred to as rejected or accused as if the Bible says that (see CCC, 597).

The Old Law of the Israelites in fact prepared the way for the Gospel. Christ's New Covenant of love establishes the Church. Through the Church, salvation is offered for all people.

**typology** the study and interpretation of types and symbols that from a theological perspective views Old Testament people and stories as foreshadowing New Testament events

**prefiguration** early indication of something, in biblical usage the coming of Jesus Christ as the Messiah

## REFLECT

**Our words and actions do matter.**

○ Identify a time in your life in which you said or did something in the heat of the moment that had much larger negative consequences than you ever intended. Explain what you have done or have been doing to make amends.

○ What can we do, alone and together, to lessen racism, prejudice, and stereotyping in school and in society? Be specific.

# Saint Gladys & Saint Gwynllyw

Saint Gladys

Saint Gwynllyw

The Church has recognized many holy men and women as saints who had received the Sacrament of Marriage. One such couple, Saint Gladys and Saint Gwynllyw (GWIN•lew) Farfog, lived in what is now the United Kingdom more than a thousand years ago.

Gladys was the eldest daughter of a Welsh King. She was united in marriage to Gwynllyw Farfog the Bearded, a powerful local chieftain. Neither Gladys nor Gwynllyw were Christians when they married. The couple's early years were tumultuous, but their lives changed when they had children. Their eldest son, Cadoc, became a priest and convinced his parents to convert to Christianity. They agreed and became good and just rulers, devoting themselves to works of charity, church-building, and peacemaking.

There they lived simply, eating a vegetarian diet and performing daily penance, such as bathing in an icy river, to atone for past sins.

Pope Benedict XVI reminds us that sainthood is something to which we can all aspire: "a host of saints . . . tell us that it is possible for everyone to take this road. In every epoch of the Church's history, on every latitude of the world map, the saints belong to all the ages and to every state of life, they are actual faces of every people, language and nation. And they have very different characters."

Many of them were even happily married.

> **Think About It** Think about a happily married Catholic couple you know. How do they treat each other? In what ways do they live out the Sacrament of Matrimony on a daily basis? What characteristics do you think are necessary to be a Saint? Gladys and Gwynllyw Farfog performed strict penances because of their former sins. What kind of Lenten penance could you perform that would help you become a better Catholic?

↗ Go to the student site at **hs.osvcurriculum.com**

## QUICK REVIEW

**1a. Analyze** How is a covenant a symbol of freedom?

**b. Connect** What images does the Nuptial Blessing contain from the Old Testament?

**c. Identify** Who are the Chosen People?

**d. Conclude** Which two qualities help a covenant endure?

**2a. List** Tell the five Old Testament figures who had major covenant relationships with God.

**b. Explain** Why do the Old Testament covenants last beyond the death of the person who made them with God?

**3. Explain** What is hidden in the Old Testament?

**Pray** As Catholics, we understand that the fullness of grace and truth is found in the Catholic Church. However, some elements of truth can be found in many other major world religions. Compose a prayer asking God to help the major world religions appreciate the truths they hold in common.

## SELF-ASSESS

Which statement best reflects where you are now?

☐ I'm confident enough about the material in this section to be able to explain it to someone else.

☐ I have a good grasp of the material in this section, but I could use more review.

☐ I'm lost. I need help catching up before moving on.

# The Covenant Promise of Abraham

The three major monotheistic religions of the world can be called "Abrahamic religions" because of the role of Abraham in each of the religious traditions. All three religions—Judaism, Christianity, and Islam—claim Abraham as an ancestor who made a covenant with God. While all three acknowledge God as Creator and claim ties to Abraham, the relationship between the Jewish People and the Catholic Church has a unique position. We trace our roots back to the Jewish faith, and our link to Judaism is special. Jesus, the Son of God and our Savior, was born and raised a Jew.

The first mention of Abraham in the Old Testament occurs in a **genealogy**, or family tree, following the final primeval story in Genesis 11. Abraham's name in the genealogy is "Abram," and he is married to "Sarai." The text specifies that "Sarai was barren; she had no child" (Genesis 11:30).

Genesis 12 begins immediately with the call and covenant promise made with Abraham, then known as Abram.

**genealogy** ancestry traced continuously in a direct line

Now the LORD said to Abram, "Go from your country and your kindred and your father's house to the land that I will show you. I will make of you a great nation, and I will bless you, and make your name great, so that you will be a blessing. I will bless those who bless you, and the one who curses you I will curse; and in you all the families of the earth shall be blessed."

—Genesis 12:1-3c

Abraham is obedient to the Lord's will. He takes Sarai and heads into Canaan. The Lord appears to Abraham again and makes an additional promise: "To your offspring I will give this land" (Genesis 12:7). At this early stage, the promise made to Abraham is that he will have a great nation, land, and descendants. He will be a blessing to all the communities of the Earth. But how could Abraham have descendants when his wife Sarai is barren and cannot have children?

## GO TO THE SOURCE

**Several other verses in Genesis repeat the promises** that God made to Abraham and his descendants in greater detail.

Read *Genesis 13:14-16*, *15:5-6*, and *17:4-8*.

○ What images are used to describe the descendants of Abraham?

○ What happens to Abraham's name, and what future events in the history of Israel are foretold?

An interreligious gathering.

# Home Altars

Altars were important to the ancient Israelites. Sacrifices took place around altars as they worshipped God. Since the early Church, altars have been important to Catholics today as they represent Christ's sacrifice as well as the table of Christ where he "gives himself to us as food from heaven" (CCC, Glossary, p. 865). Just as the altar is the focal point of any Catholic Church, home altars can serve as focal points for a family's faith.

The tradition of setting up home altars for private prayer has a rich history. May Altars, for example, honor Mary in May with a statue or image of Mary and flowers. Families often pray the Rosary near the altar. A traditional May altar might have a statue of Mary on a cloth-covered table. It is often decorated with flowers typical of the spring when Mary is honored.

The Saint Joseph Day Altar commemorates Mary's husband and Jesus' earthly father. This tradition originated long ago in Sicily and throughout Italy during periods of drought. When prayers for rain were answered, people thanked Saint Joseph, the patron saint of families. Altars feature a Joseph statue and food offered to visitors and then given to the hungry.

Another popular tradition is the Day of the Dead Altar that originated in Mexico. On November 1 and 2, the Feasts of All Saints and All Souls Day, altars display flowers and photos of deceased loved ones who are prayed for in a special way.

How are home altars valuable "expressions of faith" for families?

How can you create an altar in your home?

Sarai is the first woman named in the Bible to be unable to have children. This starts to become a pattern with the mothers of the **patriarchs**. Rebekah, the wife of Isaac; Rachel, the wife of Jacob; the mother of Samson in Judges 13:1-24; and Hannah, the mother of Samuel in 1 Samuel 1:1-28 all have problems having children. Hannah's prayer of thanksgiving after she gives birth to Samuel bears similarity to the *Magnificat*, which is the prayer Mary offers after she conceives Jesus.

In the New Testament, John the Baptist's mother, Elizabeth, an aging woman, has no children. Despite her age, she does give birth to John the Baptist. Mary, a young woman and a virgin, conceives Jesus by the power of the Holy Spirit. The miraculous nature of these birth stories emphasizes the different roles that John and

## GO TO THE SOURCE

**One version of the covenant story** with Abram (later Abraham) is recounted in *Genesis 15*.

Read *Genesis 15:7-20*.

○ This passage mentions primitive customs involving the sacrifice of animals. What kinds of animals are mentioned?

○ In this covenant story, how is God's presence represented?

○ In this covenant story, a future event is foretold. It provides a foreshadowing of what other major biblical event?

○ This passage extends the promise of the covenant beyond the life of Abraham as it points to the covenant God makes with whom?

Another passage related to God's Covenant with Abraham is found in *Genesis 17*.

○ This passage repeats the blessing found in the Creation account from the first chapter of the Book of Genesis. Identify this repeated blessing.

○ This passage also extends the promise of the covenant beyond the life of Abraham, as it points to the covenant God makes with David. Identify the passage that alludes to David.

○ What is the sign of the covenant in Genesis 17:13?

○ Make a list of the similarities and differences in the prayers of Hannah in 1 Samuel 2:1-10 and Mary in Luke 1:46-55.

○ What words can you use to praise and thank God for the blessings in your life?

Jesus have in the history of the salvation of the world.

Through their holy actions, women such as Sarah, Rebecca, Rachel, Miriam, Deborah, Hannah, Judith, and Esther sustained the hope of Israel's salvation. "The purest figure among them is Mary"[25] (CCC, 64).

Each of these accounts from the Old and New Testaments remind us that only God creates and gives new life, in any situation he chooses. Through the Resurrection of his Son, God bestows eternal life on all who believe that Jesus, whose name means "God saves," is the Savior of the world.

**Locate** Where is the first mention of Abraham in the Bible?

**Elaborate** Which women sustained the hope of Israel's salvation? How?

## The Covenant with Abraham

In Genesis 17, both Abram and Sarai have their names changed to Abraham and Sarah. A name change often reflects a new relationship with God. For example, the Lord changed Simon's name to Peter when he was named the "rock" of the Church (see Matthew 16:18). Abraham and Sarah's name changes mark a turning point in the history of Israel, and coincide with God promising a child to Abraham through his barren wife Sarah. Abraham laughs at God's promise: "Can a child be born to a man who is a hundred years old? Can Sarah, who is ninety years old, bear a child?" (Genesis 17:17).

## Lessons from Abraham

We can take the following lessons from the Abraham story:

Abraham is called by God to leave his homeland and enter a "strange" land. Often, God acts powerfully in moments of transition and change, especially when it involves a physical move to a different geographical location.

Abraham is obedient to God's will. Through his obedience, God makes an everlasting covenant with him of land and countless descendants. The promise will continue through his descendants, up to and including Jesus and his Christian followers, who receive the fulfillment of his promise through the Death and Resurrection of Jesus. For Jews, Christians, and Muslims, Abraham serves as a father and role model of faith.

Abraham continues to have faith even when faced with the impossible. God promises him many descendants, yet his wife Sarah is of an advanced age and has no children. Abraham continues to trust God, and his faithfulness is rewarded with the arrival of his son Isaac.

God tells Abraham that Sarah will give birth to a son, and they will call him Isaac. "I will establish my covenant with him as an everlasting covenant for his offspring after him" (Genesis 17:19).

Ishmael, the son born to Abraham through his Egyptian maidservant Hagar (see Genesis 16:1-15), is also blessed by God in this passage. "As for Ishmael, I have heard you; I will bless him and make him fruitful and exceedingly numerous; he shall be the father of twelve princes, and I will make him a great nation. But my covenant I will establish with Isaac" (Genesis 17:20-21).

Later on, we will see how Muslims claim Ishmael as the one with whom God makes his covenant promise. Despite differences of interpretation and tradition, it is clear in Scripture that Isaac receives the promise of the covenant beyond the life of Abraham and the lives of Isaac, Jacob, and the other Patriarchs, for it will be "an everlasting pact."

It is Sarah's turn to laugh when she overhears three messengers of God tell Abraham that she will have a son. But the Lord says to Abraham: "Why did Sarah laugh, and say, 'Shall I indeed bear a child, now that I am old?' Is anything too wonderful for the Lord? At the set time I will return to you, in due season, and Sarah shall have a son" (Genesis 18:13-14).

The child's name will be Isaac, a name that means "he will laugh." After Isaac is born, Sarah says: "God has brought laughter for me; everyone who hears will laugh with me" (Genesis 21:6). The Catechism calls the birth of Isaac one of the "divine blessings" in salvation history (see CCC, 1081).

**Identify** What is the sign of God's Covenant with Abraham?

**Explain** What does a name change usually mean for people in the Bible? Provide an example.

### REFLECT

Life has many times of transition. You have already made the transition from grade school to high school, and maybe even the transition of moving to a new neighborhood or city, developed new family relationships, felt the loss of some friendships and enjoyed the start of new ones.

○ What were some of the transition times in your life?

○ What was it like to be called out of your comfort zone to the "new land" of a transition? Did you resist or welcome it? Was it easy or tough?

**God calls to Abraham and tests him with an unusual request.**

Read *Genesis 22:1-18*.

○ What steps did Abraham take as he prepared to do as the Lord commanded?

○ What did the angel say to Abraham as he was about to sacrifice Isaac?

○ What did Abraham sacrifice?

○ What did the Lord's messenger say to Abraham the second time?

"By faith Abraham, when put to the test, offered up Isaac. He who had received the promises was ready to offer his only son, of whom said he had been told, 'It is through Isaac that descendants shall be named for you.' He reasoned the fact that God is able to raise someone from the dead—and figuratively speaking, he did receive him back" (Hebrews 11:17-20).

## REFLECT

**The sacrifice of Isaac was a test of obedience for Abraham.**

○ On a scale of 1–10, how difficult has it been to be obedient to God, your parents, or your teachers? What has it been like?

○ What do you need to help you stay obedient?

○ Share a time when you thought something was impossible, but it worked out or happened anyway.

○ When have you experienced God's mercy? How did God's mercy save you?

## The Sacrifice of Isaac

Christian hope fulfills that of the Chosen People of God, which has its origin in Abraham. Abraham's many blessings come from God's promise fulfilled in Isaac. Before any of that takes place, God tests Abraham's faithful obedience, and that test places the promise of God's covenant and the descendants of Abraham in jeopardy. God asks Abraham to sacrifice his son Isaac, the one through whom the covenant is to continue.

Abraham was purified by this test. "Hoping against hope, he believed, and thus became the father of many nations" (CCC, 1819).

Saint Paul is the first to make a connection between the sacrifice of Isaac and the sacrifice of Jesus on the Cross. Abraham acts on behalf of Israel, in obedience to God's command, and God acts on behalf of all humanity through the sacrifice of his only Son.

Scripture makes the connection between the sacrifice of Isaac and the sacrifice of Jesus on the Cross.

Saint Irenaeus uses the story to encourage Christians to carry the Cross of their faith as Isaac carried his own wood. Tertullian reinterprets the story by saying that the reason Isaac carried his own wood to the sacrifice was a mystery kept secret until Christ was asked to carry His wooden Cross to his sacrifice.

**Recall** Why does God ask Abraham to sacrifice his only son?

**Summarize** What connection does Saint Paul make between the sacrifice of Isaac and the sacrifice of Jesus on the Cross?

## GO TO THE SOURCE

**In Saint Paul's letters to the Romans and Galatians,** he makes the case that the promise made by God to Abraham is answered in Jesus. Like all Biblical authors, Saint Paul's interpretation of the promise was inspired by the Holy Spirit.

Read *Romans 3:21-4:25* and *Galatians 3:1-29*.

○ How does Saint Paul's explanation help in understanding how the promise made to Abraham is fulfilled through Christ?

## SECTION 2 REVIEW

### QUICK REVIEW

**1a.** **Link** Identify one way in which the three major monotheistic religions are joined.

**b.** **Explain** What was miraculous about God's promise that Abram would have many descendants?

**c.** **Explain** Why are births to apparently barren women important in the Bible?

**2.** **Relate** Give some examples of name changes in the Bible, and explain what a name change signifies.

**3a.** **Summarize** Tell the story of Abraham's sacrifice of Isaac.

**b.** **Analyze** Why is this story important today?

**Pray** Jesus Christ entrusted the fullness of grace and truth to the Catholic Church. Still, the three major monotheistic religions (Judaism, Islam, and Christianity) have some common elements. For example, all three recognize Abraham as a man of God and an ancestor of faith.

### SELF-ASSESS

Which statement best reflects where you are now?

☐ I'm confident enough about the material in this section to be able to explain it to someone else.

☐ I have a good grasp of the material in this section, but I could use more review.

☐ I'm lost. I need help catching up before moving on.

# The Covenant Promise of Moses

A view of Mount Sinai in Egypt.

from slavery to their "promised land." Abraham's son Jacob had twelve sons, who founded the twelve tribes of Israel. The Bible tells us they were "fruitful and prolific." But the descendants of Abraham were eventually enslaved by the King of Egypt. Then God called Moses and the birth of Israel as a nation and the acquisition of the land promised to Abraham occurred through Moses and the covenant God made with Israel in the Exodus story.

The Book of Genesis follows the covenant promise from generation to generation, from father to son: from Abraham to Isaac, from Isaac to Jacob, from Jacob to Joseph. Genesis ends with the final words of Joseph: "I am about to die; but God will surely come to you, and bring you up out of this land to the land that he swore to Abraham, to Isaac, and to Jacob" (Genesis 50:24). The promise made to Abraham will continue beyond the life of Joseph and into the Exodus story.

God's covenant with Abraham and his descendants continued when Moses led the Israelites' Exodus

## The Call Narratives

In several books of the Bible we find "call narratives," involving the call of a person for a special purpose or mission from God. These narratives consist of the following parts:

○ **An introductory word:** The pattern begins with an introductory word, with which God engages the person in a conversation, suggesting a personal relationship with him or her.

○ **Called during ordinary activity:** Usually the person is performing an ordinary task, but the setting of the story often involves a historical crisis.

○ **Mission is given:** Next, the person is commissioned for a special mission.

○ **Objections and excuses:** The person usually objects or makes excuses. Sometimes the person does not want to answer God's call. Other times the person may be overwhelmed by the call, and suggest God choose someone more suited for the job.

○ **Reassurance and sign:** This objection is followed by a reassurance by God and a sign of his support.

○ **Mission undertaken and completed.**

# JUSTICE AND DISCIPLESHIP

Jesus tells us that discipleship involves praying to the Father, studying his teachings and following his example, participating in the Eucharist, and living the virtues. He also calls us to act for justice.

**ABRAHAM, MOSES, AND JESUS** shared the common experience of being strangers in a strange land. Jesus was a refugee when he fled with his family to Egypt. Abraham and Moses each left their homelands and became immigrants.

In the United States, immigration is a frequent topic of discussion. Immigration is viewed by many as a problem, despite the fact that the majority of U.S. citizens are descendants of foreign lands (and not Native American). An immigrant is a foreign-born individual who permanently resides in another country—most often legally, though sometimes undocumented. Migrants are people who regularly move in order to find work. A refugee is a person who leaves their homeland, seeking protection against persecution. Some people argue that immigrants who are undocumented are breaking the laws of our country. The Church teaches that we must respect just civil laws (see CCC, 1899-1904). However, the *Catechism* also states, "The more prosperous nations are obliged, to the extent they are able, to welcome the *foreigner* in search of the security and the means of livelihood which he cannot find in his country of origin" (CCC, 2241).

Jesus insists that we welcome the stranger: "For I was hungry and you gave me food, I was thirsty and you gave me something to drink, I was a stranger and you welcomed me" (Matthew 25:35).

Pope Benedict XVI acknowledged that the lives of refugees and migrants are becoming more desperate. As the numbers of migrating people increase, so must the consciousness in all nations that these "people on the move" are our brothers and sisters.

"All, therefore, belong to one family, migrants and the local populations that welcome them, and all have the same right to enjoy the goods of the earth whose destination is universal, as the social doctrine of the Church teaches," the Pope said at the annual World Day of Migrants and Refugees in 2010. "It is here that solidarity and sharing are founded."

The U.S. Catholic Bishops Department of Migration and Refugee Services offers five specific guidelines for an immigration policy which respects human dignity: (1) addressing the root injustices which compel people to initially leave their homeland, (2) developing a better legal approach to keeping families intact, (3) creating programs that match workers with jobs, (4) giving undocumented immigrants who contribute to their community an opportunity to earn the right to remain here, and (5) protecting the borders from would-be terrorists while upholding humanitarian values.

**As a matter of justice:**

**Learn** more about the United States Conference of Catholic Bishops' Catholic Campaign for Immigration Reform.

**Welcome** newcomers to your community; model behavior that rejects anti-immigration racism and reach out to all ethnic communities.

**Write** a letter to elected officials, encouraging policies that respect human dignity.

Go to the student site at
**hs.osvcurriculum.com**

"All, therefore, belong to one family . . ."

You can be for justice without being a disciple, but you cannot be a disciple without being for justice.

**Identify the call narrative pattern** in one of the following: the Call of Gideon, *Judges 6:11b-17*; the Call of Jeremiah, *Jeremiah 1:4-10*; the Call of Isaiah, *Isaiah 6:1-13*; and the Call of Ezekiel, *Ezekiel 1:1–3:15*.

• One of the earliest stories that reveals this pattern is Genesis 24:34-48, which describes the time when the servant of Abraham was sent to find a wife for Isaac. Identify the call narrative pattern in this story.

Some biblical scholars point out a connection between Moses and Christ, a link between the Old and New Covenants. This connection is found in the circumstances surrounding both of their births. A new king had taken over in Egypt, knowing nothing about Joseph. The new king feared the large number of Israelites, who were being held as slaves. He viewed them as a threat to his rule and the security of his kingdom in the event of war. He ordered his taskmasters to oppress them with forced labor. Yet, the more the Israelites were oppressed, the more they multiplied and grew in number. God's covenant promise prevailed.

The king chose a drastic measure to limit the number of children born to the Israelites: he ordered midwives to kill all the boys born to the Hebrew women. When the midwives refused to carry out his orders, the Pharaoh commanded his subjects: "Every boy that is born to the Hebrews you shall throw into the Nile, but you shall let every girl live" (Exodus 1:22).

One of the Hebrew babies was placed in a basket and sent down the river, in an attempt to spare his life. His sister watched from a distance. The Pharaoh's daughter found the basket and baby, and called for a Hebrew woman to nurse the baby. That woman was actually the baby's mother, now chosen to nurse her own child. When the child grew older, the Pharaoh's daughter adopted him and gave him the Egyptian name "Moses," meaning "one drawn from the water."

**Identify** What covenant did God make with Moses?

**Connect** In what ways are the missions of Moses and Jesus reflective of each other?

**The Gospel according to Matthew uses part of the Exodus story** to portray Jesus as the "New Moses" for his Jewish audience.

Read *Matthew 2:1-23*.

○ After the birth of Jesus, what does King Herod do, and in what way does his action parallel one taken in the story of Moses?

○ Where do Jesus and his family flee to? How does this event parallel another in the story of Moses?

○ How, when, and why did Joseph know it was safe to return to Israel? Where did the Holy Family settle?

**REFLECT**

Some ways that we might hear the call of God include through Scripture, reflective prayer, encouragement from others, opportunities, and talents discovered, among others.

○ What mission is God calling you to?

○ What does God want you to accomplish over the next few years?

○ What do you have to do to accomplish this mission?

○ What objections and excuses do you have that may get in the way of completing the mission?

○ What signs and reassurances would you like to see from God?

## The Covenant of Moses

The mission of Moses is made clear. He is to go to the people of Israel and tell them that God has heard their cry, and will lead them out of their misery in Egypt to a promised land flowing with milk and honey.

After Moses shares this news with the Israelites, he must go to the Pharaoh and tell him to not only let them go, but also to offer sacrifice to God. As anyone would expect, Pharaoh is stubborn and refuses to release the Israelites. Pharaoh's response prompts God to strike Egypt with the ten plagues, until finally Pharaoh relents, and the people of Israel are freed.

Exodus 19 describes the covenant God makes with Moses at Mount Sinai. Remember that in covenants, both parties make promises. God calls Moses and reminds the Israelites of what he has done, then goes on to explain what the people will need to do now, and the benefits they will receive in return. "You have seen what I did to the Egyptians, and how I bore you on eagles' wings and brought you here to myself. Now therefore, if you obey my voice and keep my covenant, you shall be my treasured possession out of all the peoples. Indeed, the whole Earth is mine, but you shall be for me a priestly kingdom and a holy nation. These

APPLY

Psalm 136 is also read during the Easter Vigil Mass.
- Use Psalm 136 to create your own Responsorial Psalm. Decide which parts of the Psalm will be recited by the class, and which will be spoken by the leader.

## GO TO THE SOURCE

**Readings from the Book of Exodus** are used during the Easter Vigil Mass.

Read *Exodus 14:9-15:21*.
- Compare and contrast the attitudes toward God and the emotions of the people at the start of Pharoah's pursuit (Exodus 14:9-12) and after victoriously crossing the Red Sea (Exodus 14:26-15:21).
- To which passage do you feel drawn, and why?
- How do Psalms 78, 105, 106, 135 and 136 confirm this event?
- Pick one Psalm and summarize the details that it describes.

are the words that you shall speak to the Israelites" (Exodus 19:3-6). The people responded, "Everything that the Lord has spoken we will do" (Exodus 19:8).

God promises to appear in three days. Out of the clouds, thunder, and lightning God delivers the **Ten Commandments** to Moses.

The first three commandments involve love of God, and the last seven have to do with love of neighbor. These commands continue to apply to us today. Chapter 6 of the Book of Deuteronomy summarizes the first of these two aspects of the Ten Commandments.

**Ten Commandments** the fundamental moral laws given by God to his people to help them live by the covenant. They are also called the Decalogue, meaning "ten words."

Hear, O Israel: The LORD is our God, the LORD alone. You shall love the LORD your God with all your heart, and with all your soul, and with all your might.

—Deuteronomy 6:4-5

## RECALL

o Review the Ten Commandments found in Exodus 20 and Deuteronomy 5.

o How many of them can you name without looking at them?

This passage from Deuteronomy is referred to as the Shema prayer, which is considered the most important prayer in the Jewish faith. It reveals the identity of the God of Israel and explains what believers are to do in their covenant relationship with God.

Then, Leviticus 19:18 sums up the meaning of the following seven commandments: "You shall love your neighbor as yourself." In the Synoptic Gospels, a scribe/lawyer asks Jesus the question, "'Teacher, which commandment in the law is the greatest?'

He said to him, 'You shall love the Lord your God with all your heart, and with all your soul, and with all your mind'. . . . And a second is like it: 'You shall love your neighbor as yourself' (Matthew 22:36-37, 39). Jesus takes the Ten Commandments and turns them into two by quoting Deuteronomy and Leviticus (see Matthew 22:34-40; Mark 12:28-34; Luke 10:25-28). The Catechism calls these the "twofold commandment of charity" (CCC, 16).

**Blessed Pope John Paul II addressed the Jewish community in the great synagogue of Rome on April 13, 1986.** He spoke about the importance of the Jewish Scripture and the relationship between Jews and Christians, and said all people find truth and freedom in observing the Commandments. Promoting that ideal is one of the great duties of people today.

o "In doing this . . . we shall each be faithful to our most sacred commitments, and also to that which most profoundly unites and gathers us together: faith in the one God who 'loves the strangers' and 'executes justice for the orphan and the widow' (Deuteronomy 10:18-19), commanding us to love and help them (see Leviticus 19:18-34)" Pope John Paul II said.

o Pope John Paul II said that Christians learned God's love for strangers and justice for the oppressed from the Old Testament and from Jesus, who embodied the love demanded by the Torah.

o The Pope called the Jewish religion "intrinsic" and essential to Christians. This connection is one we do not have with other religions.

SOURCE: *Origins*, April 24, 1986

Throughout his papacy, Blessed Pope John Paul II reaffirmed the connection between Jews and Christians.

# Faith & Culture

⌐ Go to the student site at **hs.osvcurriculum.com**

The Book of Exodus tells us that the People of Israel ratify the covenant by saying, "All the words that the LORD has spoken we will do" (Exodus 24:3). Moses builds an altar and erects twelve pillars for the twelve tribes of Israel. He offers holocausts and sacrifices taking the blood from the bulls, and sprinkles half on the altar and half on the people, saying, "See the blood of the covenant that the LORD has made with you in accordance with all these words" (Exodus 24:8).

Today the prayers and ritual we use in the dedication of an altar reflect this ancient ritual of Moses. During the Introductory Rite, the people are sprinkled with water as a sign of repentance and Baptism. The bishop says these words before blessing the water: "But first let us ask God to bless this gift of water. As it is sprinkled upon us and upon this altar, may it be a sign of our repentance and a reminder of our baptism" (*The Rites*, Vol. 2, p. 417)

Moses, who delivered the Israelites from captivity in Egypt, was also reflected in a woman named Dorothy Day, who helped deliver people from lives of poverty in the twentieth century. Day founded the Catholic Worker movement, which still operates today, to help people find work and deal with poverty. In March of 2000, Blessed Pope John Paul II gave approval for the Archdiocese of New York to open the cause for the beatification and canonization of Dorothy Day, acknowledging her as a "Servant of God." People who loved and respected Dorothy Day have worked on her cause for canonization for this modern-day Moses.

**Identify** How many of the Ten Commandments deal with love of God, and how many deal with the love of neighbor?

**Conclude** What is the significance of the covenant God made with Moses?

## GO TO THE SOURCE

**The Letter to the Hebrews** recalls the many examples of strong faith shown in the account of Moses' life.

Read the *Letter to the Hebrews 11:23-29*.

○ Summarize the parts that describe the events in the life of Moses that foreshadowed events that took place in the life of Christ.

## SECTION 3 REVIEW

### QUICK REVIEW

**1a. Interpret** What tragedy happens to the Israelites because of the new king?

**b. Connect** How does the Gospel according to Matthew link Moses and Jesus?

**2a. List** Describe the pattern of the Call Narrative.

**b. Summarize** What was Moses' mission?

**3. Recall** How does Jesus use the Old Testament to answer, "Which is the greatest of the commandments?"

### ACT

Visit the altar in your parish church.

○ Note any decorations on the altar, such as carvings, and ask about their significance.

○ Find out when the altar was dedicated, and by which bishop.

**Pray** Compose a short prayer thanking God for the altar and other physical signs that reflect our covenant with God.

### SELF-ASSESS

Which statement best reflects where you are now?

☐ I'm confident enough about the material in this section to be able to explain it to someone else.

☐ I have a good grasp of the material in this section, but I could use more review.

☐ I'm lost. I need help catching up before moving on.

# The Covenant Promise of David

The oil of catechumens is used to consecrate altars in Catholic churches.

**shalom** Hebrew greeting meaning peace

**Messiah** literally means "the anointed one," and was the person who would bring peace and justice to the world

**consecrated** declared sacred or set aside for special purposes to serve God

The judges, kings, and prophets of the Old Testament reminded the people about the promised Messiah. The Jewish tradition contains many different understandings of the Messiah, but one common theme was that the Messiah was expected to bring **shalom**, or peace and justice, to the world. **Messiah** literally means "anointed one," as one would describe a priest or king. Once anointed, the person would be **consecrated**, or set aside for a special purpose to serve God and the people of Israel.

We find many understandings of the Messiah in the Old Testament. For instance, the Book of Deuteronomy speaks of the Messiah as a "New Moses." The Book of Daniel presents a Messiah like a "Son of Man." The prophet Isaiah describes a Messiah known as the "Suffering Servant," who represented the people of Israel.

Some of the prophets, like Malachi, look to the great prophet Elijah as the one who would announce the coming of the Messiah. The Messiah was thought of as the greatest of the kings, and this connection was made explicit through the line of King David. "Many Jews and even certain Gentiles who shared their hope recognized in Jesus the fundamental attributes of the messianic 'Son of David' promised by God to Israel"[26] (CCC, 439).

Let's look first at the Book of Genesis, which alludes to the Messiah in the Abraham story.

**Name** What is the Hebrew word for peace?

**Elaborate** How is the king from Genesis 14:18 connected with Jesus?

## GO TO THE SOURCE 📖

**The Book of Genesis** alludes to the Messiah in the Abraham story.

Read *Genesis 14*.

○ What is the name of the King of Salem?

○ Salem is later identified with the city of Jerusalem. King of Salem can also be translated "King of Peace." Explain how these details foreshadow Jesus Christ.

○ What does this king say and do in Genesis 14:18-20? How does this prefigure the actions of Christ?

Read *Psalm 110*, *Matthew 22:44*, and *Acts 2:34-35*.

○ Who is used as an example of this king and priest?

## The Son of Man

The *Catechism* contains many references to the "Son of Man" title for Jesus. The Son of God, Second Divine Person of the Blessed Trinity, became man so we may take part in the Divine nature. "For the Son of God became man so that we might become God"[27] (CCC, 460). The passage on the "Son of Man" in the Book of Daniel lends itself to prefiguring a future Messiah by describing a vision.

> As I watched in the night visions,
> I saw one like a human being
> coming with the clouds of heaven.
> And he came to the Ancient One
> and was presented before him.
> To him was given dominion
> and glory and kingship,
> that all peoples, nations, and languages
> should serve him.
> His dominion is an everlasting dominion
> that shall not pass away,
> and his kingship is one
> that shall never be destroyed.
>
> —Daniel 7:13-14

In several passages, the prophet Isaiah prophesied the coming of a suffering servant who "was wounded for our transgressions . . . and by his bruises we are healed" and who "poured out himself to death, and was numbered with the transgressors; yet he bore the sin of many, and made intercession for the transgressors" (Isaiah 53:5, 12). Catholics understand these passages as a prophecy of Christ who willingly suffered and gave his life for the sins of all.

## The Judges Before the Kings

We have discussed the Patriarchs who enter into a covenant relationship with God that promised them land and descendants. This covenant promise passes beyond the patriarchs to Moses, who is promised the land and given the Ten Commandments. After Israel enters the land and before the Israelites choose to have a king, the people are guided and led by a series of judges.

The success of the judges depends on whether they are faithful to God's Law. When the Israelites offend the Lord, they are defeated and oppressed by a foreign ruler. When Israel cries out to God for help, God raises up a judge to rescue them. Famous judges include Samuel, Deborah, Gideon, and Samson. The Book of Judges ends with this verse: "In those days there was no king in Israel; all the people did what was right in their own eyes" (Judges 21:25).

The first Book of Samuel reports that the elders of Israel are requesting a king for Israel. The text explains the tension over this request that would be similar to a request for a Temple. "But the thing displeased Samuel when they said 'Give us a king to govern us.' Samuel prayed to the Lord, and the Lord said to Samuel: 'Listen to the voice of the people in all that they say to you; for they have not rejected you, but they have rejected me from being king over

## GO TO THE SOURCE

**This passage on the suffering servant** is read every year to help us understand the suffering of Christ on Palm Sunday and Good Friday.

Read *Isaiah 50:4-6* and *Isaiah 52:13–53:12*.
○ Describe the suffering servant.
○ What will happen as a result of the servant's suffering?

## GO TO THE SOURCE

**Jesus used this image** from the Book of Daniel on the lips of Jesus during his questioning by the High Priest.

Read *Mark 14:61-64*; *Matthew 26: 63-65*; and *Luke 22:67-71*.
○ Identify the parallels between the exchange in each Gospel and the passage from Daniel 7:13-14.

The writer of Hebrews links Melchizedek with **Jesus** and interprets the promise made to Abraham in light of the high priesthood of Christ.

○ Read the *Letter to the Hebrews 4:14–7:28* to understand the link.

them. . . . Now then, listen to their voice; only—you shall solemnly warn them, and show them the ways of the king who shall reign over them'" (1 Samuel 8:6-7, 9).

The reason for the tension and underlying concern in this passage is that kings were considered divine rulers in the ancient world. In the case of the Israelites, their request for a king could be considered by many to be a dismissal of God. That results in expressed disappointment in the rejection of the God who "brought up Israel out of Egypt, and I rescued you from the hand of the Egyptians and from the hand of all the kingdoms that were oppressing you.' But today you have rejected your God, who saves you from all your calamities and your distresses; and you have said, 'No! but set a king over us'" (1 Samuel 10:18-19). Saul is appointed the first king of Israel, and is followed by David.

**Recall** When was Israel led by the judges?

**Explain** How did the success of the judges depend on their obedience to God's Law?

### Signs of the Davidic Covenant

In 2 Samuel 5:1-10, David takes over the city of Jerusalem from the Jebusites. Jerusalem then becomes the City of David. In 2 Samuel 7, David suggests a Temple for God, and once again there is a tension in this new stage of Israel's history. God had never had an earthly or symbolic house before. This change would involve a shift of focus, expressed through this message that God gives the prophet Nathan.

Go and tell my servant David: Thus says the LORD: Are you the one to build me a house to live in? I have not lived in a house since the day I brought up the people of Israel from Egypt to this day, but I have been moving about in a tent and a tabernacle. Wherever I have moved about among all the people of Israel, did I ever speak a word with any one of the tribal leaders of Israel, whom I commanded to shepherd my people Israel, saying: "Why have you not built me a house of cedar?"

—2 Samuel 7:5-7

Although God hadn't asked for—and didn't need—a house, God does grant the wish of David to build one. This is accomplished during the reign of David's son, Solomon. The Davidic Covenant is expressed in this passage:

Thus says the LORD of hosts: I took you from the pasture, from following the sheep to be prince over my people Israel; and I have been with you wherever you went, and have cut off all your enemies from before you; and I will make for you a great name, like the name of the great ones of the earth. And I will appoint a place for my people Israel and I will plant them, so that they may live in their own place, and be disturbed no more; . . . the LORD declares to you that the LORD will make you a house. When your days are fulfilled and you lie down with your ancestors, I will raise up your offspring after you, who shall come forth from your body, and I will establish his kingdom. He shall build a house for my name, and I will establish the throne of his kingdom forever. I will be a father to him, and he shall be a son to me. . . . Your house and your kingdom shall be made sure forever before me; your throne shall be established forever.

—2 Samuel 7:8-10, 11-14, 16

# Prayers of LAMENTATION

Prayers of lamentation are traditional prayer forms listed in the *Catechism* among those found in Psalms, the Old Testament's great book of prayer. They are part of the human experience expressing anger, grief, suffering, and loss. Prayers of lamentation often bring about conversion following healing from God.

> Do not forsake me, O Lord;
>> O my God, do not be far from me;
> make haste to help me,
>> O Lord, my salvation.
>
> —Psalm 38:21-22

We know that people in the Bible wept and grieved over tragedies. Suffering can be redemptive for ourselves and for others. When tragedy happens, we seek God's healing. We lament because we value life and the dignity of the person.

People of faith continue to practice lamentations every day. When people take their anger, sorrow, or frustration and turn it into a prayer, we call it lamentation. The spiritual practice of lamentation is a prayer form that involves two steps:

• Honest description of your pain, anger, frustration, or grief

• Expression of your faith and hope in God's help

You can practice lamenting for yourself, for family and friends, or for victims of famine, war, and hardship anywhere in the world. You can also practice lamentation out of your anger over someone's injustice, selfishness, or deceit.

Lamentation is different from complaining because it intentionally makes your sadness a prayerful expression of your faith. We think that we should always "grin and bear it" as if everything that happens is God's will. Our faith actually calls us to sustain our spiritual strength by telling God about our pain while still expressing our faith in his love, compassion, mercy, and help.

That is exactly what Jesus did when he was in agony in the garden, and even while dying: "And about three o'clock Jesus cried with a loud voice, 'Eli, Eli, lema sabachthani?' that is, 'My God, my God, why have you forsaken me?'" (Matthew 27:46). Then he added, "Into your hands I commend my spirit" (Luke 23:46).

Place a T for true or F for false by each of the following:

____ I usually lament for the plight of others
____ I complain instead of lament
____ I have a special place to go for my practice of lamentation
____ I want to make this practice a regular part of my spirituality

Choose one of the following and compose a lamentation using both of the proper elements: a description of your feelings, and an expression of your faith.

Family issue    Local injustice    Poverty    War
Global situation    Friend's troubles

_____

_____

_____

_____

Read *2 Samuel 7:1-17* and *1 Chronicles 17:1-15*.

○ Compare and summarize the two stories, pointing out similarities and any differences.

○ What do Psalm 89:1-5, 29-30 and 37-38, and Psalm 132:11-12 say about the promise God makes to David? Notice how Psalm 132 revisits the wish of David to build a house for God.

The Davidic covenant is the promise God makes that the throne and kingdom of David will last forever. This covenant promise is the first stage of understanding Jesus as what is known as a Davidic Messiah. The Gospel according to Matthew begins by tracing Jesus' genealogy to David. The signs of the Davidic covenant—the throne, temple, and city of Jerusalem—will prefigure the Kingdom of God that Jesus will preach about, including the throne of the Cross, the destruction of his "temple" (body) and restoring the "temple" in three days, and the new Jerusalem in Heaven.

**Name** Who finally builds a Temple for God?

**Summarize** What does God's covenant with David involve?

## The Building of the Temple

1 Kings 6 and 7 describes the building of the "Temple of the Lord," and 1 Kings 8 describes the dedication of the Temple. The passages describing the building of the Temple include a very important conditional "if."

> Now the word of the LORD came to Solomon, 'Concerning this house that you are building, if you will walk in my statutes, obey my ordinances, and keep all my commandments by walking in them, then I will establish my promise with you, which I made to your father David. I will dwell among the children of Israel, and will not forsake my people Israel.'
>
> —1 Kings 6:11-13

Solomon himself reminds the people of Israel at the dedication of the Temple, "Therefore devote yourselves completely to the LORD our God, walking in his statutes and keeping his commandments, as at this day" (1 Kings 8:61).

The "if" warning given to Solomon suggests that the Israelites will be punished if Israel is disobedient. Just as the vision of Abraham in Genesis foretold the period of slavery in Egypt, this warning can be seen as a prediction of the future exile of Israel and the destruction of the Temple and city of Jerusalem, the signs of the promise of the Davidic Covenant.

When that punishment—the exile of Israel—takes place, the pattern that results is clear. There are negative consequences for the disobedience of the Israelites. God, however, is never unfaithful to his Covenants. "For you came in mercy to the aid of all, so that those who seek might find you. Time and again you offered them covenants and through the prophets taught them to look forward to salvation" (*Roman Missal*, Eucharistic Prayer IV).

## The Messianic Prophecies

The second stage of understanding Jesus as the Davidic Messiah focuses on the royalty and kingship that runs through the line of David. These Messianic Prophecies are found in the writings of the prophets up to the time of the exile. The best examples of this are in the Book of the prophet Isaiah. "Therefore the Lord himself will give you a sign. Look, the young woman is with child and shall bear a son, and shall name him Immanuel" (Isaiah 7:14). The name Immanuel means "God with us." Isaiah continues:

> For a child has been born for us,
>     a son given to us;
> authority rests upon his shoulders;
>     and he is named
> Wonderful Counselor, Mighty God,
>     Everlasting Father, Prince of Peace.
> His authority shall grow continually,
>     and there shall be endless peace
> for the throne of David and his kingdom.
>     He will establish and uphold it
> with justice and with righteousness
>     from this time onward and forevermore.
>
> —Isaiah 9:6-7

This passage is read during the season of Advent and can also be found in many Christmas cards. It foretells a time after the Messiah when natural enemies, such as the wolf and lamb, will live in peace. "They will not hurt or destroy on all my holy mountain; for the earth will be full of the knowledge of the Lord as the waters cover the sea" (Isaiah 11:9).

**Recall** What does Solomon remind the People of Israel about at the dedication of the Temple?

**Explain** What is the Messianic Prophecy and what is an example from Isaiah?

## The Coming of Elijah

The Book of the prophet Malachi is the last book of the Old Testament before the New Testament begins. The prophet Malachi can be seen as the "bridge" to the New Testament because of the verses that reference a messenger to prepare the way for the "day of the Lord." We interpret this to mean the coming of the Messiah. As Jesus began his public ministry, believers clearly

### GO TO THE SOURCE

**The Covenant** made to David and Solomon is addressed.

Go back to *Psalm 89* and read verses *39-52*.
○ Summarize the thoughts expressed in the psalm.
○ Describe a time in your own life when you felt the kind of hopelessness and disappointment described in the Psalm.

Read about the sins of Solomon in *1 Kings 11:1-43*.
○ Describe and summarize the sins of Solomon in 1 Kings 11:1-10.
○ Describe and summarize the punishment of Solomon and Israel in 1 Kings 11:11-40.

Notice the repeating of the promise to David in *1 Kings 11:38* and the hope God still holds in David's descendants in *1 Kings 11:39*.
○ What does this discussion tell you about God?

must have understood this messenger to be John the Baptist, because he prepared the way for the coming of Jesus, the Messiah, the Christ—meaning the Anointed One—and Savior of the world.

> See, I am sending my messenger to prepare the way before me, and the Lord whom you seek will suddenly come to his temple. The messenger of the covenant in whom you delight—indeed, he is coming, says the LORD of hosts. But who can endure the day of his coming, and who can stand when he appears? . . . Lo, I will send you the prophet Elijah before the great and terrible day of the LORD comes. He will turn the hearts of parents to their children, and the hearts of children to their parents, so that I will not come and strike the land with a curse.
>
> —Malachi 3:1-2; 4:5-6

The Gospel according to Mark includes a passage from Malachi, which also connects to a verse from Isaiah: "The voice of one crying out in the wilderness: 'Prepare the way of the Lord, make his paths straight'" (Mark 1:2-3). Following this passage, we see John the Baptist proclaiming a baptism of repentance for the forgiveness of sins, highlighting his role as the Elijah figure who announces the coming of the Messiah. And Mark's description of John the Baptist's physical appearance mirrors the description of Elijah (see 2 Kings 1:8; Mark 1:6).

**The miracles of Elijah** and his successor Elisha prefigure those performed by Jesus in the Gospels.

Identify the parallels between the prophets and Jesus in the following passages:

○ *1 Kings 17:17-24, Luke 7:11-17,* and *2 Kings 4:31-37*

○ *2 Kings 4:42-44* and *Matthew 14:13-21; Mark 6:32-44; Luke 9:10b-17;* and *John 6:1-15*

## Fulfillment of the Promise

The disciples of Jesus eventually understood that he was the Messiah and the Son of Man. They also came to understand his kingship to be that of a different kind of leader. He was a servant leader, not a political or kingly ruler. "Jesus accepted his rightful title of Messiah, though with some reserve because it was understood by some of his contemporaries in too human a sense as essentially political"[28] (CCC, 439). His authority came from God, and demanded the total covenant loyalty and obedience to God that the Davidic king embodied on Earth.

Jesus, the Son of God, Second Person of the Blessed Trinity, embodies the God of the Covenant with Israel, and the New Covenant that will last forever.

**Identify** Which book of the Old Testament is the last one before the New Testament?

**Explain** How is Jesus different from an earthly king?

## SECTION **4 REVIEW**

> ### QUICK REVIEW

**1a. Interpret** How was Melchizedek a foreshadowing of Jesus?

**b. Link** How did Isaiah's suffering servant prefigure Jesus?

**2a. Identify** Who is the messenger mentioned in the Book of Malachi, and why is he important?

**b. Recall** How did Elijah and Elisha prefigure Jesus' coming?

**3a. Identify** What were Israel's rulers called before the people demanded to have a king?

**b. Explain** Why was it considered problematic to have a king ruling the People of Israel?

**4a. Interpret** What was the Davidic Covenant, and why was it important?

**b. Name** Who built the Temple in Jerusalem?

**c. Infer** What does God's warning to Solomon mean?

**Listen and Discuss** Close your eyes and listen as a classmate reads some of Isaiah's prophecies about the coming of the Messiah.

○ Concentrate on forming vivid mental images as you listen.

○ Talk with a few classmates about the images you created from the readings.

○ Discuss how different life would be if Isaiah's images dominated the world.

> ### SELF-ASSESS

Which statement best reflects where you are now?

☐ I'm confident enough about the material in this section to be able to explain it to someone else.

☐ I have a good grasp of the material in this section, but I could use more review.

☐ I'm lost. I need help catching up before moving on.

# PRAYER

**Give us, O Lord,**
a steadfast heart,
which no unworthy affection
may drag downwards;
give us an unconquered heart,
which no tribulation
can wear out;
give us an upright heart,
which no unworthy purpose
may tempt aside.
Bestow upon us also,
O Lord our God,
understanding to know you,
diligence to seek you,
wisdom to find you,
and a faithfulness
that may finally embrace you;
through Jesus Christ our Lord.

—Saint Thomas Aquinas

## TERMS

Use each of the following terms in a sentence that shows you know what the term means. You may include more than one term in a sentence.

| | |
|---|---|
| New Covenant | patriarch |
| Magisterium | Ten Commandments |
| typology | shalom |
| prefiguration | Messiah |
| genealogy | consecrated |

## PEOPLE

Use information from the chapter to tell why each person or term is significant.

1. Abram/Abraham

2. Sarai/Sarah

3. Isaac

4. Ishmael

5. Saint Irenaeus

6. Moses

7. Melchizedek

8. Suffering Servant

9. Isaiah

10. David

11. Solomon

## UNDERSTANDING

Answer each question and complete each exercise

### SECTION 1

1. **Analyze** What is the importance of studying covenant relationships?
2. **Explain** Why is the New Covenant, established through Jesus, the last one that will be established?
3. **Explain** Why does the Church venerate the Old Testament?
4. **Summarize** Describe the Christian interpretation of the story of Abraham and the sacrifice of his son Isaac.

### SECTION 2

5. **Tell** What was God's promise to Abram?
6. **Explain** Why is Ishmael important?
7. **Summarize** Tell some lessons that are taught through the story of Abraham.

### SECTION 3

8. **Compare** What are some similarities between the early lives of Moses and Jesus?
9. **Connect** What is the relationship between the Ten Commandments and the two-fold commandment of charity?
10. **Recall** What is the Shema prayer?

11. **Connect** What is the connection between Melchizedek and today's priests?

12. **Identify** Who wrote about the suffering servant, and why are these readings important?

13. **Restate** How did Israelites come to be ruled by a king?

14. **Explain** Tell why David and Solomon were important leaders of Israel.

## CONNECTING

**Visual** This artwork, painted in about 1500 by Absolon Stumme, shows the Tree of Jesse. Jesse was the father of King David, from whom Jesus descended.

Explain the symbolism of having the tree grow from Jesse's chest. What does the painting teach about the lineage from Jesse to Jesus? Is the dress of the people consistent with Biblical times? What might account for any differences?

**Challenge** You are at the mall with a group of friends, one of whom is Jewish. Some in the group ask your Jewish friend some questions.

    **Friend 1:** Do you like being Jewish?

    **Jewish Friend:** It's who I am.

    **Friend 2:** Do you read the Bible?

    **Jewish Friend:** We read the Old Testament.

    **Friend 3:** Well, I read the New Testament because the Old Testament doesn't really concern Christians.

    **You:** Of course it concerns Christians!

○ Use information from the chapter to explain your objection to what your friend said.

**Question** After working through this chapter, how would you outline God's plan for salvation as you know it?

## SELF-ASSESS

**On Your Own** Make a list of the most important things you learned from this chapter, then select three things that represent your growth in understanding. Write a paragraph explaining your choices.

**With a Partner** List what you found most helpful or interesting in this chapter, as well as any other questions that have surfaced.

○ What might the person in this photo be expressing?

○ When do you feel closest to God?

# The Messiah and Redemption

 Go to the student site at
**hs.osvcurriculum.com**

# WHAT DOES IT MEAN?

## To sacrifice for others.

**A religion teacher** read the following story to her sophomore religion class.

A high school student developed a rare blood disease. His family was devastated, but fortunately, the teen's 5-year-old brother had miraculously survived the same disorder and had developed antibodies against the disease. The father sat his younger son down and explained to him that they could use his blood to save his older brother's life. "I'll do it," the child agreed. The young boy was quiet on the way to hospital to donate blood, but his family did not notice. When they arrived, they took him into the donor room and he was prepped for the procedure. As his blood began to transfer to the clear plastic bag, the boy turned to his parents with tears in his eyes and asked, "How long will it be before I die?" The 5-year-old had misunderstood. The boy agreed to save his brother's life thinking they needed all of his blood.

The teacher taped the story to the board and wrote underneath it in large letters:

*P-A-S-C-H-A-L M-Y-S-T-E-R-Y*

Why did she write this term?

Check the answer that best matches where you are today.

*I can explain the Incarnation*
☐ Quite a bit   ☐ Somewhat   ☐ Not at all

*I know what Salvation is all about*
☐ Quite a bit   ☐ Somewhat   ☐ Not at all

*I've experienced being spiritually "lost"*
☐ Quite a bit   ☐ Somewhat   ☐ Not at all

*I see why humanity needs Redemption*
☐ Quite a bit   ☐ Somewhat   ☐ Not at all

*I trust that Jesus' name has power*
☐ Quite a bit   ☐ Somewhat   ☐ Not at all

*I am clear about who Jesus is*
☐ Quite a bit   ☐ Somewhat   ☐ Not at all

# The Incarnation

*What do the titles given to Jesus say about his mission?*
*What about Redemption?*

*Have you ever struggled to find the words to explain something to someone?*

The Old Testament tells us of the promise of the Messiah and **Redemption**. As followers of Christ, we know that promise is fulfilled in Jesus Christ: the Messiah, our Savior, and our Redeemer. As Catholics, we use those terms a lot. They have become integral to understanding who Jesus is and what that means for our lives.

> Peter said to them, 'Repent, and be baptized every one of you in the name of Jesus Christ so that your sins may be forgiven; and you will receive the gift of the Holy Spirit.'
>
> —Acts 2:38

Every time we say the Nicene Creed, we profess our faith in the Incarnation, "For us men and for our salvation he came down from heaven, and by the Holy Spirit was incarnate of the Virgin Mary, and became man." The *Catechism of the Catholic Church* gives four reasons for the Incarnation: The Word became flesh in order to save us by reconciling us with God; so that we might know God's love; to be our model of holiness; and to make us partakers of the divine nature (see CCC, 457-460).

Saints throughout the ages have recognized the purpose of the Incarnation:

- "For this is why the Word became man, and the Son of God became the Son of Man: so that man, by entering into communion with the Word and thus receiving divine sonship, might become a son of God" (Saint Irenaeus). The Son of God did not lose his divine nature when he took on human nature.

- "For the Son of God became man so that we might become God" (Saint Athanasius).

- "The only-begotten Son of God, wanting to make us sharers in his divinity, assumed our nature, so that he, made man, might make men gods" (Saint Thomas Aquinas).

**Redemption** the action of being saved from sin, or God's plan made possible through the life, Death and Resurrection of Jesus, by which our sins are forgiven and we are reconciled to God

**kenosis** the self-emptying of the Son of God

## DISCUSS

Since the Son of God became man so that we might become one with God, how have we done as people made in God's divine image and likeness?

○ Evaluate three human accomplishments over the centuries, for the better or for the worse. Give concrete examples of the best and worst that humanity has accomplished.

○ Make a list of human qualities that reflect God's influence in our lives.

**Saint Paul expresses his understanding of the Incarnation** in this great hymn about Jesus. This passage is about the **kenosis**, or the self-emptying, of the Son of God. This is what we need to do as disciples. We must imitate the divine humility of Jesus.

Read *Philippians 2:5-11*.
○ How does this passage depict the relationship between Jesus and God the Father?

○ How then can you move in the direction of God?

Saint Gregory of Nyssa, reflecting on the flaws of human nature throughout history, speaks of the need for humanity to be saved through the Incarnation:

> Sick, our nature demanded to be healed; fallen, to be raised up; dead, to rise again. We had lost the possession of the good; it was necessary for it to be given back to us. Closed in the darkness, it was necessary to bring us the light; captives, we awaited a Savior; prisoners, help; slaves, a liberator. Are these things minor or insignificant? Did they not move God to descend to human nature and visit it, since humanity was in so miserable and unhappy a state?[29]
>
> —Saint Gregory of Nyssa (CCC, 457)

**Define**  What does Redemption mean?

**Connect**  What are four reasons for the Incarnation?

## APPLY

Here again are the parallel images Saint Gregory used around A.D. 375 to describe the state of humanity and God's motivation to save us: sick—to be healed; fallen—to be raised up; dead—to rise again; lost it—to be given it back; in darkness—to be brought into the light; and captives, prisoners, slaves—to be liberated.

○ Come up with two new parallel images that Saint Gregory might use if he were alive today. Use his format: _____ to be _____.

## The Identity of Jesus

The Old Testament provided the Jewish faithful with the notion of the Messiah, describing both the purpose and identity of the Promised One. The Gospels recognize Jesus as the fulfillment of the promise. As we understand what it means to confess that Jesus is the Messiah, it is important to remember the context and continuity of Messiah from the Jewish tradition.

> A shoot shall come out from the stump of Jesse,
>     and a branch shall grow out of his roots.
>
> The spirit of the LORD shall rest on him,
>
>     the spirit of wisdom and understanding,
>     the spirit of counsel and might,
>     the spirit of knowledge and the fear of the LORD.
>
> —Isaiah 11:1-2

Jesse is the father of the boy who would become known as King David. Jesus is a descendant of these important figures in Jewish history. This is significant since the Old Testament prophesizes that the Messiah would be a descendent of King David. The Old Testament also foretells the virgin birth in Bethlehem, Jesus' suffering for our salvation, and the Resurrection.

## COMPARE

Examine each of the following Scripture passages, and identify which Book, Chapter, Verse matches with the quoted phrases in paragraphs 422-423 from the *Catechism*.

- Mark 1:1
- 1 John 4:2
- Galatians 4:4-5
- John 13:3
- Mark 1:11
- John 1:14, 16
- John 3:13; 6:33

We believe and confess that Jesus of Nazareth, born of a Jew of a daughter of Israel at Bethlehem at the time of King Herod the Great and the emperor Caesar Augustus, a carpenter by trade, who died crucified in Jerusalem under the procurator Pontius Pilate during the reign of the emperor Tiberius, is the eternal Son of God made man. He "came from God,"[30] "descended from heaven,"[31] and "came in the flesh."[32] For "the Word became flesh and dwelt among us, full of grace and truth; we have beheld his glory, glory as of the only Son of the Father . . . And from his fullness have we all received, grace upon grace."[33]

—CCC, 423

So how did Jesus live his life on Earth? The Gospels tell us quite a bit. He lived a simple life, identifying with those in need. He healed people. He preached with authority. He performed miracles. He prayed the Psalms and went to the Temple and synagogue.

From his birth until his Death on the Cross, Jesus shared the life of the poor, enriching us with his poverty. His experience included thirst, hunger, and lack of sleep. "Foxes have holes, and birds of the air have nests; but the Son of Man has nowhere to lay his head" (Luke 9:57). Jesus always identified with the poor and actively loving and helping the poor is a condition he gave for entering God's Kingdom. "Truly I tell you, just as you did it to one of the least of these who are members of my family, you did it to me" (Matthew 25:40; see CCC, 544).

We know Jesus traveled throughout the Holy Land and performed miracles and preached to crowds. His miracles include healing the blind, the paralyzed, and even those with leprosy. "Moved with pity, Jesus stretched out his hand and touched him, and said to him, 'I do will it. Be made clean!'" (Mark 1:41:NAB).

In Jesus' preaching, summarized in the Sermon on the Mount, he told crowds that the lowly were blessed; that the most vulnerable would be heirs to the Kingdom and would receive God's grace. He told people how to live and how to deal with anger, oaths, retaliation, and even enemies, but his teachings were different from what people were used to hearing: "But I say to you, Love your enemies and pray for those who persecute you" (Matthew 5:44). Jesus also pointed people to the Father urging us to be perfect as the Father is (see Matthew 5:48). He also taught us how to pray, fast, and to trust God the Father for the things we need.

In his family life and in his ministry with the disciples, Jesus followed Jewish laws, traditions, and customs. Jesus had a deep reverence for the Torah.

## GO TO THE SOURCE

**Look up the following passages** about the religious feasts that Israel, and therefore Jesus, celebrated:

The Sabbath Day, *Leviticus 23:1-3*; Passover, *Leviticus 23:4-14*; Pentecost, *Leviticus 23:15-22*; The New Year/Rosh Hashanah, *Leviticus 23:23-25*; the Day of Atonement/Yon Kippur, *Leviticus 23:26-32*; Tabernacles, *Leviticus 23:33-44*; *Deuteronomy 16: 13-17*; *Exodus 23:16*.

Then read the *Letter to the Hebrews* and see how the Jewish rituals were reinterpreted in light of Christ and the Christian faith.

- Compare and contrast the Letter to the Hebrews with the Old Testament writings. List the parallels and differences that you notice.

# Saint Edith Stein

## (1891–1942)

Jesus and all of his first followers were devout Jews. It wasn't until Saint Paul began his missionary journeys to Asia Minor that Gentiles began to convert to the new religion. Most of the Catholics you know were probably born into Catholic families, but some people leave the religion of their ancestors and convert to Catholicism, finding both the promise and mystery of Redemption.

Saint Edith Stein experienced such a conversion. The youngest of eleven children, she was born in 1891 in Breslau, Germany, into a devout Jewish family. Her father died when she was 2 and though her mother tried to pass on her Jewish faith, Edith wasn't interested in religious matters. She stopped praying and, by the age of 14, she regarded herself an atheist.

She was an exceptional student and completed her university studies at a time when few women were given an opportunity to continue their education past elementary school. In 1921, she read Saint Teresa of Avila's autobiography and found her heart and her mind drawn toward the Catholic Church. She was baptized on January 1, 1922, and acknowledged both her Jewish roots and her new-found faith,

saying, "I had given up practicing my Jewish religion when I was a 14-year-old girl and did not begin to feel Jewish again until I had returned to God."

She wished to enter a convent, but her spiritual mentors encouraged her to keep teaching and writing instead. It wasn't until 1933, when new Nazi laws forbid those of Jewish descent to teach, that she finally joined a Carmelite convent in Cologne.

Edith continued her academic work as best she could although the growing Nazi threat against Jews caused her to move to the Netherlands for protection. Even there she was not safe. On August 2, 1942, the Nazis came to her convent and rounded up all the Jewish Christians, including Edith and her sister Rosa who had also converted. They were sent to Auschwitz where they were killed along with thousands of others.

This home in Wroclaw, Poland, belonged to the Stein family until it was taken by the Nazis in 1939. Today, it is the home of the Edith Stein Society, an organization devoted to Jewish-Christian understanding.

Edith saw herself as both a child of the Jewish people and a child of the Catholic Church. Her conversion did not lead her to reject the faith of her ancestors, but rather to see Jesus as the fulfillment of the Jewish Scriptures, the long-awaited Messiah. At the time of her canonization, Pope John Paul II called her "a daughter of Israel," who remained faithful both to "the crucified Lord Jesus Christ and, as a Jew, to her people in loving faithfulness."

Like those first Jewish converts 2,000 years ago, Edith Stein embraced both her Jewish roots and her Christian convictions, becoming a modern-day martyr for both faiths.

**Think About It** Do you know someone who has converted to Catholicism from another religion? Ask them what it was about the Catholic faith that drew them to inquire and be received into the Church. What is your family's religious background? Has your family always been Catholic or did someone convert from a different faith? Why do you think that Saint Edith is considered both a Jewish and Christian martyr?

Go to the student site at
**hs.osvcurriculum.com**

In his teaching, Jesus reflected a Jewish understanding of the nature of God through his relationship with his Father. The Jews understood God as the Lord of history, extending justice to all people, as a loving and merciful Father. The Jewish people viewed God as both **transcendent**, going beyond the realm of human lives, and **immanent**, very much within the lives of humans and human history.

The relationship between Christ and the Father is unique because they are one, the first and second Persons of the Blessed Trinity. The Son of God assumed human nature while remaining God. Everything he does in his human nature communicates the divine ways of the Trinity (see CCC, 470). In his teaching, praying, and preaching, Jesus indicated his unique relationship with God the Father, calling him by the Hebrew title "Abba," which is a more personal form of "Father." As people united with Christ, we can call out to God in this intimate manner, "Abba," as one would to a beloved father.

**transcendent** above, beyond, and outside the realm of normal human lives

**immanent** existing or operating within the human realm and human history

**Tell** Give an example of how God is both immanent and transcendent.

**Describe** What are some things Jesus taught in his preaching and time with his disciples?

---

## SECTION 1 REVIEW

### QUICK REVIEW

**1a.** **Explain** What is Redemption?

**b.** **List** What are four reasons for the Incarnation?

**c.** **Define** What does the Incarnation mean for us?

**2a.** **Infer** Why is Jesus' Jewish heritage important?

**b.** **Describe** What was Jesus earthly life like?

**Pray** Compose a short prayer remembering God's great deeds in salvation history and his presence in your life.

### SELF-ASSESS

Which statement best reflects where you are now?

☐ I'm confident enough about the material in this section to be able to explain it to someone else.

☐ I have a good grasp of the material in this section, but I could use more review.

☐ I'm lost. I need help catching up before moving on.

# Ancient Jewish Prophecies and the Gospels

We have seen in the previous chapter that the Father's preparation for the coming of his Son, Jesus, took centuries. God causes everything to converge in Christ, including the "First Covenant," and all the rituals and sacrifices. The prophets announced Jesus' coming and God awakened in the hearts of non-believers a "dim expectation" of his time on Earth (CCC, 522). The virgin birth of Jesus indicates the miraculous nature of the Messiah's arrival.

> The gospel accounts understand the virginal conception of Jesus as a divine work that surpasses all human understanding and possibility:[34] "That which is conceived in her is of the Holy Spirit," said the angel to Joseph about Mary his fiancée.[35] The Church sees here the fulfillment of the divine promise given through the prophet Isaiah: "Behold, a virgin shall conceive and bear a son."[36]
>
> —CCC, 497

The prophet Isaiah tells us that the child's name shall be **Emmanuel**, which means "God with us" (Isaiah 7:14). This references the birth of a messianic king and finds fulfillment in the Christian Tradition, through the birth of Jesus.

Saint John the Baptist was the greatest and final prophet whose prophecies announced the coming of the Messiah. John welcomed the coming of Christ even before he was born, leaping in his Mother's womb at the news. John declared Jesus to be the "Lamb of God who takes away the sin of the world!" (John 1:29). He also called upon all believers to prepare their lives for the coming of the Messiah through repentance. Through his preaching, baptizing, and calls to **repent**, John the Baptist gave witness to and prepared for Christ (see CCC, 523).

John the Baptist explained to others that he was not the Messiah. When Jewish leaders insisted on knowing who he was, he referred to the Old Testament: "I am the voice of one crying out in the wilderness, 'Make straight the way of the Lord'" (John 1:24).

In the Gospel according to John, the final witness and testimony of John the Baptist is a profound statement of humility: "He must increase, but I must decrease" (John 3:30).

**repent** to feel or communicate sincere remorse for one's sin

**Emmanuel** name given to the Messiah by the prophet Isaiah meaning *God with us*

# Advent

The liturgical year begins with Advent on the last weekend in November or first in December. It is a time of anticipation and preparation for the coming of Christ. Advent echoes the preparation that took place among the Chosen People and ultimately the coming of God's Son, the Messiah, to Earth. God foretells the coming of his Son through the Israelite prophets and creates an expectation of this immense happening among the Gentiles (see CCC, 522).

During Advent, we really prepare for three events or three comings. First, the Christ child is conceived through the Holy Spirit. Mary's yes to God's plan provides the vessel through which the mystery of the Incarnation takes place. "That first coming is the essence of our Christmas celebration," wrote Bishop William P. Callahan in an essay on Advent. "The Word made Flesh is visible for all the world, all the ages, and all human history to see, study, evaluate, and emulate."

The second coming is Jesus present to us now. It is how we experience the Lord in our own lives as baptized sons and daughters of God. It is reflected in Jesus' words when he said: "Those who love me will keep my word, and my Father will love them, and we will come to them and make our home with them" (John 14:23). While the Incarnation signaled our Redemption, the second coming becomes the path that leads to the third coming for which we also prepare during Advent.

Advent gives us an opportunity to prepare for and anticipate, in a special way, Jesus' coming again at the end of time for the final judgment. We don't know when or how that will happen, but we know that Christ will come again and Advent is a time that reminds us of that fact. It is a time when we can refocus our attention on the return of Jesus and living in a way that prepares us.

As we share this long preparation for the celebration of the Incarnation, we renew our desire for Christ to come again at the end of time. We share in John the Baptist's proclamation on the first arrival of Jesus: "He must increase, but I must decrease" (John 3:30). And so Advent is a time to ready ourselves for the liturgical year. We renew our commitment to reflect those words of John the Baptist, namely, to participate in and spread the news of the Kingdom of God.

**What are some examples of family customs during Advent?**

**How can the celebration of Advent help you to connect the three comings of Christ?**

**What more can you do to make Advent a time of preparation?**

**How have you decreased so that Christ could increase?**

## GLOBAL PERSPECTIVES

### An Epiphany Custom

**In Eastern European churches, those who attend Mass on the Feast of the Epiphany receive an envelope with a piece of chalk and incense.**
At home, the chalk is used to write above the doorways, the initials of the traditional names of the magi: Caspar, Melchior, and Bathazar in between the numbers of the date of the New Year: 20 + C + M + B + the last two numbers of the year. These letters also represent the Latin words "Christus Mansionem Benedicat," which means "May Christ bless the dwelling." This saying is fitting since Epiphany is also a customary day to have one's home blessed with holy water and incense.

○ What other story does marking the doors remind you of?

○ What else could chalk and incense symbolize?

→ Go to the student site at **hs.osvcurriculum.com**

The preparation for the coming of Jesus is a key theme in the season of Advent, which marks the beginning of our **liturgical year**. In the course of the liturgical year, the Church celebrates the entire story of our salvation. "In the liturgical year the various aspects of the one Paschal mystery unfold" (CCC, 1171). We remember and celebrate the whole of Christ's Paschal Mystery through the various seasons and feasts, each with a particular emphasis on a different aspect of Christ's life and saving work, always seen in relationship to the whole Paschal Mystery. Through this structure we claim the passage of time as a sacred experience of God's abiding presence in the Church.

**Describe** Why do we refer to Saint John the Baptist as the last or final prophet?

**Conclude** What does John the Baptist tell leaders about who he is?

**liturgical year** the cycle of liturgical seasons and feasts which comprise the annual Church calendar.

### REFLECT

John the Baptist was very popular among the Jews of his time, yet he remained humble. Instead of taking the spotlight for himself, John understood God's plan and insisted that his role be one of preparation, not fulfillment.

○ What does John the Baptist teach us about being both a leader and a follower?

○ Describe a time when you (or someone close to you) had an experience of humility. Was the attention of the spotlight preferred or the role of helping, assisting, and preparation? To which role is God calling you?

## GO TO THE SOURCE

**John the Baptist sends his followers** to ask Jesus if he is the one who is to come, or if they should look for someone else.

Read what Jesus tells John's disciples in *Luke 7:18-23* and *Matthew 11:2-6*.

○ Identify the parallels between those Gospel passages and a messianic prophecy in Isaiah 35:5-6.

○ Jesus refers to two Old Testament prophecies in Luke 7:27-28. About whom is Jesus referring?

○ Read Isaiah 40:3-5 and Malachi 3:1-2 and identify how these two readings describe the one about whom Jesus is speaking.

○ How do these prophets describe that person's purpose?

According to the Gospel of Luke, when Jesus spoke in the synagogue, he had just returned from a forty-day retreat in the desert. He had already become known as a wise thinker who spoke profoundly about God and challenged some people's perceptions of the world. Imagine sitting and listening to Jesus. His reputation as someone that many people admire proceeds him, therefore you hang on his words as a special message for you.

○ How are you poor?

○ On a scale of 1 to 10 how do you rate your willingness/past history of helping the poor around the world?

○ In what way are you a captive?

○ Who in your social network could use your help because they are held captive? How are you blind?

○ How are others around the world oppressed?

○ How are you oppressed?

○ Given your responses here, to what degree is the message of Jesus good news to you? Explain.

## The Fulfillment of the Promise

The Old Testament revealed the promise of a Messiah to the Jewish faithful and some Gentiles at the time of Jesus' birth knew it as well.

An account of the Visit of the Magi, which we celebrate at the end of the Christmas Season on the **Feast of the Epiphany**, is found in the Gospel of Matthew. The Magi or Wise Men—also known as kings—were aware of a prophecy based on cosmic signs in the sky. They followed a star in order to pay homage to the newborn King of the Jews. The Book of Psalms and the prophecies of Isaiah foretell images reflected in the Epiphany story. They refer to kings bearing gifts and coming from faraway lands. This story is also important because the Magi represent the Gentiles, and their bringing gifts shows their acceptance of Jesus as the Messiah.

The magi's three gifts reflect important dimensions of Jesus' identity: gold as king; frankincense as priest; and myrrh (oil) as prophet. By our Baptism we have a share in Christ's identity and mission as priest, prophet, and king. Through Baptism we are called to live as priest, a life of prayer and loving sacrifice; as prophet, a life of speaking God's truth and standing up for justice; and as king, a life of humble service promoting the Kingdom of God and leading others to Christ.

> The God of power and Father of our Lord Jesus Christ has freed you from sin and brought you to new life through water and the Holy Spirit. He now anoints you with the chrism of salvation, so that, united with his people, you may remain for ever a member of Christ who is Priest, Prophet, and King.
>
> —*Rite of Baptism for Children*, para. 62

**Feast of the Epiphany** name for the feast day that commemorates the Magi or Wise Men visiting the infant Jesus

## GO TO THE SOURCE

**King Herod the Great hears about the visit of the magi,** and attempts to find out where the newborn king is located.

Read *Matthew 2:1-15*.

○ Identify the parallels between Matthew 2:5-6 and Micah 5:2.

○ Who was present at Herod's secret meeting and what was it about?

○ Why did Herod's plans not work out?

○ *Exodus 29:7, 30:26-29*

○ *Leviticus 8:12*

○ *1 Samuel 9:16, 10:1, 16:1, 12-13*

○ *1 Kings 1:39, 19:16*

As we read in Luke's Gospel, Jesus makes his anointing as the Messiah perfectly clear when he enters the synagogue, reads the words of the prophet Isaiah, and tells those gathered that this Scripture passage was fulfilled. Imagine you are sitting in the synagogue in Nazareth with the people who have known Jesus all his life. The scroll of the Prophet Isaiah is handed to Jesus. As you read the following, think carefully about why the coming of Jesus is "Good News" to you.

'The Spirit of the Lord is upon me,
    because he has anointed me
        to bring good news to the poor.
He has sent me to proclaim release to the captives
        and recovery of sight to the blind,
            to let the oppressed go free,
to proclaim the year of the Lord's favor.'
And he rolled up the scroll, gave it back to the attendant, and sat down. The eyes of all in the synagogue were fixed on him. Then he began to say to them. 'Today this scripture has been fulfilled in your hearing.'

—Luke 4:18-22

**Identify** What do the three gifts from the magi reflect about Jesus' identity?

**Infer** Why is the story of three magi from afar visiting the Christ child important?

## SECTION **2 REVIEW**

### QUICK REVIEW

**1a. Tell** Why is the name Emmanuel important?

**b. Identify** Which prophet said, "Behold, a virgin shall conceive and bear a son"?

**2a. Explain** Why is John the Baptist considered the last prophet?

**b. List** What three events, or three comings, do we prepare for during Advent?

**c. Link** How is John the Baptist a fulfillment of Old Testament prophecies?

**3. Connect** Explain how the feast of the Epiphany is connected to Isaiah's prophecies.

### ACT

Look through the Bible quotations in this section of the chapter and select one as your favorite.

○ Write the quotation with artistic handwriting, or use a word processing program to print it with a decorative typeface.

○ Display the finished artwork in a place where you can share it with others or where you will see its message often.

### SELF-ASSESS

Which statement best reflects where you are now?

☐ I'm confident enough about the material in this section to be able to explain it to someone else.

☐ I have a good grasp of the material in this section, but I could use more review.

☐ I'm lost. I need help catching up before moving on.

# In Jesus' Name

The idea that names have meaning was prevalent in ancient Israelite culture. From Isaiah, the Israelites knew the Messiah as Emmanuel, "God is with us." Then in the New Testament, there is a new name because "the Holy Spirit completes in Mary all the preparation for Christ's coming among the People of God" (CCC, 744). At the Annunciation, the angel Gabriel gave him the name Jesus as his proper name, which expresses both his identity and mission. In Hebrew, the name *Jesus* means "God Saves." By the Holy Spirit's action in Mary, the Father gives us Emmanuel, his Son.

The name Jesus is significant. It is the name of God's Son, the second Person

## GO TO THE SOURCE

**Compare and contrast** the details in these two Gospel passages about the Annunciation.

Read *Luke 1:26-38* and *Matthew 1:18-25*.
○ Distinguish what is unique in each passage from what is common to both.

○ How does the angel address Joseph and Mary's fear and awe?

of the Blessed Trinity. This divine name brings Redemption and salvation to the world. We are all united to Jesus through his Incarnation. There is no other name by which we can be saved. And all salvation comes from Christ through the Church, his Body (see CCC, 432).

The Gospels and the Letters of the New Testament used special names for Jesus. The titles Lord, Son of God, Christ, Messiah, Son of David, and Son of Man help us understand who Jesus is and how he is the promised Redeemer.

The early Church not only preached in the name of Jesus but also suffered in his name, as evidenced by the following passage, "As they left the council, they rejoiced that they were considered worthy to suffer dishonor for the sake of the name. And every day in the temple and at home they did not cease to teach and proclaim Jesus as the Messiah" (Acts 5:41-42).

**Name** Other than Jesus, what are two names or titles by which he is known?

**Distinguish** Why is the name Jesus important?

*The Annunciation* by Dante Gabriel Bossetti

## The Power of a Name

The name Jesus Christ so deeply reflects who he is as the Son of God and Messiah, that through the power of his name, the disciples were able to perform miracles.

Acts 4:11 makes reference to Psalm 118, a Hymn of Thanksgiving, "I thank you for you answered; you have been my savior. The stone that the builders rejected has become the cornerstone" (Psalm 118:21-22). The "stone" may have originally meant the foundation stone of the temple, while Peter's Christian interpretation referred to the Death and Resurrection of Christ, the Paschal Mystery. Jesus makes a reference to this passage when he is speaking to the chief priests and elders in the temple area in Matthew 21:41, Mark 12:10-11, and Luke 20:17.

"The name of Jesus is at the heart of Christian prayer. All liturgical prayers conclude with the words 'through our Lord Jesus Christ'. The *Hail Mary* reaches its high point in the words 'blessed is the fruit of thy womb, Jesus.' The Eastern prayer of the heart, the *Jesus Prayer*, says, 'Lord Jesus Christ, Son of God, have mercy on me, a sinner.' Many Christians, such as St. Joan of Arc, have died with the one word 'Jesus' on their lips" (CCC, 435).

We learn of the importance of praying in the name of Jesus from the Gospel according to John: "You did not choose me but I chose you. And I appointed you to go and bear fruit, fruit that will last, so that the Father will give you whatever you ask him in my name" (John 15:16).

### DISCUSS

- In your daily life, who do you know that is rejected or brushed off as being insignificant?
- What wisdom do these Scripture passages offer for those who are rejected? How about for those who do the rejecting?

### GO TO THE SOURCE

**In the Acts of the Apostles,** Peter testifies before the same High Priests that called for the Crucifixion of Jesus.

Read *Acts 4:7-12*.

- During Jesus' Passion and Crucifixion, Peter was so frightened that he denied knowing Jesus three times. What gave Peter such courage to speak so boldly before the High Priests?
- Peter credits the name of Jesus for the power to perform what miracles?
- What is the warning the High Priests give to the disciples? What are they specifically told not to speak?
- How do Peter and John respond to their warning?

Forgiveness was also received through the name of Jesus. "All the prophets testify about him that everyone who believes in him receives forgiveness of sins through his name" (Acts 10:43).

**Recall** How did the Apostles Peter and John respond to the High Priests warning them not to speak Jesus' name?

**Explain** How does the Resurrection glorify the name of Jesus?

### GO TO THE SOURCE

The *Catechism* tells us that the name of Jesus holds such power because of the Resurrection. The Resurrection glorifies the name of the Savior God. After the Resurrection, we refer to the name of Jesus as the "name which is above every name"[37] (CCC, 434).

Read *Mark 1:21-28*; *John 15:16*; *Acts 10:43*; and *Acts 16:16-18*.

- List the types of power found in the name of Jesus.
- What would you say to someone to encourage them not to take Jesus' name in vain?

Traditional site of the Crucifixion of Jesus in Jerusalem, Israel.

**Messianic Secret** Jesus' request for people not to tell anyone that he was the Messiah until it was time to reveal it

### The Messianic Secret

We find examples in the Gospels where Jesus heals someone and tells them not to tell anyone. Theologians refer to Jesus' request not to tell anyone as the **Messianic Secret**. The person in each story, however, is often unable to follow Jesus' command and proceeds to tell many people. One story is about a leper who believed Jesus could heal him of his illness. The accounts say that Jesus healed the man and then gave him a stern warning saying, "See that you say nothing to anyone; but go, show yourself to the priest, and offer for your cleansing what Moses commanded, as a testimony to them" (Mark 1:45). The man told so many people, however, that Jesus couldn't even go into town. Nevertheless, people came to see him in the countryside.

Jesus knew that it was not yet his time to be revealed as the Messiah. That time would come after his suffering, Death, and Resurrection. Many lost faith in Jesus

### GO TO THE SOURCE

**Summarize what is happening each time Jesus is called "Son of David":**

Read *Matthew 9:27, 12:23, 15:22, 20:30, 21:9, 21:15*.
○ Compare Matthew's version of 9:27-31 and 20:29-34 to *Mark 10:46-52* and *Luke 18:35-43*.

### GO TO THE SOURCE

**A stranger walks with two disciples of Jesus** on the road to Emmaus.

Read *Luke 24:13-35*.
○ How did Jesus explain that they should have known the Messiah had to suffer?
○ How did the two disciples come to recognize Jesus?
○ Describe a time when a conversation with a close friend or relative helped you gain insight into a difficulty.

during his suffering and Death. They expected a messiah from the line of the mighty King David who would deliver Israel from the oppression of the Romans. This messiah would establish a political and religious kingdom that would bring peace throughout the world.

Jesus was not this kind of Messiah. He did not want false expectations to spread due to his miracles and the expectations of the people. Some references to these expectations can be found in the New Testament. For example, in the last chapter of Luke's Gospel, the Resurrected Jesus walks with the two disciples on the road to Emmaus. They do not recognize Jesus and are devastated at his Death. Along their journey, Jesus explains to them that the Messiah had to suffer.

**Perhaps the most direct statement Jesus made** about his unity with God the Father can be found in the Gospel of John's account of the Last Supper.

Read *John 14:1-11*.
○ How would you summarize what Jesus is saying?
○ What does this do to doubt?

## The Lord God Himself

The Hebrew name for God is translated into Greek as **Kyrios**, which means "Lord." This is often the way Jesus was addressed and indicates his divinity. The New Testament uses this word to refer to the Father and the Son, Jesus (see CCC, 446). This is another example of the importance and power of names in our Judeo-Christian tradition.

The title of Lord shows the trust of people who ask Jesus for help or healing. It recognizes his unity with the Father and the Holy Spirit. It is also used as a title of adoration: "My Lord and my God!" The love expressed in the title of Lord remains part of our Christian tradition (see CCC, 448). As the angels announce the birth of Jesus to the shepherds, they use the words Savior, Messiah, and Lord (see Luke 2:11).

One of the most direct New Testament passages that acknowledges Jesus as Lord and God comes from the Apostle Thomas. Thomas is not in the room when the Risen Jesus appears to the other Apostles. In a famous account in the Gospel of John, Thomas refuses to believe unless he examines the wounds in Jesus' hands and side. A week later, Thomas is with the disciples and Jesus appears again. This time Thomas believes, saying: "My Lord and my God!" Jesus replies, "Have you believed because you have seen me? Blessed are those who have not seen and yet have come to believe" (John 20:25).

**Describe** What happens when Jesus tells the healed leper not to say anything?

**Connect** How does the title of "Lord" connect the Father and the Son

**Kyrios** a Greek word meaning Lord, that is the translation of the Hebrew name for God

**Look up the following passages** that involve Jesus being addressed as Lord and summarize what takes place in each passage:

○ *Matthew 8:2, 14:30, 15:2*
○ *Luke 1:43*
○ *John 21:4-16*
○ *Revelation 11:15*

### ANALYZE

Thomas was also called "Didymus" which means "twin." Some scholars consider his name to mean that he had a twin, or it may be used here to indicate the two qualities of doubt and faith in the same person.
○ What role do you think doubt plays in someone's spiritual life?
○ What tensions between doubt and faith play out in your own life?

# PRIMARY SOURCES

A Jewish scholar named Flavius Josephus lived during the first century. He was one of the first non-Christian authors to write about the early Christian community, which was closely tied to the Jewish community. He also chronicled the first Jewish-Roman War and the destruction of Jerusalem.

Like many works from antiquity, scholars have debated whether later authors may have contributed to Josephus' writings, specifically to a passage describing Jesus. While there is not a general consensus on this passage, several Jewish scholars have published translations.

*"At this time there was a wise man who was called Jesus, and his conduct was good, and he was known to be virtuous. And many people from among the Jews and the other nations became his disciples. Pilate condemned him to be crucified and to die. And those who had become his disciples did not abandon their loyalty to him. They reported that he had appeared to them three days after his crucifixion, and that he was alive. Accordingly they believed that he was the Messiah, concerning whom the Prophets have recounted wonders."*

> ❝At this time there was a **wise man** who was called Jesus . . .❞
>
> —*Flavius Josephus*

Make a list of what Josephus' writing confirms about what we know about Jesus.

If you were writing a contemporary response to Josephus, what would you add about Jesus?

How does this exchange between Josephus and you reflect your relationship with Jesus? Explain.

➜ Go to the student site at **hs.osvcurriculum.com**

# My Faith

**WHEN JESUS BEGAN** his public life, the people of Nazareth, his hometown, were stunned.

"On the Sabbath he began to teach in the synagogue, and many who heard him were astounded" (Mark 6:2).

Here are some teachings from Jesus that surprised people:

**The greatest in God's Kingdom are humble, like children.** When his disciples wanted to know who was the greatest in God's Kingdom, Jesus told them they have to become like children or they will never enter eternal life with God (see Matthew 18:3-4).

**The happiest people are not the people who have everything.** When Jesus said, "Blessed are the poor in spirit," he meant that people who put God first will find the greatest joy. In ancient Israel, people thought that wealth was a sign of God's approval.

**We should treat everyone as neighbors.** In the Good Samaritan story, Jesus said that we're all neighbors and should treat each other well.

↗ Go to the student site at **hs.osvcurriculum.com**

## SO HERE'S THE QUESTION

*Which teachings from Jesus are still "surprising" in our world? Which teachings from Jesus are challenging for you or your friends to understand or accept?*

Reflect on the "Parable of the Good Samaritan" (see Luke 10:29-37). Who is the modern-day victim, Levite, priest, and Good Samaritan?

*Discipleship ... within the Body of Christ ... for the glory of God and the good of the world.*

---

## SECTION 3 REVIEW

### QUICK REVIEW

**1a. Tell** What does the Hebrew name "Jesus" mean?

**b. Explain** What did the early Christian community think about suffering because they followed Jesus?

**2a. Relate** How is Jesus like the rejected stone that became the cornerstone?

**b. Infer** What can help readers of the Bible see that Jesus' name is powerful?

**3a. Define** What does the word "Christ" mean?

**b. Explain** Tell why Matthew's Gospel begins by saying that Jesus is the Messiah.

**4a. Tell** Where does the term "Lord" come from, and what does it imply in using it for Jesus?

**b. Summarize** Retell the story of Doubting Thomas.

**Pray** Compose a short prayer asking for help when the things that distract you from Jesus are stronger than your faith in him.

### SELF-ASSESS

Which statement best reflects where you are now?

☐ I'm confident enough about the material in this section to be able to explain it to someone else.

☐ I have a good grasp of the material in this section, but I could use more review.

☐ I'm lost. I need help catching up before moving on.

# The Mystery of Redemption

Jesus' teaching through parables points out truths about the nature of God, the Kingdom of God, and the mystery of Redemption. Jesus emphasized that his parables were designed to allow his disciples and followers to understand what others could not. His goal was to show others the right way to live and love God. However, to understand the meanings behind the parables, one has to devote time and care to their study.

## The Mystery of Redemption

The mystery of Redemption is at work throughout Christ's life:

**1** "in his Incarnation through which by becoming poor he enriches us with his poverty"[38]

**2** "in his hidden life which by his submission atones for our disobedience"[39]

**3** "in his word which purifies its hearers"[40]

**4** "in his healings and exorcisms by which 'he took our infirmities and bore our diseases'";[41]

**5** "and in his Resurrection, by which he justifies us."[42]

—CCC, 517

The Gospel writers all had faith that Jesus was the Son of God and the Messiah. That is why they took such care in recording his teachings. They wanted their contemporaries and future followers to recognize the importance of Jesus' words.

## Throughout His Life

Through Christ, we have been redeemed. Our sins are forgiven through the grace God generously gave us. The *Catechism* reminds us that, "Christ's whole life is a mystery of *redemption*. Redemption comes to us above all through the blood of his cross,[43] but this mystery is at work throughout Christ's entire life" (CCC, 517). The Resurrection of Jesus means that Redemption is accomplished and the promise fulfilled.

Jesus certainly taught us about who God is. In fact, his whole life was a teaching. In it he also gave us the perfect model of humanity. Through Jesus we better understand how to act in moral and just ways and how to work toward spiritual wholeness.

## GO TO THE SOURCE

**Look at the following passages** about the mystery of Christ's Redemption.

Read *Ephesians 1:8-10, Colossians 1:13,* and *1 Peter 1:18-19.*

○ Describe how the following words taken from the above Scripture passages help you to understand the mystery of Christ's Redemption: saved, forgiveness, wisdom, insight, mystery, rescued, darkness, ransomed, precious blood of Christ and lamb without defect or blemish.

Everyday life challenges you to think about right and wrong, to sort out the good from the bad, and to inform and form your conscience. Here's an example. . . .

A huge fight breaks out among students in a large city. An innocent student bystander is beaten to death. Everyone sees it. The death is even recorded on someone's cell phone and uploaded to the Internet. Despite all the people who saw the incident, police can't find any witnesses. The killers are free. No one wants to speak up. Those who would speak up are afraid of being targeted as snitches. What would you do if you witnessed it?

If I talk to the cops, people will think I'm a snitch.

Mind my own business!

Speak up, for the family's sake.

If I don't talk to the cops, the same people could do this again.

Don't speak up, for my family's sake!

The people who did this are a threat to the whole community.

What would you want people to do if it was your brother who was killed?

What do you say?

# Going Moral

Read the Tradition that Saint Paul handed down to the Church at Corinth in *1 Corinthians 15:3-11*.

○ Summarize the reading in your own words.

> In humbling himself, he has given us an example to imitate, through his prayer he draws us to pray, and by his poverty he calls us to accept freely the privation and persecutions that may come our way.[44]
>
> —CCC, 520

Yet Christ is not someone we should learn about from afar. Part of this saving mystery is that we are each personally invited to become his disciples and follow him. Salvation happens *for* us; and it happens *with* us. As we respond to the Holy Spirit's action in our lives and come to know, believe, and live our faith, the gift of our Redemption takes further root in our lives.

Recall in the Gospel of Luke that Jesus meets the tax collector Zacchaeus, who then experiences a conversion. Zacchaeus promises to give to the poor and repay anyone he cheated. After the visit Jesus says, "Today salvation has come to this house because this man too is a descendent of Abraham. For the Son of Man has come to seek and to save what was lost" (Luke 19:9-10).

The First Letter of Peter gives us this: "And baptism, which this prefigured, now saves you—not as a removal of dirt from your body, but as an appeal to God for a good conscience, through the resurrection of Jesus Christ" (1 Peter 3:21).

What began with the Incarnation reaches its fulfillment in the Resurrection: As our sins are forgiven and we are made whole, we actually partake in the divine nature.

Our dignity, value, and worth as humans have been realized and we participate in the mystery of Redemption through the sacramental life of the Church, especially the Eucharist.

**Recall** What did Jesus say was the purpose of his speaking in parables?

**Conclude** What did the writers of the four Gospels believe about Jesus?

## SECTION 4 REVIEW

### QUICK REVIEW

**1a. Explain** What is the purpose of a parable?

**b. Infer** Why must a parable fit the culture of the parable's audience?

**2a. Discuss** How does Saint Peter's use of "ransomed" describe how Jesus saved humanity from sin and death?

**b. Describe** How do we participate in the mystery of Redemption?

### ACT

Write your own parable. Share your work with the larger group if time permits.

○ You may want to begin with the basic lesson of the parable and work backward.

○ Be certain to use ideas that parallel the lesson that you want to teach.

○ Consider writing down your parable, illustrating it, and sharing it with younger children, if appropriate.

### SELF-ASSESS

Which statement best reflects where you are now?

☐ I'm confident enough about the material in this section to be able to explain it to someone else.

☐ I have a good grasp of the material in this section, but I could use more review.

☐ I'm lost. I need help catching up before moving on.

# PRAYER

**Opening Prayer**

O Jesus, through the Immaculate Heart of Mary, I offer you my prayers, works, joys, and sufferings of this day for all the intentions of your Sacred Heart, in union with the holy sacrifice of the Mass throughout the world, in thanksgiving for your favors, in reparation for my sins, for the intentions of all my relatives and friends, and in particular for the intentions of the Holy Father.
Amen.

We thank you, God,
that you have revealed yourself
among us in Jesus, your living Word.
We thank you that his light continues
to shine throughout this world.
Make yourself known to us.
Help us to hear your word, share your love,
and shine your light to the ends of the earth.
We pray in the name of Jesus and his eternal light. Amen.
"Let anyone with ears hear!"

## TERMS

Use each of the following terms in a sentence that shows you know what the term means. You may include more than one term in a sentence.

| | |
|---|---|
| Redemption | repent |
| kenosis | liturgical year |
| transcendent | Feast of the Epiphany |
| immanent | Messianic Secret |
| Emmanuel | Kyrios |

## PEOPLE

Use information from the chapter to tell why each person or term is significant.

1. Zacchaeus

2. John the Baptist

3. Saint Edith Stein

4. Elijah

5. Kyrios

6. Thomas the Apostle

## UNDERSTANDING

Answer each question and complete each exercise.

### SECTION 1

1. **List** What terms have become integral to understanding who Jesus is and what that means for our lives?
2. **Recall** Give one example of how Saints through the ages have recognized the purpose of the Incarnation.
3. **Summarize** Why is it important to know about the Jewish expectation and understanding of the Messiah?
4. **Compare** How does Jesus indicate his unique relationship with God the Father?

### SECTION 2

5. **Recount** How did the life of John the Baptist fulfill Old Testament prophecies?
6. **Explain** Why is it appropriate to use readings from Isaiah and about John the Baptist during Advent?
7. **Connect** Explain the significance of the gifts that the Magi gave Jesus.

### SECTION 3

8. **Summarize** Why was Jesus named Jesus?
9. **Explain** What shows that Jesus' name is powerful?
10. **Connect** Why would it be a political statement for Jesus to call himself a Messiah?
11. **Infer** What does Thomas' statement "My Lord and my God" tell us about Thomas?

### SECTION 4

12. **Infer** Why did Jesus teach using parables?
13. **Analyze** How do Catholics partake of the mysteries of Christ?

## CONNECTING

**Visual** This photograph is of stone figures that are near one of the doors of Chartres Cathedral in France. The figures depict the Prophet Simeon (holding the infant Jesus), John the Baptist (holding a lamb), and Saint Peter (holding a key).

Explain the symbol each man carries, why each man is important enough to be depicted on the cathedral, and why the figures might be in this order.

**Challenge** You ask a friend to proofread a paper that you have written for religion class.

> **Friend:** This is getting confusing. Are all these names for Jesus?
>
> **You:** Where?
>
> **Friend:** Well, it looks like Jesus is called Lord, the Messiah, the Son of God, and the Savior.
>
> **You:** Yes, that's right. He is all of those things.
>
> **Friend:** What do they mean?
>
> **You:** Each name means something specific about Jesus.
>
> **Friend:** So what do the names mean?

○ What is your next reply?

○ Then continue the conversation anticipating at least two more questions that your friend might ask. Anticipate also how you would answer. Use information from the chapter to explain Jesus' names.

**Question** After working through this chapter, how would you describe Jesus' earthly life?

**Imagine** You want to write and illustrate the story of Doubting Thomas. You want to show how Thomas changed from doubting Jesus' Resurrection to saying "My Lord and my God!"

○ Which sources would you consult to read the story?

○ What scenes would you include in the story?

○ Which characters would be useful to include?

○ How would you show the thoughts of the people in the story?

## SELF-ASSESS

**On Your Own** Make a list of the most important things you learned from this chapter. Select three things that represent your growth in understanding as you worked through this chapter. Write a paragraph explaining your choices.

**With a Partner** List what you found most helpful or interesting in this chapter as well as any other questions that have surfaced.

# The Mystery of Redemption

 Go to the student site at
**hs.osvcurriculum.com**

## YOU WILL

○ Reflect on the baptism of Jesus and Wedding at Cana.

○ Learn how the Transfiguration reveals Jesus as the fulfillment of the Law and Prophets.

○ Explore how the Resurrection was met by Jesus' first followers.

○ Examine how the post-Resurrection accounts in the Bible emphasized the fulfillment of the Word of God.

○ Learn how the Sacraments are key to our salvation.

○ Find out how taking up one's cross reconciles us to Christ and to each other.

○ Explore how the Assumption of the Blessed Virgin Mary is a singular participation in her Son's Resurrection.

○ Discover how the life of Mary is linked to major events in the Paschal Mystery of her Son.

○ Understand the virtue of hope as a means of transforming the world.

○ Explain how the Church makes Christ visible in the world today.

## DEFINE

| | |
|---|---|
| temptation | Assumption |
| *Roman Missal* | hope |
| omnipotence | grace |
| filial | justification |
| Transfiguration | Seven Sacraments |
| Ascension | sacramental grace |

# WHAT DO YOU SAY?

Students in a religion class were asked: *What does it take to get to Heaven?* and *What about Hell?* The majority of the students said getting to Heaven required following the Ten Commandments. Here are a few other written responses:

- "It takes forgiveness to get to Heaven because God forgives us, then we should forgive others and ourselves."

- "Heaven: repent, be truly sorry, and act out God's word by your actions. Hell: not believing in God, ignoring the Church, sinning."

- "I think what it takes to get to Heaven is to accept Christ and try to be a better Catholic. I think to get to Hell you reject God and completely do your own thing."

- "Being kind and being loving. Being ruthless."

- "The only way to get to Heaven is to totally die to yourself and live for God, building a relationship with Christ. There are many ways to get to Hell. You can curse, deny, distrust God, and not claim him as your savior."

# WHERE ARE YOU?

**Check the answer that best matches where you are today.**

I understand that Jesus redeemed us through his life, Death, and Resurrection.
☐ Quite a bit ☐ Somewhat ☐ A little ☐ Not at all

I can relate the Temptation of Christ in the desert to issues I face in my own life.
☐ Quite a bit ☐ Somewhat ☐ A little ☐ Not at all

I recognize the importance the Seven Sacraments have in the Church.
☐ Quite a bit ☐ Somewhat ☐ A little ☐ Not at all

I see how hope and grace relate to my Catholic faith.
☐ Quite a bit ☐ Somewhat ☐ A little ☐ Not at all

# God's Plan for Redemption

*What is the defining moment of God's plan of Redemption?*
*How do we overcome fear?*

*How did Jesus' prediction of his Death and Resurrection impact his disciples?*

God has unfolded the mysteries of our faith over time. Gradually as we learn more, we get a better idea of a mystery's depth and meaning. "Christ's whole life is a mystery of *redemption*" (*Catechism of the Catholic Church*, 517). Through "the divine missions of the Son and the Holy Spirit, God the Father fulfills the 'plan of his loving goodness' of creation, redemption, and sanctification" (CCC, 235).

Human sinfulness—choosing to freely and intentionally turn away from God and his love, to hurt ourselves and others—has damaged humanity's relationship with God. It was the sin of Adam and Eve, our first parents, that created the need for Redemption. That first sin had so badly damaged this relationship with God that there was no conceivable way we could aptly reconcile. Redemption required a Savior.

God has never stopped caring for and loving us. He made covenants with the ancient Israelites. He continued to call his people back to him and his way through the prophets. He did not abandon us. His plan for our Redemption—and ultimately our restored friendship with him—was realized through the birth and life of Jesus, his only Son. Out of love, the Father willingly gave his Son to us knowing that he would have to suffer in order to free us from the power of sin. Christ willingly died on the Cross to ransom us, free us from sin, and bring about our Redemption.

Before Jesus, humans were defined by a broken relationship, but through Jesus we are defined by his love for the Father, for his people, and for his Creation. Though we may still falter and sin, we are no longer *identified* by the sin. Through faith, the Church, and the Sacraments, especially the Eucharist, we enter into the Paschal Mystery. This becomes the defining moment for all time, for all people, and for all Creation.

While Christ's whole life achieved our Redemption, four events in his life signal the final elements of God's unfolding plan: the baptism of Jesus, the Temptation of Jesus, the miracle at the Wedding of Cana, and the Transfiguration.

The accounts of Jesus' baptism include allusions or connections to the Old Testament. "O that you would tear open the heavens and come down, so that the mountains would quake at your presence" (Isaiah 64:1). Something different occurs when the sky opens at Jesus' baptism. Instead of the mountains quaking, the Holy Spirit, in the form of a peaceful dove, comes out of the sky. God the Father's voice from Heaven tells us, "'This is my beloved Son'"[45] (CCC, 535). This is the sign that Jesus is the Messiah of Israel, the

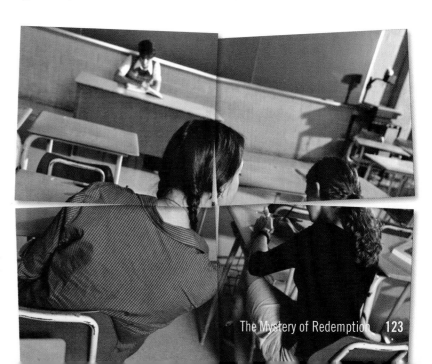

**Read the account of the baptism of Jesus** in *Matthew 3:13-17*.

○ Describe John the Baptist's reaction in verses 14 and 15.

○ What does the voice of God say?

○ Imagine you were directing a movie that included this scene from Scripture. How would you capture its details and significance?

Son of God. Just as one man's sin (Adam's) closed the way to Heaven, one man's act of righteousness (Jesus') opened it to life for all.

Jesus' baptism indicates God's plan for our Redemption and the beginning of his public life. Through this event, we see:

• the manifestation of Jesus as the Messiah of Israel and Son of God

• that Jesus allows himself to be numbered among sinners (even though he himself has no sin)

• that John the Baptist calls Jesus the Lamb of God who takes away the sins of the world

• that Jesus refers to his baptism with anticipation of the Crucifixion, yet still "fulfilling all righteousness" by submitting himself to his Father's will

• the Father's voice proclaiming his entire delight in his Son

• the Holy Spirit, whom Jesus possessed in fullness from his conception, coming to "rest on him"

• the opening of the heavens that had been closed by Adam's sin

• the waters sanctified by the presence of Jesus and the Holy Spirit (see CCC, 536)

We know the baptism offered by John was a sign of one's desire to repent, to turn from sin and toward God. It was not sacramental (bringing about what it signified) as the Sacraments instituted by Christ are. From the very beginning, followers of Christ who believed in him and desired to join the Church were offered Baptism. For them and for all of us baptized through the centuries, our Redemption in Christ began with our Baptism. Christ paid the price with his life so that we could be free from the consequences of Original Sin. In Baptism, we die and rise with Christ. We are connected to the Paschal Mystery of Jesus, through which he achieved our Redemption. The Church celebrates the Paschal Mystery in the liturgy. "Christ's work in the liturgy is sacramental: because his mystery of salvation is made present there by the power of the Holy Spirit" (CCC, 1111).

> Do you not know that all of us who have been baptized into Christ Jesus were baptized into his death? Therefore we have been buried with him by baptism into death, so that, just as Christ was raised from the dead by the glory of the Father, so we too might walk in newness of life.
>
> —Romans 6:3-4

The Letter to the Galatians speaks of Baptism as "putting on" or "clothing oneself" with Christ. When we are baptized we become one in Christ. We are no longer male or female or, as it says in Galatians, Jew or Greek, slave or free. "If you belong to Christ, then you are Abraham's offspring, heirs according to the promise" (Galatians 3:29).

Baptism begins Christian life and leads us to the other Sacraments. Through our Baptism:

• we are freed from personal and Original Sin

• we are reborn as sons and daughters of God

• we become members of Christ

• we are incorporated into the Church

• we are made sharers in her mission (see CCC, 1213)

• we become temples of the Holy Spirit

As we are initiated, freed, reborn, and incorporated into the Church, we are invited to participate in our Redemption. The Sacrament of Baptism calls us to cooperate with the grace of God throughout our lives.

## The Temptation of Jesus

Jesus is tempted by the devil three times in the desert. His forty days in the desert recall the testing of the People of Israel in the desert for forty years. Unlike the Israelites, who complained and lost faith in God, Jesus overcomes the **temptation** by Satan. Jesus represents a "new Israel," who remains faithful to God and triumphs over evil.

Recorded in the Gospels of Matthew, Mark, and Luke, we find common elements in the three accounts of Jesus' temptation:

- the Spirit leads Jesus into the desert/wilderness, where he stays and fasts for forty days

- Jesus is tempted three times by Satan

- Jesus prevails over the temptations

The temptation of Jesus recorded in the three Synoptic Gospels is always proclaimed during the Liturgy of the Word on the first Sunday of Lent. The **Roman Missal**—the ritual book used in the celebration of the Mass—includes the presider's prayers, the responses and acclamations of the people, special prayers for each liturgical season, including feast days of saints. In 2000, Blessed Pope John Paul II (who was beatified in 2011) announced a revised Third Edition of the *Roman Missal* in Latin. It includes prayers for newly canonized saints, more prefaces for the Eucharist Prayers, updated rubrics (instructions for the celebration of the Mass), and more. The English translation of the revised edition of the Latin *Roman Missal* began to be used during Advent 2011. It includes new translations of some existing prayers and responses. These translations are closer to the Latin text and show more clearly how our prayers are rooted in Scripture.

The preface prayer, which is the first part of the Eucharistic Prayer, for the first Sunday of Lent, contains a theological summary of how the temptations of Jesus reveal the unfolding of Redemption in our lives:

## GO TO THE SOURCE

**Read about Jesus' temptation** as described in *Matthew 4:1-11*; *Mark 1:12-13*; and *Luke 4:1-13*.

- What do we learn about Jesus from these accounts?

- The temptation stories contain what can be called the triple-play of sins: pleasure, popularity, and power. Which of the three "Ps" match up with which of the three temptations?

- Jesus responds to each temptation by quoting the Book of Deuteronomy. Look up each of the following passages and identify which response pairs with which temptation: Deuteronomy 6:13, 6:16, and 8:3.

- What does James 1:12-16 say about temptation?

By abstaining forty long days from earthly food, he consecrated through his fast the pattern of our Lenten observance and, by overturning all the snares of the ancient serpent, taught us to cast out the leaven of malice, so that, celebrating worthily the Paschal Mystery, we might pass over at last to the eternal paschal feast.

—*Roman Missal*

**temptation** an attraction from within or from outside that is contrary to right reason and to God's Commandments

The preface prayer provides a meaning for the season of Lent. It is a season of self-denial and sacrifice—denying our own interests, desires, or pleasures. We are meant to reject the devil's temptations. That way we more worthily participate in the Eucharist as the source of our strength on our journey to Heaven.

The *Catechism* explains that the unfolding of redemption is reflected in the temptations of Jesus in the following ways:

- Jesus is the new Adam who remains faithful and just, whereas the first Adam gave in to temptation.

- Jesus fulfills Israel's vocation perfectly, in contrast to the Israelites who challenged

**Roman Missal** the ritual book for the celebration of the Mass; it includes the presider's prayers, the responses and acclamations of the people, special prayers for each liturgical season, including feasts day of saints.

## APPLY

In Chapter 2, we discussed the acronym H.A.L.T. We are more vulnerable to temptation when we are: hungry, angry, lonely, and tired.

- How does H.A.L.T apply to Jesus in the account of his temptation by Satan?

**omnipotence** characteristic of being all-powerful, which is attributed to God

and questioned God's **omnipotence** during their forty years in the desert.

- Christ reveals himself as God's Servant, totally obedient to the divine will.

- Jesus conquers evil.

- "Jesus' victory over the tempter in the desert anticipates victory at the Passion, the supreme act of obedience of his **filial** love for the Father" (CCC, 539).

**filial** describes the love of a child for a parent

**List** What three things that start with the letter "P" does Jesus reject?

**Elaborate** What do we learn about Jesus and our Redemption from the temptations in the desert?

### Announcing the Kingdom

After Jesus' time in the desert and the arrest of John the Baptist, Jesus entered Galilee to begin preaching the Good News that the Kingdom of God was at hand. He announced the Kingdom through parables and miracles. He told people to repent and believe the Good News. The purpose of this was to gather people around the Son to share the divine life of the Father. "This gathering is the Church" (CCC, 541).

It is the Paschal Mystery that brings about the Kingdom of God. Jesus used signs and words to draw people to himself and ultimately to eternal happiness and life with God the Father. "And I, when I am lifted up from the earth, will draw all people to myself" (John 12:32). We are all called to this union (see CCC, 543).

The Kingdom belongs to those with humble hearts, and Jesus' message reminds us that the poor are blessed because the Kingdom of God is theirs. Only a humble heart that identifies with the poor can begin to understand God's revelation. The humble heart is that of the sinner who has come to realize his or her need for God. Jesus invites us to such a conversion by pointing out "the vast 'joy in heaven over one sinner who repents'"[46] (CCC, 545).

Jesus spent his public ministry spreading his invitation to the Kingdom. With the Beatitudes and the other teachings from the Sermon on the Mount, he gave us a guide for being in relationship with God and others. By his own life, the Son showed us how to trust in God's reign and rule in our lives. We need to be open to God's way and will for us, to seek God's forgiveness and not to lose sight of eternal life that God offers to those who believe and live in his grace.

Jesus performed miracles that represent the victory of Christ's Kingdom over evil. And Jesus invites us to the Kingdom through parables that reveal the mystery of the Kingdom. Through Jesus, the Kingdom is here, but it's not yet complete. It is present in the Church, and will be complete when Jesus returns in glory.

Jesus' words, signs, and actions show that he is the Messiah, the Son of God sent by the Father and one with the Holy Spirit. His invitation to the Kingdom requires a "radical choice" from us: "to gain the kingdom, one must give everything.[47] Words are not enough; deeds are required"[48] (CCC, 546). Jesus' parables help us to understand this. When we hear the Word of God, will we be good soil on which the Word can grow? What will we make of the gifts we have been given?

> Jesus and the presence of the kingdom in this world are secretly at the heart of the parables. One must enter the kingdom, that is, become a disciple of Christ, in order to "know the secrets of the kingdom of heaven."[49]
>
> —CCC, 546

### DEVELOP

- As a class, put together a collage of pictures from magazines, newspapers, or the Internet that symbolize a faithful response to temptations of pleasure, popularity, and power in our world today.

- What do you make of James' insight (see James 1:12-16) that temptation can be a blessing in disguise?

We can see a pattern in the Gospel according to Matthew of how Christ teaches his Kingdom of love, mercy, justice, and Redemption. This is just one of many parts of Scripture that describe the Kingdom.

| Chapters | Content | Summary |
|---|---|---|
| 5 to 7 | Sermon on the Mount | Guide to living in the Kingdom |
| 8 and 9 | Ten miracles | Representing the victory of Christ's Kingdom over evil |
| 13, 18-19, 21-22 | Ten parables | Stories that disclose the mystery of the Kingdom of God and its embodiment in the Church |

**Connect** Make a list of the teachings of the Sermon on the Mount, the ten miracles, and the ten parables, then write in your own words a description of the Kingdom.

The Kingdom that Jesus preached is the reign of God, in which his grace is present in the world, but reaches its fulfillment in Heaven.

**Tell** Name one parable that helps you understand the Kingdom of God and explain why.

**Identify** To whom does the Kingdom of God belong?

## The Wedding at Cana

Christ's life, mission, and ministry confirm God's plan for Redemption. The miracle at Cana is the first that Jesus performs to reveal his glory as God's Son and Messiah, "and his disciples believed in him" (John 2:11).

## GO TO THE SOURCE

**The miracle of Jesus changing the water into wine is** familiar to most of us.

Read the story about the Wedding at Cana in *John 2:1-11.*

○ With whom did Jesus attend the wedding?

○ What is Jesus' response when Mary tells him that the wedding party has run out of wine?

○ Describe the directions Jesus gives to the servants.

○ What is the significance of the chief steward's comment to the bridegroom?

○ What do we learn about Jesus in this event?

The miracle of changing water into wine at Cana was the first of seven signs, or miracles, in the Gospel according to John. By calling them signs, John emphasizes their role in marking the divine glory of Christ to foster the growth of faith in his disciples. Just as the miracles in the Gospel according to Matthew are part of Christ's revelation of the relationship between the Kingdom and God's plan of Redemption, so the sign/miracles in John are also part of Christ's revelation of his identity as part of his plan to redeem us.

> The time is surely coming, says the LORD,
> > when the one who plows shall overtake
> > > the one who reaps,
> > and the treader of grapes the one who
> > > sows the seed;
> the mountains shall drip sweet wine,
> > and all the hills shall flow with it . . .
> they shall plant vineyards and drink their wine,
> > and they shall make gardens and eat their
> > > fruit.

—Amos 9:13-14

In the Scriptures, we are invited to consider which wedding banquet we wish to attend: the one that lasts for a day, or the one that starts today and lasts for all eternity. Jesus teaches several parables about wedding banquets. Jesus' miracle at the wedding in Cana announces what is to come at the Last Supper when Jesus offers himself to us: "It makes manifest the fulfillment of the wedding feast in the Father's kingdom, where the faithful will drink the new wine that has become the Blood of Christ"[50] (CCC, 1335). Through

this miracle and others, the Redemption unfolds.

**Recall** What does Mary tell the stewards to do about the wine shortage at the wedding?

**Identify** What does Jesus' miracle at the wedding in Cana announce?

## The Transfiguration of Jesus

Just as the baptism of Jesus began his public life, the **Transfiguration** of Jesus set the stage for his Passion, Death, Resurrection, and Ascension—and, ultimately, our Redemption.

In the Transfiguration, God makes it perfectly clear that Jesus is "my Son, the Beloved." The presence of Moses and Elijah

**Transfiguration** the culmination moment in the public life of Jesus in which his appearance changed in the presence of the Apostles, and Elijah and Moses appeared beside him to reveal him as the true Messiah

is like a neon sign blinking above the head of Jesus, one that reads "Messiah!"

Moses represents the "Law" that he received from God and Elijah represents the "Prophets" who foretold the coming of the Messiah. Jesus fulfills both the Law (i.e. the Torah) and the writings of the prophets. Jesus used the Law and prophets in the Gospel of Luke to explain why he had to suffer and die: "Then beginning with Moses and all the prophets, he interpreted to them the things about himself in all the scriptures" (Luke 24:27).

Recall too from the Gospel of Matthew that "All this took place to fulfill what had been spoken by the Lord through the prophet: 'Look, the virgin shall conceive and bear a son, and they shall name him Emmanuel'" (Matthew 1:22-23/see Isaiah 7:14). Elijah was also the prophet who announced the coming of the Messiah in the Book of the prophet Malachi.

God the Father has anointed Jesus the Christ with the Holy Spirit for a divine mission. We see this at Jesus' baptism by John and something similar at Jesus' Transfiguration, as we get a glimpse into the life of the Trinity. The Father and the Holy Spirit were with Jesus at the beginning and throughout his ministry. The work of the three Persons of the Holy Trinity cannot be separated. Where one is, there are the other two. The Trinity is

## GO TO THE SOURCE

**Read the three accounts of the Transfiguration** in *Matthew 17:1-13*, *Mark 9:2-8*, and *Luke 9:28-36*.

○ Who was present? What happened? Who appeared?

○ What were the Apostles' responses to what they saw?

○ What did the voice from the cloud declare?

○ This scene should look and sound familiar when compared to the theophany stories. Read *Exodus 19:16-20:18* as well as *Matthew 3:13-17*. How does God appear in both stories, and what does the voice of God say?

present in the story of the Transfiguration in the same way as at Jesus' baptism: "the Father in the voice; the Son in the man; the Spirit in the shining cloud"[51] (CCC, 555).

The Transfiguration of Jesus is proclaimed during Mass on the second Sunday of Lent. The Preface on this Sunday further elaborates on its theological meaning for the Church.

> On the holy mountain he manifested to them his glory, to show, even by the testimony of the law and the prophets, that the Passion leads to the glory of the Resurrection.
>
> —*Roman Missal*

God's plan for Redemption in the Transfiguration unfolds through:

## CONNECT

Look at the Scripture passages that are read along with the Transfiguration story on the second Sunday of Lent. Make a connection between the passages and the Transfiguration. Choose Year A, B, or C readings as listed in the *Lectionary*:

○ Year A: Genesis 12:1-4; Psalm 33: 4-5, 18-19, 20, 22; 2 Timothy 1:8-10; Year B: Genesis 22:1-2, 9, 10-13, 15-18; Psalm 116: 10, 15, 16-17, 18-19; Romans 8:31-34; Year C: Genesis 15:5-12, 17-18; Psalm 27: 1, 7-8, 8-9, 13-14; Philippians 3:17-4:1.

○ Why is the Transfiguration passage so appropriate during the season of Lent?

○ Why do you think the account of the Transfiguration is proclaimed on a Sunday after the temptation of Jesus?

○ What connections can be made between the two accounts?

• Jesus disclosing his divine glory and confirming Peter's confession that he is the Messiah

# My Faith

**SAINTS PETER, JAMES, AND JOHN** witnessed the Transfiguration of Jesus on top of the mountain and it surely must have been a significant moment in their faith. Their emotions probably included both fear and excitement.

Take some time and recall some of your "mountaintop" moments.

After you answer the main question, be sure to respond to each of the four specific questions as well. Remember that you may use your reflections here as part of the final report you give at the end of this course.

### SO HERE'S THE QUESTION

*When have you felt closest to God in your life so far?*

○ Was it because of the individual(s) you were with, or was it a solitary experience?

○ Was it due to a certain activity, or a certain place?

○ What emotions did you have?

○ What understanding or knowledge did it leave you with?

- Jesus revealing that he will have to suffer greatly before dying and rising from the dead

- Moses and Elijah appearing, representing the Law and the Prophets

- Christ's Passion being the will of the Father and the Son

- the cloud indicating the presence of the Holy Spirit

## DISCUSS

○ How does the Transfiguration help us better understand Jesus' suffering and Death?

○ How does it help us deal with the inevitable reality of suffering in our own lives?

○ God tells us to listen to Jesus. What is Jesus saying to us that we are to hear, understand, and obey?

## GO TO THE SOURCE

**Elijah, who appears with Moses** during Jesus' Transfiguration, had an experience of his own on a mountaintop during his lifetime.

Read *1 Kings 19:11-13*.

○ What is the lesson of Elijah's experience of God on Mount Horeb?

○ Why is God present in "sheer silence" instead of the typical signs of theophany?

○ How would you answer the question that God asks Elijah, "What are you doing here?"

- a foretaste of Christ's glorious return, when he "will transform the body of our humiliation that it may be conformed to the body of his glory" (Philippians 3:21).

- recalling that "it is through many persecutions that we must enter the kingdom of God"[52] (CCC, 555 and 556).

**Tell** What does God say from the cloud to the Apostles at the Transfiguration of Jesus?

**Select** Of the bulleted items that detail how God's plan for Redemption unfolds in the Transfiguration, which one speaks to you most in your life now, and why?

## SECTION 1 REVIEW

### QUICK REVIEW

**1a. Connect** How is Jesus' baptism linked to the Old Testament?

**b. Recall** How does the baptism of Jesus unfold God's plan for Redemption?

**c. Identify** How does one come to know the secrets of the Kingdom of Heaven?

**2a. Tell** Relate the story of the wedding at Cana.

**b. Integrate** What are three common elements in the Temptation accounts in the Gospels?

**3a. Summarize** Tell the story of the Transfiguration.

**b. Explain** Why are Moses and Elijah present at the Transfiguration?

**c. List** Tell three ways in which the Transfiguration points to Jesus' role in human Redemption.

**Listen and Discuss** Consider how Saints Peter, James, and John must have felt during the Transfiguration.

○ How it would feel to see Jesus with Moses and Elijah?

○ Discuss how these Apostles would have recognized the Old Testament figures.

○ Contemplate what you would do or say if you had been present.

### SELF-ASSESS

Which statement best reflects where you are now?

☐ I'm confident enough about the material in this section to be able to explain it to someone else.

☐ I have a good grasp of the material in this section, but I could use more review.

☐ I'm lost. I need help catching up before moving on.

# Jesus' Suffering and Death

Have you ever experienced a defining moment in your life? Some event that left you thinking, "Things are never going to be the same again." Maybe it was graduating from middle school or moving to a new city. Other examples could be the death of a parent, grandparent, or close friend; a separation or divorce in a family; the birth of a baby brother or sister; a new romantic relationship; winning an athletic championship; or even your first concert.

We all have these defining moments. Even nations have times that define what they stand for or what they believe. For example, people could debate the defining moments of the United States: were they the writing of the Declaration of Independence, the influx of immigrants, the Industrial Revolution, various wars, the election of presidents, or the assassinations of leaders? Moments of suffering and pain can define a nation just as much as celebrations of joy and hope for the future.

A defining moment may involve emotional pain or struggling with the mystery of suffering and death. Other times it is a joyful experience of hope and love. A defining moment changes you, affecting the way you think, feel, and act in the world.

The Passion, Death, Resurrection, and Ascension of Jesus were defining moments for the first followers of Christ and the early Church. Two thousand years later, we continue to reflect on the meaning of the Paschal Mystery in our lives, but it is more than defining moments. The Paschal Mystery is the source of our Redemption, the ultimate story that defines us as sons and daughters of God. (see CCC 1067)

## LIST

○ Think about events that helped define who you are today. Then list them.

○ Make a timeline to illustrate these stories and note those that were sad, that involved sickness, suffering, and/or death, and those that were joyful.

○ How old were you when these events happened? Who were the people involved who made the story so prominent?

○ Indicate how aware you were of God's presence or action in those times, what role your faith played before, during, or after.

The Paschal mystery of Christ's cross and Resurrection stands at the center of the Good News that the apostles, and the Church following them, are to proclaim to the world. God's saving plan was accomplished 'once for all'[53] by the redemptive death of his Son Jesus Christ.

—CCC, 571

Jesus did not keep his knowledge of his impending suffering and Death a secret during his lifetime. On three occasions, he tells his disciples he will have to suffer and die and after three days rise again. Three times he discloses the Paschal Mystery, yet the disciples don't understand until the events happen. Even afterward, they still need time to believe, and some choose not to.

○ To more fully appreciate the Passion Narratives, read and reflect on the following: Mark 14:32-15:47; Matthew 26:36-27:66; Luke 22:39-56; and John 18:1-19:42.

○ Look up these Scriptures and summarize what each says about the Death of Jesus: Matthew 26:52-56; John 19:1-12; Acts 3:17-26; Acts 26:12-23; Acts 8:32-35; Luke 24:13-27; 44-47.

○ What have you learned about Jesus' suffering and Death that you had not realized before?

> Then he began to teach them that the Son of Man must undergo great suffering, and be rejected by the elders, the chief priests, and the scribes, and be killed, and after three days rise again. He said all this quite openly.
>
> —Mark 8:31-32

At the Last Supper, Jesus instituted the Eucharist as the memorial of his suffering and sacrifice. He also made the Apostles priests of the New Covenant by washing their feet and giving them the commandment of love (see CCC, 1337). The Last Supper becomes the new Passover and fulfills the Jewish Passover while also pointing to the final Passover of the Church into the Kingdom of God (see CCC, 1340). Jesus tells the Apostles to repeat his words and actions until he comes again. It is not just to remember Jesus, but to remember the Paschal Mystery—the Passion, Death, Resurrection, and Ascension of Jesus to the Father.

Since then Christians have met on Sunday, the first day of the week, the day of the Resurrection, to celebrate the Eucharist—the center of the Church's life (see CCC, 1343). "The pilgrim People of God advances, 'following the narrow way of the cross,'[54] toward the heavenly banquet, when all the elect will be seated at the table of the kingdom" (CCC, 1344). All love is sacrificial. Christ's love is the supreme sacrifice, and the Eucharist is the Sacrament of the sacrifice and Resurrection of Christ.

Throughout our Church's history, the Mass has consisted of a gathering, the Liturgy of the Word, the Liturgy of the Eucharist, and a sending forth. "Is this not the same movement as the Paschal meal of the risen Jesus with his disciples? Walking with them he explained the Scriptures to them; sitting with them at table 'he took bread, blessed and broke it, and gave it to them'"[55] (CCC, 1347).

## The Passion of Jesus

All four Gospels contain accounts of the Passion of Jesus. These accounts were written from the perspective of a post-Resurrection faith that had been deepened through the experience of the Resurrection of Jesus. The Gospel writers knew that Jesus' Death was not the end of the story. While the four Gospels differ in what they highlight, each presents Jesus' sufferings and Death as:

• a sacrifice which expresses Jesus obedience to God the Father, his virtue, and his mission of Redemption

• the result of commitments Jesus made as part of his mission

• the struggle between the power of life and the power of death

We know that Christ truly suffered and died. He really died and was buried, for the benefit of all. He endured the human pain and anguish of carrying the Cross to the site of his Crucifixion. He endured the human pain and anguish of hanging from that same Cross. And, "His human soul united to his divine person, the dead Christ went down to the realm of the dead. He opened heaven's gates for the just who had gone before him" (CCC, 637).

## Mystery of Suffering and Evil

Though we may witness suffering from natural and man-made disasters, the selfless response by many to help those in need gives us hope and inspires us to loving action as well. Suffering and death can be positive parts of the Kingdom of God. While seeking suffering and death is intrinsically evil, when our endurance or response to it brings about something good, we are making our faith a lived reality, and sharing in the divinity of Christ.

As logical, rational beings, we often have a hard time with the idea that Jesus knew about his impending suffering and Death. This difficulty can prompt believers to come to a number of false conclusions, especially when we use phrases like "Jesus *had* to die." Some of the common theological misunderstandings include:

- that God the Father *needed* Jesus to die, as if God caused it to happen.

- that God the Father *wanted* Jesus to suffer, as if suffering would somehow *appease* God.

In faith, we understand that Jesus' Death was part of the mystery of God's plan for Redemption. We also know that God is all-loving, and does not cause evil. God the Father sent his Son to pay for our sins. Jesus freely offered himself for that purpose. God the Father allowed his Son, Jesus, to suffer and die the way he did in order to show us the gravity and seriousness of sin and the extent of God's love for us.

> God is in no way, directly or indirectly, the cause of moral evil.[56] He permits it, however, because he respects the freedom of his creatures and, mysteriously, knows how to derive good from it:
>
> > For almighty God, . . . because he is supremely good, would never allow any evil whatsoever to exist in his works if he were not so all-powerful and good as to cause good to emerge from evil itself.[57]
>
> —CCC, 311, Saint Augustine

Several Scripture passages speak of the Death of Jesus as a sign of God's love for us.

> God's love was revealed among us in this way: God sent his only Son into the world so that we might live through him. In this is love, not that we loved God but that he loved us and sent his Son to be the atoning sacrifice for our sins. . . . We love because he first loved us.
>
> —1 John 4:9-10, 19

## RECALL

- Remember a time in your life when you let the actions or words of others deter you from doing the morally right thing. What provoked you?

- How about remembering a time when you were able to do the morally right thing despite the actions or words of others. How were you able to do so?

- God's choice to love us does not depend on anything we say or do. Do you think you primarily *react* to others or do you *choose* how you will act, independent of others, most of the time?

Many of us may wonder why would Jesus accept what he knew would happen to him at the Crucifixion. But Jesus knew the purpose of his life. In speaking about his impending Death, Jesus even asks, "And what should I say—'Father, save me from this hour'?" (John 12:27). No, Jesus says, he was meant to redeem us through his Death and Resurrection. "The desire to embrace his Father's plan of redeeming love inspired Jesus' whole life,[58] for his redemptive passion was the very reason for his Incarnation" (CCC, 607).

Jesus, true God and true man, accepts his suffering and Death to freely show the Father's divine love for us. The Father wants to redeem us, and Jesus' love for the Father and for us results in our salvation. Jesus' dedication to the will of his Father, despite knowing that it would end in his Death, reflects God's love for us. Human sinfulness led to the Crucifixion. God did not let the reality of that sinfulness deter him from his plan for our salvation. That, too, reflects God's love for us. We need to accept and live the grace of Redemption.

**Identify** What is the ultimate story that defines us as sons and daughters of God?

**Conclude** Why did God the Father permit the Crucifixion of his only Son?

# PRIMARY SOURCES

**A**rchbishop Oscar Arnulfo Romero was appointed archbishop of San Salvador, the capital city of El Salvador, in 1977. A short time after his appointment his friend, Father Rutilio Grande, was assassinated for his work with the poor.

Jesus described the path his followers were to follow, "He calls his disciples to 'take up [their] cross and follow [him],'[59] for 'Christ also suffered for [us], leaving [us] an example so that [we] should follow in his steps'"[60] (CCC, 618). Archbishop Romero took up his cross.

*I must tell you, as a Christian, I do not believe in death without resurrection. If I am killed, I shall arise in the Salvadoran people.*

*—Archbishop Romero*

Archbishop Romero talked about service to the poor in a prophetic sermon. Here is a portion of what he said:

*Those who surrender to the service of the poor through love of Christ will live like the grain of wheat that dies. It only apparently dies. If it were not to die, it would remain a solitary grain. The harvest comes because of the grain that dies. We know that every effort to improve society, above all when society is so full of injustice and sin, is an effort that God blesses; that God wants; that God demands of us. I am bound, as a pastor, by divine command to give my life for those whom I love, and that is all Salvadorans, even those who are going to kill me.*

Not long after that sermon, Archbishop Romero suffered his own passion and death when he was assassinated while celebrating Mass in the chapel of San Salvador's Hospital of Divine Providence on March 24, 1980.

> "**When I looked at Rutilio** lying there dead I thought 'if they have **killed** him for doing what he did, then I too have to **walk** the same **path**.'"
>
> *—Archbishop Romero*

How do the words of Archbishop Romero help you understand the Death and Resurrection of Jesus?

How does the following image Jesus uses with the grain of wheat help you understand his Death? "Unless a grain of wheat falls into the earth and dies, it remains just a single grain; but if it dies, it bears much fruit" (John 12:24).

➜ Go to the student site at **hs.osvcurriculum.com**

## QUICK REVIEW

**1a. Identify** What were the defining moments for the early Christian community?

**b. Explain** Why is it wrong to say Jesus had to die, needed to die, or wanted to die?

**2a. Conclude** Why did Jesus accept what he knew would happen to him on the Cross?

**b. Summarize** What or who did Archbishop Romero liken to a grain of wheat?

## ACT

Discuss with a group how you can be like the grain that Archbishop Romero described. Make a list of examples of this idea in your own life or in the lives of people you have read or know about.

## SELF-ASSESS

Which statement best reflects where you are now?

☐ I'm confident enough about the material in this section to be able to explain it to someone else.

☐ I have a good grasp of the material in this section, but I could use more review.

☐ I'm lost. I need help catching up before moving on.

# The Resurrection and Ascension of Jesus

The Resurrection of Jesus is part of God's plan for Redemption played out in the Paschal Mystery. Without the Resurrection and the entire Paschal Mystery, we would have no central reason for hope, much less lasting hope; the story would end. The Resurrection also confirms Jesus' divinity. He is the "'I Am,' the Son of God and God himself" (CCC, 653). Through his Death, Christ frees us from sin, and through his Resurrection, he shows us the way to new life. The Resurrection makes us brothers and sisters of Jesus because we now have a share in the life of Christ (see CCC, 654). Saint Paul writes that our faith is futile without the Resurrection of Jesus.

> But in fact Christ has been raised from the dead, the first fruits of those who have died. For since death came through a human being, the resurrection of the dead has also come through a human being; for as all die in Adam, so all will be made alive in Christ.
>
> —1 Corinthians 15:20-22

## GO TO THE SOURCE

**Mary Magdalene and the holy women** who visit the tomb to anoint the body of Jesus were "the first to encounter the Risen One.[61] Thus the women were the first messengers of Christ's Resurrection for the apostles themselves"[62] (CCC, 641).

Read the Resurrection account in *John 20:1-18*.

○ What stands out to you or what was God saying to you in your reading of this passage today?

○ What do you think is the significance of the Risen Christ first appearing to Mary Magdalene?

Being "dead," even though our bodies are alive, means that we live in *fear* instead of in the *hope* of everlasting life. The consequence of Original Sin was the experience of death. We are already dead if the fear born out of our painful past events and mistakes dominates our thoughts, actions, and spirit. Once we have reached that point, we have lost hope in a new life of abundant love that Jesus' Resurrection represents. We are still alive, however, if we overcome the fear of future pain and future loss. We can't allow these fears to dominate our thoughts, actions, and spirit. Instead, we have hope in the joy beyond the pain and in life beyond the loss we experience. Jesus' empty tomb is a symbol of that hope. Followers of Jesus Christ know that suffering is never in vain because it can help us move toward Heaven and eternal life. In our suffering, we can help make up to some degree for the hurt and harm we cause by our sin.

The empty tomb is also the primary symbol of Jesus' Resurrection, and the first sign that led the disciples to recognize that the Resurrection had taken place. The disciples of Jesus confirmed the Risen Christ because they actually encountered him. Many were martyred for preaching about Jesus' Resurrection. They would not have died for something they knew to be a fraud. We can be confident in the Resurrection because the first disciples of Christ were.

## GO TO THE SOURCE 📖

**The risen Jesus** scolds his disciples for their lack of faith after the Resurrection takes place.

Read *Mark 16:11-14*.

○ How does Jesus describe the faith of the eleven?

○ What parallels do you find between the Apostles' reaction to the Resurrection and your own?

**After the Crucifixion, Jesus' Body was laid to rest in a tomb that belonged to Joseph of Arimathea, a member of the Sanhedrin.**

Church of the Holy Sepulchre

○ The Gospel of John describes the location of the tomb as near the Crucifixion in a garden (see John 19:41).

○ In the year A.D. 326, Roman Emperor Constantine had a basilica built on the spot where today the Church of the Holy Sepulchre sits in the city of Jerusalem.

○ A series of church buildings have occupied the space. The familiar dome over the rotunda was rebuilt in 1868. The rotunda houses the monument where the Tomb of Christ is located.

○ What do the empty tomb mean to you?

○ Many call the site of the Church of the Holy Sepulchre the holiest place on Earth. Why do you think they do so?

# Faith & Culture

↗ Go to the student site at **hs.osvcurriculum.com**

The empty tomb is no proof of the resurrection, that much is undeniable. Conversely, though, one might ask: Is the Resurrection compatible with the body remaining in the tomb? Can Jesus be risen if he is still lying in the tomb? What kind of resurrection would that be? . . . In Jerusalem at the time, the proclamation of the Resurrection would have been completely impossible if anyone had been able to point to a body lying in the tomb. . . . We have to say that the empty tomb as such, while it cannot prove the Resurrection, is nevertheless a necessary condition for Resurrection faith, which was specifically concerned with the body, and consequently, with the whole of the person.

—Pope Benedict XVI, *Jesus of Nazareth*, p. 254

The discovery of the empty tomb by the holy women and the disciples is a real, historical event involving Christ's physical body. The New Testament bears witness to the disciples' encounters with the risen Jesus, and the empty tomb verifies that witness.

Saint Paul writes to the early Christians in Corinth on what he knew to be true about the Paschal Mystery.

> Christ died for our sins in accordance with the scriptures, and that he was buried, and that he was raised on the third day in accordance with the scriptures, and that he appeared to Cephas [Peter], then to the twelve. Then he appeared to more than five hundred brothers and sisters at one time, most of whom are still alive, though some have died. Then he appeared to James, then to all the apostles. Last of all, as to one untimely born, he appeared also to me.
>
> —1 Corinthians 15:3-8

**Recall** What is the primary symbol of Jesus' Resurrection?

**Explain** What does the Resurrection ensure that we will have?

### The Response to the Resurrection

When we remind ourselves how incredible the reality of the Resurrection must have been for even Jesus' closest followers, it makes sense that the Apostles' acceptance of the Resurrection went through a process of unfolding. Although Jesus had told the Apostles that the Resurrection would take place, they were still doubtful when they faced the reality of it. They doubt the women who brought them the news (see Mark 16:11 and Luke 24:11), and believe they witnessed a ghost when Jesus came to them (see Luke 24:37).

### DISCUSS

- How and why is it that Christians believe in the Resurrection of Jesus?
- Give your own personal statement of faith as to why you believe in the Resurrection.

### GO TO THE SOURCE

Look at the following passages from the Gospels of Luke and John that take place following the Resurrection.

Read *Luke 24:13-35* and *36-49*.
- What point comes across most to you in these two stories?

Read *John 20:1-18* and *21:1-19*.
- How would you describe Jesus' actions/emotions in these two accounts?

One of the reasons for the Apostles' difficulty accepting the Resurrection was that no one had ever seen, experienced, or envisioned anything like it. Jesus' risen life was completely different from those, like Lazarus, whom Jesus himself raised from the dead. Lazarus and the daughter of Jairus weren't *resurrected*; they were *resuscitated* and *returned* to earthly life. One day Lazarus and the daughter of Jairus would die again, but in his risen body, Jesus "passes from the state of death to another life beyond time and space" (CCC, 646).

It is important to remind ourselves that the Resurrection was a physical, bodily experience. Jesus' whole body was resurrected. Jesus ate and drank with the Apostles after his Resurrection. No one saw exactly how Christ's Resurrection happened. We see the aftermath in the empty tomb and in the Apostles' meetings with the risen Jesus, but the Resurrection itself is a mystery— "something that transcends and surpasses history" (CCC, 647).

The Resurrection bears tremendous meaning for our faith. We referenced Saint Paul's Letter to the Corinthians when we explained that the Resurrection is the reason for our faith and the reason for our hope. It fulfills the Covenant promises from the Old Testament, as well as the promises made by Jesus while he lived among us. Moreover, the "truth of Jesus' divinity is confirmed by his Resurrection" (CCC, 653).

# CATHOLIC LIFE

# Saint Mary Magdalene

Mary Magdalene has an important role in the New Testament. Over the centuries, thousands of pages have been written about her even though she is mentioned by name only thirteen times in all four Gospel accounts.

Many people over the years have thought Mary Magdalene was a reformed prostitute who secretly entered the house of a rich man named Simon and used her long hair to anoint Jesus' feet with precious oil, prompting Jesus to say, "Your faith has saved you; go in peace" (Luke 7:50).

But that view of Mary Magdalene is most likely incorrect. The idea that she was a reformed prostitute comes from a sixth century sermon by Pope Gregory the Great. Gregory described a figure who was a combination of Mary Magdalene, Mary of Bethany (sister of Lazarus), and the unnamed "sinner" who anointed Jesus' feet with oil. By assuming the unnamed woman's sin was sexual, Gregory may have inadvertently introduced the idea that Mary Magdalene had been a prostitute. In 1969, the Vatican issued a statement stating that the three were different women.

So what do we know about Mary Magdalene? We know that Jesus healed her from seven demons. Those demons might have been illnesses, psychological problems, or sins. Since seven is a symbolic number in Judaism indicating completeness, it might mean that she was truly sick or troubled. All we know for certain is that Jesus healed her and she became one of his devoted followers. We also know that she must have had wealth since Luke says that she and others helped support Jesus and the disciples "out of their own means" (Luke 8:3).

If those were the only things we knew about Mary Magdalene, she might have been forgotten. However, she is remembered for her unique role in the history of Redemption. On the first day of the week after Jesus was laid to rest, Mary Magdalene went to his tomb and discovered that the stone had been rolled back. As she sat crying, a man she thought was a gardener asked who she was looking for. She responded, "Sir, if you have carried him away, tell me where you have put him, and I will get him" (John 20:15). At that moment, the man called her by name and she recognized him as Jesus, crying out "Rabboni"—Teacher!

The Resurrection was a historical event involving Christ's physical body that was testified by those who saw the Risen Jesus, including Mary Magdalene, and was verified by the empty tomb. Since Jesus' Resurrection lies at the heart of Christian faith, we know that someone had to be the first to see him in his glorified body and risen state. That someone was Mary Magdalene. Her witness reveals that salvation did not end on the Cross, but only began with it. It is only in and through the Resurrection and our response to it that our own personal Redemption ensues.

> **Think About It** How did Mary respond when Jesus healed her? And then when she saw him after his Resurrection? How do you think you would have reacted if you had seen the Risen Jesus?

➚ Go to the student site at
**hs.osvcurriculum.com**

This painting shows Christ (dressed as a traveler) appearing to Cleopas and another disciple on the road to Emmaus.

The Resurrection above all constitutes the confirmation of all Christ's works and teachings. All truths, even those most inaccessible to human reason, find their justification if Christ by his Resurrection has given the definitive proof of his divine authority, which he had promised.

—CCC, 651

In the Gospel of Luke, the disciples on the road to Emmaus were mourning the Death of Jesus and fearful for themselves and their community. During the breaking of the bread, the Paschal Mystery was revealed and the disciples received the eternal hope of Christ. It's not enough to talk about Jesus, think about Jesus, read about Jesus, or learn about Jesus. To receive the hope of the Paschal Mystery, the disciples had to experience Jesus for themselves by hearing his voice, seeing his Resurrected body, and sharing a meal with him. The hope of the Paschal Mystery that takes away the fear we experience in life is revealed to you when you experience Jesus in the Eucharist and the gathering of the Church for all the Sacraments, the intimacy of relationships, the reading of Scriptures, the quiet of prayer, the loving acts of those you don't even know, and in service to others.

The Resurrection of Jesus then ensures our Redemption from sin. The *Catechism* puts it this way: "The Paschal mystery has two aspects: by his death, Christ liberates us from sin; by his Resurrection, he opens for us the way to a new life" (CCC, 654). Christ's Resurrection, and in fact the Risen Christ himself, is the source our own future resurrection.

## The Ascension of Jesus

The final event in the earthly life of Jesus, his **Ascension** into Heaven, is closely linked to the first, his descent from Heaven in the Incarnation. "Only the one who 'came from the Father' can return to the Father: Christ Jesus.[63] 'No one has ascended into heaven but he who descended from heaven, the Son of man'"[64] (CCC, 661; John 3:13).

Christ's ascension marks the definitive entrance of Jesus' humanity into God's heavenly domain, whence he will come again (cf. *Acts* 1:11); this humanity in the meantime hides him from the eyes of men (cf. *Col* 3:3).

—CCC, 665

How does Jesus' returning to the Father make us stronger and help further the Kingdom of God? Think about something in your own life. For example, if a teacher takes our tests for us, we will not learn. No one will benefit from knowledge we do not have. A coach has to step off the field or court to allow his or her players to play. An author of a book reaches thousands more people than he or she would if the same information or story were only given to a live audience. Word of the Ascension of Jesus spread with an explosion of people going to every corner of the Earth, sharing his Good News so that all may be saved.

Jesus, who was truly man while remaining truly God, assumed a human nature and soul. He never lost his divine nature, as we know from the Incarnation, which is the mystery of the union of the divine and human natures. The Ascension brings Jesus' humanity into Heaven, from where he will return (see CCC, 665). The Ascension and glorification of Jesus culminate in Jesus sending the Holy Spirit to his Apostles at Pentecost.

**Recall** What does the Ascension mark?

**Contrast** What was the difference between Christ's Resurrection and that of Lazarus, who was raised from the dead by Jesus?

## GO TO THE SOURCE

**There are several accounts** of the Ascension in *Acts 1:9-11*; *Luke 24:50-53*; and *Mark 16:14-20*.

Read the Resurrection account in *John 20:1-18*.
- What stands out to you or what was God saying to you in your reading of this passage today?
- What do you think is the significance of the Risen Christ first appearing to Mary Magdalene?

## SECTION 3 REVIEW

### QUICK REVIEW

**1a. Tell** What does Jesus' empty tomb symbolize?
  **b. Identify** To whom did Jesus appear first after the Resurrection?

**2a. Summarize** How did Jesus' followers react to his Resurrection?
  **b. Connect** How is Jesus' Resurrection linked to his Incarnation?

### ACT

Write a short journal entry from the point of view of one of Jesus' followers.

- You've heard about Jesus' Resurrection from another follower. Would you believe it?
- How would your thoughts be affected by seeing Jesus after the Resurrection?
- What could you conclude about your faith, based on these two reactions?

### SELF-ASSESS

Which statement best reflects where you are now?

☐ I'm confident enough about the material in this section to be able to explain it to someone else.

☐ I have a good grasp of the material in this section, but I could use more review.

☐ I'm lost. I need help catching up before moving on.

# Hope and Grace

As Jesus prepares to leave the Earth to sit at the right hand of his Father, we are reminded of his words that give us profound hope. He has not abandoned us.

> Do not let your hearts be troubled. Believe in God, believe also in me. In my Father's house there are many dwelling places. If it were not so, would I have told you that I go to prepare a place for you? And if I go and prepare a place for you, I will come again and will take you to myself, so that where I am, there you may be also.
>
> —John 14:1-3

The unfolding of God's plan for Redemption is meant to give us hope during our time on Earth. The Resurrection contains a promise of our own resurrection. We can even take some hope in the confusion and doubt experienced by Jesus' own disciples, who witnessed the Paschal Mystery with their own eyes. Much like God's plan for Redemption and the Apostles' faith in the Resurrection, our own faith unfolds and grows over time. We should not fear this.

The reason we do not need to be afraid is offered by Jesus in the Acts of the Apostles, "But you will receive power when the Holy Spirit has come upon you; and you will be my witnesses in Jerusalem, in all Judea and Samaria, and to the ends of the earth" (Acts 1:8). Jesus promised and sent the Holy Spirit, who gives us courage to persevere in faith.

The events of Pentecost fulfilled Jesus' promise. The Apostles were no longer afraid to share the Good News of Christ because they were filled with the Holy Spirit, the Third Person of the Holy Trinity. Many people became followers of Jesus on that first Pentecost. The Holy Spirit filled, inspired, and acted through Saint Peter and the Apostles. The new believers quickly devoted themselves to the Apostles' teachings on Jesus, to prayer, and to the communal breaking of the bread. They grew in number every day. This set a perfect example of the power available to us through the Gifts of the Holy Spirit.

It is said that the phrase "Do not be afraid" appears 365 times in the Bible, often at important times such as Mary's pregnancy and in the Resurrection Narratives.

○ Why might this phrase be repeated so often in the Bible?

○ List five things that frighten you, then apply the phrase "Do not be afraid" to each one, explaining how God can lessen your fear.

○ Is there anything that God says not to fear? Research in the Bible to find out.

With God's help, put into practice the Gifts of the Holy Spirit—wisdom, understanding, right judgment, courage, knowledge, piety, and fear of the Lord, and you will be amazed by the realization of God's presence in your daily life. The Holy Spirit renews our hearts and leads us to truth. Our ultimate fulfillment awaits us in Heaven. It is a perfect life with the Holy Trinity, the Virgin Mary, the saints, and all holy people. "Heaven is the ultimate end and fulfillment of the deepest human longings, the state of supreme, definitive happiness" (CCC, 1024). It is the Holy Spirit that allowed saints to be filled with joy even as they faced persecution. It is the same Holy Spirit today who gives us the courage and grace to enable us to live holy lives.

## The Assumption of Mary

Mary the Mother of God needed the same courage from the Holy Spirit to accept her role in the plan for Redemption. Her free decision brought us everlasting hope. Everything the Catholic Church teaches about Mary comes from what the Church believes about Christ. What we know about Mary shines a light on our faith in Christ. Mary's "yes" to God's call allowed her to be used by God for his plan of salvation. Her consent to be the Mother of God came from her love for God. Mary wholeheartedly supported the Father's will, Jesus' work of Redemption, and the prompting of the Holy Spirit.

Mary is our model of faith and love, and a unique member of the Church (see CCC, 967). Her whole life was part of God's plan. Each year we celebrate the Feast of the Immaculate Conception on December 8. Some confuse this feast day with the conception of Jesus, but it commemorates the Immaculate Conception of Mary herself. She was conceived without Original Sin from the first moment of her conception, and through God's grace she remained pure from all personal sin throughout her life.

Through Jesus, God sums up his salvation history. God created the world not because he needed to or because of any accident. He created everything from his own will to share himself, his wisdom, and his goodness (see CCC, 295). He makes use of his Creation to carry out this plan, and Mary's life played a unique part. Mary is joined to her Son's Resurrection through her **Assumption**.

> Finally the Immaculate Virgin, preserved free from all stain of original sin, when the course of her earthly life was finished, was taken up body and soul into heavenly glory, and exalted by the Lord as Queen over all things, so that she might be the more fully conformed to her Son, the Lord of lords and conqueror of sin and death.[65]
>
> —CCC, 966

As the Ascension of Jesus relates to other events of the Paschal Mystery, the life of Mary is joined with her Son's throughout his life, from conception to death and his Resurrection and up to the coming of the Holy Spirit at Pentecost. She is the Mother of God; Mother of the Redeemer. Mary is also the Mother of the Church.

Her husband, Joseph, played an important role in the lives of Jesus and Mary. He faced the dilemma of being about to marry a woman who became pregnant. An angel spoke to Joseph in a dream and assured him of taking Mary as his wife. He married Mary, protected her, and found a place for her to give birth. Then he avoided violence by fleeing to Egypt and later settled his family in Nazareth where he provided for his wife and foster son.

**Assumption** the teaching affirming that at the end of her life, Mary was taken up, body and soul, into Heaven

The Assumption of Mary is celebrated on August 15, and the Preface for the Assumption helps us to understand this event as a sign of hope and comfort for all Christians.

> For today the Virgin Mother of God was assumed into heaven as . . . a sign of sure hope and comfort to your pilgrim people; rightly you would not allow her to see the corruption of the tomb since from her own body she marvelously brought forth your incarnate Son, the Author of all life.
>
> — *Preface, The Assumption of the Blessed Virgin Mary, Roman Missal*

### The Virtue of Hope

Mary, throughout her life, modeled **hope** and trust in God. "Hope is the theological virtue by which we desire the kingdom of heaven and eternal life as our happiness, placing our trust in Christ's promises and relying not on our own strength, but on the help of the grace of the Holy Spirit"(CCC, 1817). Hope helps us live out the Paschal Mystery of Christ in our world through the power of the Holy Spirit. Hope relates directly to God, as do the other two theological virtues: faith and charity (love). Hope, along with faith and love, allows us to live in a relationship with the three divine Persons of the Holy Trinity. Hope keeps us from drowning in discouragement and sustains us when times are difficult.

> Certainly, Jesus Christ is the true light, the sun that has risen above all the shadows of history. But to reach him we also need lights close by—people who shine with his light and so guide us along our way. Who more than Mary could be a star of hope for us? With her "yes" she opened the door of our world to God himself; she became the living Ark of the Covenant, in whom God took flesh, became one of us, and pitched his tent among us.
>
> —Pope Benedict XVI, *Spe Salvi* (*In Hope We Were Saved*), November 30, 2007

Hope is distinct from wishing because it actively involves placing one's trust in God. Trusting in God's promises for the future of our salvation impacts how we live our daily lives.

> It affords us joy even under trial . . . Hope is expressed and nourished in prayer, especially in the Our Father, the summary of everything that hope leads us to desire.
>
> —CCC, 1820

Hope can be expressed in the goals we have set for ourselves and our dreams for the future, personally and collectively as the Church. It can be expressed in the desire God has for us to live in his love.

> Empowered by the Spirit, and drawing upon faith's rich vision, a new generation of Christians is being called to help build a world in which God's gift of life is welcomed, respected and cherished—not rejected, feared as a threat and destroyed. A new age in which love is not greedy or self-seeking, but pure, faithful and genuinely free, open to others, respectful of their dignity, seeking their good, radiating joy and beauty. A new age in which hope liberates us from the shallowness, apathy and self-absorption which deaden our souls and poison our relationships. Dear young friends, the Lord is asking you to be prophets of this new age, messengers of his love, drawing people to the Father and building a future of hope for all humanity.
>
> —Blessed Pope John Paul II

**Explain** How does Jesus give us hope?

**Describe** How is Mary a model of hope for us?

### The Gift of Grace

Have you ever been given an assignment, project, or job that seemed impossible to achieve on your own? To a certain extent, accomplishing huge tasks requires self-confidence, hard work, and discipline. Yet we also know when we are in over our heads. When faced with a seemingly insurmountable task, some choose to shut down. Why bother trying if you know you will fail? Others wisely ask for help.

We are called to become the children of God, so that we become partakers of his divine nature and have everlasting life (see CCC, 460 and 1996). This is impossible to do on our own, but fortunately for us, God's **grace**, or favor from God, is freely given.

God's plan for Redemption results in our **justification**, that is, God's gracious action that frees humans from sin and bestows his righteousness through their belief in Jesus Christ (CCC, Glossary). It is the act of God's grace, which frees us from sin and sanctifies and renews us. Justification involves the free gift of grace and our willingness to accept this grace. The one and only way to be justified or redeemed is to cooperate with the grace of God. In so doing, we turn away from sin and turn toward God, accepting his forgiveness. These two aspects of justification are similar to the aspects of conversion that we will address in later chapters.

This grace is free; it's like getting divine help. We haven't done anything to earn or deserve this grace, but like a loving parent aiding a child, God gives us the divine help we need to respond to him in love. By his willingness to suffer and die for us, Jesus merited or won this justification, and it's granted through Baptism. This grace of being justified joins us to the Paschal Mystery of Jesus in a special way because we actually share in Christ's life, thanks to the Holy Spirit within us. This most excellent work of God's mercy gives glory to God and Christ and offers the gift of eternal life.

God knows that we place the burden of sin on ourselves, and that it creates a downward spiral in our lives. We wonder why we keep making the same mistakes and doing the things we know are wrong. This dilemma brings us to our dependence on God's free gift of grace. There is no way to earn or make up for God's infinite love. Once we realize the Paschal Mystery was for us, then

## GLOBAL PERSPECTIVES

**The Church celebrates Mary and many of the Saints as patrons of various countries.**

Mary is honored with many different titles.

Mary, under the title Our Lady of the Immaculate Conception, is the patroness of United States, and her feast day is celebrated on December 8. In Brazil and Portugal she is also honored under the title Our Lady of the Immaculate Conception. Other titles of Mary are honored by nations around the world. For example, Mexico honors Our Lady of Guadalupe (December 12); Slovakia honors Our Lady of Sorrows (September 15); Chile honors Our Lady of Mount Carmel (July 16); and the Dominican Republic commemorates Our Lady of High Grace (April 4).

➔ Go to the student site at **hs.osvcurriculum.com**

the direction of that downward spiral can begin to change and we can begin to feel—and become—truly free.

## The Seven Sacraments

Justification comes from Baptism, the first of the Sacraments. Each of the **Seven Sacraments** in its own way celebrates Passion, Death, Resurrection, and Ascension of Jesus—his Paschal Mystery. Christ instituted the Seven Sacraments so that we might have life through him. "They bear fruit in those who receive them with the required dispositions" (CCC, 1131). The Holy Spirit prepares us for the Sacraments by predisposing our hearts to welcome God (see CCC, 1133). Through the Sacraments, Christ communicates his Holy Spirit to us (see CCC, 739). This is called **sacramental grace**. The actions and words—the form and matter—of each Sacrament are vital, but it is Christ and the Holy Spirit who give sacramental grace. Christ himself is at work in the Sacraments through the Holy Spirit. "As fire transforms into itself everything it touches, so the Holy Spirit transforms into the divine life whatever is subjected to his power" (CCC, 1127).

**grace** undeserved gift from God that helps us respond to our calling in life to become his children, to take part in his divine nature, to do good and avoid evil (see CCC 1996)

**justification** God's gracious action that frees humans from sin and bestows his righteousness through their belief in Jesus Christ

**Seven Sacraments** effective signs of grace, instituted by Christ and entrusted to the Church, by which divine life is shared with us through the work of the Holy Spirit

**sacramental grace** "the grace of the Holy Spirit, given by Christ and proper to each sacrament" (CCC, 1129)

**In the account of Thomas' encounter with Christ,** one can make connections to the Sacraments.

Read *John 20:19-29*.

○ Where are the disciples when the Risen Jesus appears to them?

○ What one line does Jesus repeat three times? What is the context in which Jesus says this? What is happening?

This understanding is key for Catholics, because we need the Sacraments and the grace they bring for our salvation, which Christ accomplished through his suffering, Death, Resurrection, and Ascension. The Apostle Thomas' encounter with Christ after the Resurrection helps us understand the sacraments as celebrations of the Paschal Mystery of Christ.

The *Catechism* also describes the action of the Holy Spirit in the seven Sacraments that form the heart of the Church's worship: "In the liturgy the Holy Spirit is teacher of the faith of the People of God and artisan of 'God's masterpieces,' the sacraments of the New Covenant" (CCC, 1091).

"The Spirit heals and transforms those who receive him by conforming them to the Son of God" (CCC, 1129). In our daily life, we conform to Christ through acts of sacrifice, trust in the Father, and reconciliation. These acts include concern for the poor, defending justice, admitting our faults to others, examining our lives, and correcting our sins against others. We experience this conversion to become more like Christ in our acceptance of suffering or when we face persecution. Scripture calls this taking up our cross and following Jesus (see Luke 9:23; CCC, 1435).

The fullness of Christian life and the perfection of charity are achieved through the celebration—and the living out—of the Eucharist and other Sacraments. "Spiritual progress tends toward ever more intimate union with Christ. This union is called 'mystical' because it participates in the mystery of Christ through the Sacraments—'the holy mysteries'—and, in him, in the mystery of the Holy Trinity. God calls us all to this intimate union with him . . ." (CCC, 2014).

**Define** What is sacramental grace?

**Apply** What do acts of reconciliation and the sacramental life do for our relationship with Christ?

## SECTION 4 REVIEW

### QUICK REVIEW

**1a. Conclude** What does Mary's Assumption mean to us?

**b. Analyze** What is Mary's relationship to us?

**c. Define** What is a virtue?

**d. Elaborate** What does hope prepare us for?

**2a. Explain** Why is the Church called a "sacrament"?

**b. Conclude** Why do we need Sacraments and grace?

### ACT

Read through the rites, or official prayers, of at least one Sacrament.

○ When and how is the Holy Spirit mentioned in the prayers?

○ What sort of power does the Holy Spirit have, as witnessed by these prayers?

### SELF-ASSESS

Which statement best reflects where you are now?

☐ I'm confident enough about the material in this section to be able to explain it to someone else.

☐ I have a good grasp of the material in this section, but I could use more review.

☐ I'm lost. I need help catching up before moving on.

## The Nicene Creed

**I believe in one God,**
the Father almighty,
maker of heaven and earth,
of all things visible and invisible.
I believe in one Lord Jesus Christ,
the Only Begotten Son of God,
born of the Father before all ages.
God from God, Light from Light,
true God from true God,
begotten, not made, consubstantial with the Father;
through him all things were made.
For us men and for our salvation
he came down from heaven,

*At the words that follow up to and including* and became man, *all bow.*

and by the Holy Spirit was incarnate of the Virgin Mary,
and became man.
For our sake he was crucified under Pontius Pilate,
he suffered death and was buried,
and rose again on the third day
in accordance with the Scriptures.
He ascended into heaven
and is seated at the right hand of the Father.
He will come again in glory
to judge the living and the dead
and his kingdom will have no end.
I believe in the Holy Spirit, the Lord, the giver of life,
who proceeds from the Father and the Son,
who with the Father and the Son is adored and glorified,
who has spoken through the prophets.
I believe in one, holy, catholic and apostolic Church.
I confess one Baptism for the forgiveness of sins
and I look forward to the resurrection of the dead
and the life of the world to come. Amen.

## TERMS

Use each of the following terms in a sentence that shows you know what the term means. You may include more than one term in a sentence.

| | |
|---|---|
| temptation | Assumption |
| Roman Missal | hope |
| omnipotence | justification |
| filial | grace |
| Transfiguration | Seven Sacraments |
| Ascension | sacramental grace |

## PEOPLE

Identify why each of these people is significant.

1. Lamb of God

2. Amos

3. Satan

4. Peter, James, and John

5. Moses and Elijah

6. Archbishop Romero

7. Mary Magdalene

8. Mary the Mother of God

9. Thomas

## UNDERSTANDING

Answer each question and complete each exercise.

### SECTION 1

1. **Explain** Why is Jesus' baptism by John a significant moment?
2. **Connect** How did Jesus' baptism reveal Redemption?
3. **Infer** What does the account of the wedding at Cana reveal about Jesus' mission?
4. **Distinguish** Tell the role of each person in the Transfiguration story: Moses, Elijah, Jesus, and Peter.

### SECTION 2

5. **Recall** Why does Saint Paul say that Christian faith is futile without the Resurrection of Jesus?
6. **Develop** How do the reactions of Jesus' followers to his Resurrection provide us with evidence that it actually happened?
7. **Infer** What implications do Jesus' Death and Resurrection have for people today?
8. **Explain** What is the significance of the empty tomb?

### SECTION 3

9. **Reflect** What effect does Jesus' Ascension have on us?
10. **Infer** How do the Apostles' and disciples' initial confusion and doubt concerning the Resurrection give us hope?
11. **Connect** How does the Assumption conform Mary more fully to her Son?
12. **Relate** What role did Mary play in bringing about the Redemption?

13. **Define** What is grace?
14. **Connect** What can we take from the disciples' reaction to the Resurrection that compares to our own understanding of our faith?
15. **Recall** Mary's "yes" allowed her to cooperate with what important work of God?
16. **List** Name three acts of reconciliation that conform us to Christ in our daily life.

## CONNECTING

**Visual** This illustration by the British poet and artist William Blake is called "The Third Temptation." Study the illustration and then answer the questions.

Which elements of the Gospel story can you find in this picture? What part of the story does the artwork show? What does the artist convey about Satan? How does the artist use form and lines to tell the story?

**Challenge** Your friend is talking with you about a current events report you gave in history class about a life long criminal who was recently sentenced to life in prison.

> **Friend:** That guy's going to Hell for sure.
>
> **You:** You don't know that.
>
> **Friend:** You gave the report. Didn't you hear yourself talk about his criminal life?
>
> **You:** He still has a chance at Redemption.
>
> **Friend:** I don't think so.

○ What is your next reply?

○ Continue the conversation, anticipating at least two more points your friend might make about the criminal's fate.

**Question** After working through this chapter, what advice would you give someone who seems to have lost hope?

## SELF-ASSESS

**On Your Own** Make a list of the most important things you learned from this chapter. Select three things that represent your growth in understanding as you worked through this chapter, then write a paragraph explaining your choices.

**With a Partner** List what you found most helpful or interesting in this chapter, as well as any other questions that have surfaced.

# Experiencing the Paschal Mystery

Go to the student site at
**hs.osvcurriculum.com**

- Explore the mystery of suffering.

- Reflect on suffering in your own life and/or the lives of people you know.

- Examine how suffering can affect body, mind, and spirit.

- Identify the relationship between suffering and love, happiness and pain.

- Clarify aspects of the Spirituality of Suffering.

- Recognize the dynamics of resolving grief.

- Explore the other experiences of loss in life.

- Discuss the spirituality of Abandonment to Divine Providence.

- Evaluate your own level of resiliency and how openness to God's grace can increase your ability to weather struggles and suffering.

- Apply the experience of the Paschal Mystery to your own life.

sacrifice

paradise

paradox

passion

compassion

eschatology

Particular Judgment

Heaven

Hell

Purgatory

Parousia

resiliency

# WHAT DO YOU SAY?

At the beginning of their sophomore year, students were asked to describe the hardest part about their freshmen year in high school:

"**The hardest part for me** started the first day of school. The teacher asked me my name. I stutter, so it took me a few seconds to get it out. Before I could say it, a lot of kids started laughing. They thought I was so nervous I forgot my name. All year, people teased me whenever I tried to answer a question and stuttered."

"**Stupid people.** That's the hardest thing so far in high school. I like indie music. And I read a lot. So some people think I'm a loner. They spread rumors about me and make comments behind my back. It's frustrating and it hurts. I'm getting used to it though. It doesn't bother me as much. But stupid people, that's the hardest part."

"**Honestly?** Leaving a lot of my friends from grade school. Only like three or four of us came to this high school. I didn't know anybody here freshmen year, but everybody else was here with all their friends. I hated it actually, but I didn't say anything. At first, I still saw my old friends on weekends and over break, but now we hardly hang out. Everyone is into their own school activities and stuff. I have two new friends instead of a whole class of old friends."

# WHERE ARE YOU?

**Check the answer that best matches where you are today.**

I think we should do everything we can to avoid suffering.
☐ Quite a bit ☐ Somewhat ☐ A little ☐ Not at all

I have questions about Heaven, Hell, and Purgatory
☐ Quite a bit ☐ Somewhat ☐ A little ☐ Not at all

I often wonder why God doesn't stop my suffering or the suffering I see in the people I love.
☐ Quite a bit ☐ Somewhat ☐ A little ☐ Not at all

I accept suffering as a part of life.
☐ At Mass ☐ In Thoughts ☐ In Nature ☐ Not at all

# The Experience of Suffering

People dying in wars. People without enough food. Not enough money to pay the bills.

Why would a loving God allow his followers to suffer?

The Catholic faith accepts suffering as a part of life. We do not seek it out, but we realize everyone will experience it at some point. Suffering is a consequence of Original Sin. Some Christians emphasize God's desire to bless believers with wealth, health, and happiness. Others may even think that if you follow Christ you will not have any problems. But the Catholic Church has always seen Christ's suffering, Death, Resurrection, and Ascension as a sign that as followers of Christ, we too will face suffering, but we have hope of resurrection and renewal.

> My grace is sufficient for you, for power is made perfect in weakness.
>
> —2 Corinthians 12:9

The Paschal Mystery is at the center of the Good News and of our Catholic spirituality. Our faith will help us get through tough times, but there is no expectation that our faith will prevent those times. Christ wasn't shielded from tough times, why should we expect our lives to be different? The Apostles gave up everything to follow Christ, and they weren't exempt from suffering either.

> The days aren't always sunny . . . sometimes, we must cross through dark valleys.
> Even then, though, we can remain joyous and human—but only if heaven is open for us, only if we can be strengthened in the certainty that God loves us in full, that God is good and, through this, in the certainty that it's good to be human.
>
> —Pope Benedict XVI, remarks to a group from Traunstein (Bavaria), Castel Gandolfo 30 July 2011

At times we may want to deny that "sometimes, we must cross through dark valleys." We live in a culture that is very focused on, almost obsessed with, being comfortable. Sometimes we avoid hard work because it's hard. Then later we are disappointed in ourselves because we haven't accomplished what we wanted. This chapter will discuss how to appropriately embrace our own sufferings so we can know and show that true joy can be in our lives.

## The Mystery of Suffering

Why wouldn't a loving God reward us in this life for our faith by protecting us from pain and suffering? This is really one of the big mysteries of our faith. The Catholic Church admits that there is no easy answer. "The world we live in often seems very far from the one promised us by faith. Our experiences of evil and suffering, injustice, and death, seem to contradict the Good

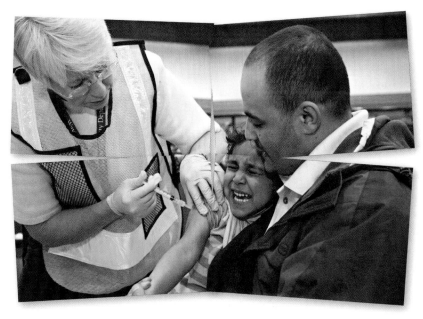

News; they can shake our faith and become a temptation against it" (CCC, 164). Only in the afterlife will the mystery of suffering on Earth be understood and God's reward be given to those who endured suffering with faith. Let's look at the story of the late Cardinal Joseph Bernardin.

Cardinal Bernardin said he had three fears in life: the fear of being falsely accused, the fear of getting cancer like his father, and the fear of dying. All that he feared happened to him. He was falsely accused of sexual abuse by a man named Steven Cook, who later retracted his accusation. Cardinal Bernardin met with him, forgave him, and anointed Mr. Cook, who was dying.

In 1995, Cardinal Bernardin was diagnosed with pancreatic cancer and the prospect of a painful dying process. He noticed that illness tended to pull him inside himself to focus on his pain. He felt sorry for himself and depressed. He wanted to withdraw from people.

He learned to turn outward to Jesus and his message and to open himself to God's grace. Christ helped him to begin to think of other people and their needs. He decided to walk with them in their trials. When he began his treatment, he took time to be with his fellow patients.

He comforted each one and followed up with phone calls and notes. In the last three months of his life, he acquired a "special parish" of six hundred people like himself, and he gave them hope and love. For him, death was not the end. It was the transition to life eternal.

Cardinal Bernardin taught us that approaching death meant learning new lessons of faith to share with others. He was well prepared. "I know that just as God called me to serve him to the best of my ability throughout my life on earth, he is now calling me home."

We have a whole history of witnesses to our faith, including Abraham, who hoped against hope, and Mary, who saw the suffering and Death of her Son. We turn to them as we "lay aside every weight, and sin which clings so closely, and . . . run with perseverance the race that is set before us, looking to Jesus the pioneer and perfecter of our faith"[66] (CCC, 165).

It is natural to try to avoid suffering. However, when faced with hardships, we have choices. We can choose to give up and act powerless. Or, we can face our suffering and try to learn from it. Hard times can teach us things about ourselves and reveal our strengths and weaknesses.

Like suffering, sacrifice is not something people look forward to. Yet, whether we want to or not, we still do it. Why? **Sacrifice** means surrendering one thing for the sake of something, or someone, else. We don't sacrifice something because we want to get rid of it. We sacrifice because we are committed to something, or someone, greater, and the same goes for God. Sacrifice is a core concept for us Catholics. Making sacrifices and living with suffering are not signs of weakness, but they actually require a great deal of courage.

The Catholic embrace of the Paschal Mystery is a spiritual acceptance of the pain that comes to our door. It is about the strength of faith and the embrace of hope. People respond to suffering in different ways. Some of us choose to succumb to suffering and then pass it on. Have you known someone who takes out their anger at friends or family members? Have you ever done this yourself?

As Catholics, we do not celebrate suffering, but we do recognize it as an inevitable part of life. When possible, it is to be avoided. When this is not possible, our suffering can be united to the suffering of Christ. Saint Paul points out that we are all parts of Christ's Body in the world today (see I Corinthians 12:27). Jesus used his own suffering to accomplish good—the salvation of humankind. To show the mercy and kindness of God, he also worked to alleviate the suffering of others. Because we are the Body of Christ, we can unite our suffering to his and through our relationship with him,

**sacrifice** surrendering one thing for the sake of something else; literal Latin meaning is "to make holy"

trust that God can use this suffering for good. Embracing suffering also means that we recognize the pain of others and through compassionate acts try to transform their suffering into healing.

Accepting the reality of suffering is important so that we can move beyond expecting our lives to be free of it, and actually live life.

Webster's Dictionary defines the word "suffer" in this way: "to endure death, pain, or distress, to sustain loss or damage, to be subject to disability or handicap." Suffering is a spiritual experience of life as well which results from Original Sin and personal sins. It was Original Sin that wounded our human condition and brought about imperfections, including suffering, a tendency toward sin, and the need for salvation.

## Salvific Meaning

Shortly after the 2011 earthquake and tsunami in Japan, Pope Benedict XVI was answering questions on a live television show when a seven-year-old girl from Japan asked him why people had to suffer as her people were suffering. He responded this way:

> I also have the same questions: why is it this way? Why do you have to suffer so much while others live in ease? And we do not have the answers, but we know that Jesus suffered as you do, an innocent, and that the true God who is revealed in Jesus is by your side.

In the book *Crossing the Threshold of Hope,* Blessed Pope John Paul II says the following about Jesus' presence with us when we are suffering:

> The scandal of the Cross remains the key to the interpretation of the great mystery of suffering, which is so much a part of the history of mankind. Even contemporary critics of Christianity are in agreement on this point. Even they see that the crucified Christ is proof of God's solidarity with man in his suffering. God places Himself on the side of man . . . God is always on the side of the suffering.

Saint Paul and others speak about what the Catholic faith calls the *salvific meaning of suffering:*

> I am now rejoicing in my sufferings for your sake, and in my flesh I am completing what is lacking in Christ's afflictions for the sake of his body, that is, the church.
>
> —Colossians 1:24

In this passage, Saint Paul is choosing to offer his suffering for the good of the Church. Christ's suffering brings Redemption to humanity. Because he is an incarnate, Divine Person, Christ has united himself to us in a way we can't fully understand. Still the possibility of becoming like him, the possibility of sharing in his own life, is offered to us all through his Paschal Mystery. Our own suffering gives us an opportunity to be further conformed to the image of Christ. It is necessary for us to take up our cross and be his disciples, "for 'Christ also suffered for [us], leaving [us] an example so that [we] should follow in his steps'"[67] (CCC, 618).

The seven Gifts of the Holy Spirit include fortitude, which allows us to resist temptations, overcome challenges, and follow Christ's example. With fortitude, we can conquer fear, even fear of death (see CCC, 1808 and 1831). In the verse from Colossians, Saint Paul recognizes that he now is part of Christ's Body, the Church. Therefore, when he suffers, he continues the saving work of Christ.

# Saint Pio of Pietrelcina
## (1887–1968)

Why do we have to suffer? It is an age-old question. Blessed Pope John Paul II, in his Apostolic Letter, *Salvifici Doloris,* "On the Christian Meaning of Human Suffering," gives a partial answer when he says that we can find meaning in our suffering because it unites us with the redemptive suffering of Christ. Suffering allows us to share in the process by which Christ's merits are offered to all. Pio of Pietrelcina, better known as Saint Padre Pio, spent his entire life doing just that.

Francesco Forgione was born in 1887 to a farming family in southern Italy. His parents were devout Catholics and Francesco grew up in a deeply religious family. When he was ten, he expressed a desire to become a monk. To help him fulfill his dream, his father traveled to America to earn money to support his education. When he was 15, Francesco entered a Capuchin monastery and took the name Pio in honor of Pope Saint Pius V, who was the patron of his hometown of Pietrelcina.

Soon after his ordination, Padre Pio had a vision in which Jesus and Mary appeared to him and gave him the stigmata, the marks of Christ's Passion, which he bore for the rest of his life. The suffering he experienced from the wounds in his hands, feet, and side was intense and he prayed daily to be relieved of his pains. His prayer was answered, at least for a while, as the outward signs ebbed and flowed during his life. However, through the years, he faced many other kinds of physical pain, including typhoid fever, migraines, asthma, and ulcers.

The Convent Shrine of Saint Padre Pio is located in San Giovanni Rotondo, Italy.

Despite his willingness to join his own pain to that of Jesus, Padre Pio understood that we must do our best to relieve the suffering of others. With this in mind, he built a Home to Relieve Suffering at San Giovanni Rotondo. Its purpose was to be "a place that the patient might be led to recognize those working for his cure as God's helpers, engaged in preparing the way for the intervention of grace."

On the fiftieth anniversary of his reception of the stigmata, Padre Pio celebrated Mass, but by the next day he felt his life slipping away. In the early hours of September 23, 1968, he went to confession and reviewed his vows of poverty, chastity, and obedience before dying in his room. In the years that followed, thousands of pilgrims visited his burial site. On June 16, 2002, Blessed Pope John Paul II declared him Saint Pio of Pietrelcina. At his canonization Mass, the Pope said, "The life and mission of Padre Pio prove that difficulties and sorrows, if accepted out of love, are transformed into a privileged way of holiness, which opens onto the horizons of a greater good, known only to the Lord."

**Think About It** We all experience suffering in our lives. What kind of suffering is the most difficult for you, physical, emotional, or mental? When have you offered comfort and support to someone going through a period of pain and suffering? How important do you think it is for a Christian to suffer? How does joining your suffering to the Passion of Jesus change the experience?

Go to the student site at
**hs.osvcurriculum.com**

People experience human suffering that may come from the following:

- Natural causes including tornadoes, hurricanes, earthquakes, and tsunamis.

- Human causes such as car accidents, war, violence, terrorism, crime, faulty construction of buildings and bridges, etc.

- Interpersonal causes such as rejection, death of a loved one, family conflict, arguments, or the end of a friendship.

- Personal causes including failure in school, sports, or other personal ambitions and goals.

- Health related causes such as illness, injury, or conditions related to aging.

- Greed, violence, immorality, and human sins.

Suffering can bring three different forms of pain: physical, psychological, and spiritual. Pain can be acute, which means it comes on fast, sharp and severe. Pain can be chronic, which means it last a long time and never seems to completely go away.

Physical pain is the body's way of telling us that something is wrong with a muscle, bone, or nerve. Psychological pain is emotional pain like sadness, fear, or anxiety. Spiritual pain refers to the way we feel in our relationship with God or our religion. Many saints, like John of the Cross, talk about spiritual pain as "dark nights of the soul" when we feel

**paradise** a perfect place; a state of friendship with God and of original holiness and justice enjoyed by our first parents

## GO TO THE SOURCE

**Read each of these Old Testament passages** and describe the type of pain reflected in each one: physical, psychological, or spiritual.

*Tobit 10:1-7, Psalm 22, Psalm 38, Psalm 137, Sirach 37:1-6, Lamentations 3:1-17.*

## REFLECT
### Pain is a part of life.

- Considering the three different forms of pain caused by suffering, give an example of each before reading the next paragraph.

disconnected from God or guilty about a moral mistake. Mother Teresa wrote about her own experiences of spiritual pain in her journal. One kind of suffering can cause another. For example, physical suffering can cause psychological suffering. Spiritual pain can cause physical pain and so forth.

**Restate** What is suffering?

**Elaborate** How do Catholics view suffering?

## Spirituality of Suffering

Can you imagine a world without suffering? The Book of Genesis begins with a description of Adam and Eve in **paradise**. Philosophers and writers through the centuries have used paradise as a key theme in their works. Plato's *Republic*, Sir Thomas More's *Utopia*, and Jonathan Swift's *Gulliver's Travels*, all describe a vision of utopia, an ideal society with limited suffering.

Many notions of utopia are based on the idea that happiness comes from lack of pain and suffering. The Paschal Mystery tells us otherwise. Pain and suffering are part of real living. Christ endured his Passion and Death out of love for us, and God the Father allowed his Son to suffer and die this way because of his love for all humans. Happiness doesn't depend on an easy life. True happiness comes from living God's plan for our lives. When, united with Christ, we act out of love for God and others even in the midst of suffering, we are living out God's plan. This would be very difficult, perhaps impossible, to do on our own, but Jesus shares his own life with us through the Sacraments, and in this gift we are given the grace to do what God asks of us.

What has been the source of some of the suffering in your own life?

Choose one or more of the following categories and take some time listing those sources of pain. You may have more than one situation within any of the categories, and you may also have more than one category apply to a given experience. Use a symbol, word, or abbreviation to categorize it.

**Cause** Natural Causes, Human Causes, Interpersonal Causes, Personal Causes, Health Related Causes

_____ _____ _____ _____

**Form** (Physical, Psychological, or Spiritual)

_____ _____ _____ _____

**Duration** (Acute or Chronic)

_____ _____ _____ _____

**Responsibility:** Me / Others / Both / Neither

_____ _____ _____ _____

**Level of Pain:** Low / Med / High

_____ _____ _____ _____

• What experiences of suffering have you seen others go through?

---

If I were to choose between pain and nothing, I would always choose pain.

—William Faulkner

The presence of pain and suffering, despite God's love for humanity, is a **paradox**, something that seems contradictory, yet is true. The Latin word, "passio," is generally translated as "suffering." The English word, **passion**, comes from "passio." It may relate to an emotion like love or hate. Often, it is used to describe love. We also say that someone's passion may be a certain sport, subject, or hobby. We use the word passionate to describe how intensely someone cares about something. The paradox is that we often suffer over something we greatly love. We endure hardships for the things we love. We endure pain for the people we love. No wonder the Latin word for both love and suffering is passion. No wonder we use the word passion to describe the first element of the Paschal Mystery. Christ's Passion refers to the suffering he endured out of his love for all of us.

But we also suffer when the people we care about suffer. We often refer to suffering with another as **compassion**. Loving people suffer when they can do nothing to relieve the suffering of someone they care about. The point is that much suffering comes because we love. Think about it: Would we suffer as much in life if we didn't have any love for any thing or any person? Love is part of the paradox of suffering. Love is part of the spiritual nature of suffering.

> Suffering is, in fact, guaranteed for anyone who takes on the task of loving. Persons who love will suffer, but they will also find a fullness of life and a personal experience of the Spirit's presence.
>
> —Eugene Kennedy, _The Pain of Being Human_

Remember that the Paschal Mystery refers to the Passion, Death, Resurrection and Ascension of Christ. Our faith offers us the promise that suffering and death are not the end of the story; rather, Jesus' Resurrection gives us hope in our own resurrection. He gives us the example of accepting the Father's will even when it involves suffering. When we realize that Christ's Paschal Mystery is not just referring to Jesus but also pointing to a reality in our own lives, we can find a form of spirituality.

**paradox** something that seems contradictory, yet is true

**passion** from a Latin word which means "to suffer' and also to love

**compassion** a feeling of empathy for another who is suffering that results in solidarity or a "suffering with" the other

## DISCUSS

○ Discuss the reasons for supporting or not supporting each of these statements.
_Happiness depends largely on the lack of pain and suffering._
_Happiness depends on a person's relationship with God and how they live it out._

○ Then make a case for the one that comes closest to your own view.

**When Jesus was dying on the Cross** he made a statement that could be interpreted as a paradox.

Read *Matthew 27:46* and write out the statement. Then read *Psalm 22*, and identify which verse Jesus was quoting.

○ Would you categorize the ending of Psalm 22 as that of "despair and abandonment" or "faith and confidence"?

○ What does that tell you about the struggles with suffering and faith in God?

The spirituality of the Paschal Mystery carries the belief that God will not abandon us in times of suffering. This spirituality includes the deep hope that God will accompany us through tough times. As we realize that God accompanies us in our suffering, his grace—in prayer, the actions of another, the Sacraments, bitter tears—transforms our pain. Suffering is never in vain because it can help us move toward eternal life. By offering to God the patient endurance of our suffering, we can help make up in some degree for the hurt and harm caused by sin.

The *Catechism* affirms this notion of God's presence through our suffering. "God does not abandon his creatures to themselves. He not only gives them being and existence, but also, and at every moment, upholds and sustains them in being, enables them to act and brings them to their final end" (CCC, 301).

Jesus' real human experience of the Paschal Mystery leads us to these three spiritual truths.

• Suffering does not separate us from God. Instead, it unites us with the Passion of Christ.

• God's grace is sufficient and available to us, giving us strength and hope. God does not let us face our suffering alone.

• Suffering is not the end. It does not have to rob us of happiness—in this life and in the next.

**Define** What is compassion?

**Imagine** What would life be like without pain and suffering?

## SECTION 1 REVIEW

### QUICK REVIEW

**1a. Define** What is suffering?
 **b. List** What are the different kinds of pain mentioned in this section?
 **c. Summarize** What is the paradox of Suffering?

**2a. Define** What is passion?
 **b. Describe** What is the paradox of passion?

**3a. Explain** Why do we call the first aspect of Christ's Paschal Mystery his Passion?
 **b. Summarize** How is the mistaken view of happiness found in the concept of utopia?

**4. Outline** In your own words, explain the salvific meaning of suffering.

### ACT

Complete one of the following.

○ Provide two songs, along with their printed lyrics, which illustrate the spirituality of suffering. Include a brief explanation of how each song reflects spirituality.

○ Interview one person who has found the spiritual strength to embrace suffering and get through it. Be sure to identify exactly the kind of spiritual strength that the person tapped into.

### SELF-ASSESS

Which statement best reflects where you are now?

☐ I'm confident enough about the material in this section to be able to explain it to someone else.

☐ I have a good grasp of the material in this section, but I could use more review.

☐ I'm lost. I need help catching up before moving on.

# The Pain of Death

Nothing hurts us more than the death of a loved one. Jesus cried when he heard of his friend Lazarus' death. And perhaps you too have already felt what it is like to have a family member or friend die.

Why does this type of pain hurt so much? Because death means an end to our physical experiences with a person that we love. We will no longer laugh with that person or hear their voice. There will be no more conversations, advice, or hugs.

> Let us hold fast to the confession of our hope without wavering, for he who has promised is faithful.
>
> —Hebrews 10:23

The Church teaches that death came into the world as a result of Original Sin. God's plan for the first humans was an earthly life in paradise. However, God does not send death to someone because he or she is living a sinful life. God does not bring direct punishment to someone like that. Likewise, natural disasters are not God's way of punishing people who live in a certain area.

No one can live in a way that guarantees how long they will live or how peacefully they will die. Good people sometimes die after a long period of suffering. While there are no guarantees, the Church has always invited us to "pray for a happy death."

Earlier in this chapter, we recognized the various causes of suffering—some are due to our choices, while others are beyond our control. However, when viewed in the context of the Paschal Mystery, suffering has merit. Suffering can enable people to deepen their reliance on others and God. It can lead to a more authentic prayer life. It can enable friends and family to step out of their comfort zone and offer more care and more prayer to those who are suffering. But one person's suffering will not automatically save another person or family member from potential suffering.

The *Catechism* tells us that those who are dying should be given attention and care to help them live their last moments in dignity and peace. They are helped by our prayers, and it is our responsibility to see to it that they receive the proper Sacraments that help them prepare to meet God (see CCC, 2299).

Those Sacraments include Reconciliation and Anointing of the Sick. The Church also offers those at the end of their lives the Eucharist, called viaticum. The Eucharist, given at the end of one's life, "is the seed of eternal life and the power of resurrection" (CCC, 1524).

> Now before the festival of the Passover, Jesus knew that his hour had come to depart from this world and go to the Father. Having loved his own who were in the world, he loved them to the end.
>
> —John 13:1

The burial of the dead is a corporal work of mercy that the Church expects us to be responsible for because it honors the dead.

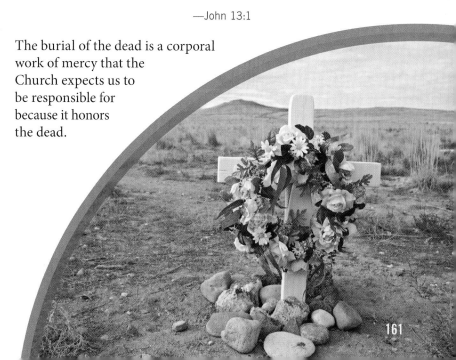

## Attitudinal Survey

| Circle your response to each statement. | I agree | I disagree | I'm not sure |
|---|---|---|---|
| 1. It's hard for me to accept that one day I will die. | A | D | NS |
| 2. Most people are uncomfortable talking about death. | A | D | NS |
| 3. Modern society treats death realistically. | A | D | NS |
| 4. Death makes life more meaningful. | A | D | NS |
| 5. I'm afraid of funeral homes, cemeteries, and things related to death and dying. | A | D | NS |
| 6. Death is a form of punishment for our sins. | A | D | NS |
| 7. Good people will die a happy death. | A | D | NS |
| 8. Someone who suffers a long, terminal illness spares their loved ones by allowing them to say goodbye. | A | D | NS |
| 9. Someone who suffers a quick death enables loved ones to be spared. | A | D | NS |
| 10. I am responsible to help bury the dead. | A | D | NS |
| 11. Sacrificing your life for an ideal isn't worth it. | A | D | NS |
| 12. It's best not to cry at funerals. | A | D | NS |
| 13. Time heals the pain of grief. | A | D | NS |
| 14. There really isn't anything you can do to lessen someone's grief. | A | D | NS |
| 15. Once a loved one dies your life will never be the same. | A | D | NS |
| 16. Grieving a loved one's death never ends. | A | D | NS |
| 17. If I had a terminal illness, I'd want someone to tell me. | A | D | NS |
| 18. If a person is cremated, his/her body will not rise on the last day. | A | D | NS |
| 19. It's important to visit the graves of family members. | A | D | NS |
| 20. Open coffins make me uncomfortable. | A | D | NS |

> The bodies of the dead must be treated with respect and charity, in faith and hope of the Resurrection. The burial of the dead . . . honors the children of God, who are temples of the Holy Spirit.
>
> —CCC, 2300

As Catholics, it is our responsibility to give the deceased a proper funeral. At the end of time, our bodies will become incorruptible when God reunites body and soul (see CCC, 1016). These realities stem from Christ's Passion, Death, Resurrection, and Ascension.

At the same time, honoring the dead does not mean that the Church prohibits autopsies, organ donation, or cremation of a deceased body. Autopsies can be permitted for either legal or scientific purposes. Organ donation has tremendous merit because so many lives can be saved. The Church also permits cremation so long as it is not someone's way of denying faith in the Resurrection of the body (see CCC, 2300-2301). The respect given to any human body should be extended to cremated remains. The ashes should be contained and buried or entombed. Scattering cremated remains does not meet required reverent containment of the ashes.

**Recall** What kind of death does the Church invite us to pray for?

**Conclude** What is our responsibility to give to deceased people?

# The Vigil

**W**akes are events where people gather to pray for someone who has recently passed away, in the presence of the person's body and family. During a wake, Catholics often hold a vigil service where prayers are offered. The vigil service is part of the Church's Order of Christian Funerals. Family and friends gather in the presence of the body, usually at a funeral home or a church; sometimes in a home. A priest or deacon often presides at the vigil, but lay leaders or any Catholic who has been prepared can lead.

Most wakes include an open coffin. Generally, the body has been embalmed and dressed in formal clothes. Sometimes one or two of the deceased person's favorite items are placed in the open coffin.

If the deceased has been cremated, there is usually a shrine where people can pay their respects. Photos, scrapbooks, and mementos of the deceased are on display.

Here are some suggestions when attending a wake:

- Offer your condolences to the family, for example, say, "I'm sorry for your loss," or "I'm praying for you." If possible, share something you admired or respected about the person who has passed away. Try to avoid clichéd phrases, such as saying that the deceased is "in a better place." Don't ask questions about the cause of death or what the family's immediate plans are.

- Stand or kneel at the coffin and offer a prayer over the body of the deceased. Some people offer a prayer of thanksgiving to God for all the things the deceased brought to their life. Others speak directly to the deceased, expressing gratitude or the desire to model something learned from that person.

- The vigil service offers prayers for the soul of the deceased as an expression of the faith we have in eternal life. It is also a faith-filled celebration of that person's life: poetry is read, stories recalled, and heartfelt praises are given.

## The Act of Grieving

We all react to death and the loss of life in different ways. Grief often embraces many different emotions. Fear is one of the emotions we often feel when we think of losing a loved one.

In addition to strong feelings of fear, there are a range of emotions we can go through when faced with the effect someone's death has on us. Grieving is the initial reaction to a loss, while mourning is the process of coping with a loss over time. In her work, Therese Rando presents a "6 'R' Process of Mourning."

1. **Recognize** the loss—be willing to acknowledge who (or what) has been lost and the consequences of this.

2. **React** to the loss—Allow yourself to feel the feelings you have in response to the loss.

3. **Recollect** and **re-experience** what was lost (remember what things were like before the loss). It is important here to remember objectively—the positives and the negatives about what (or who) is lost.

4. **Relinquish** your attachment to object of your loss (the person who has died or the situation that has changed)

5. **Readjust** so you can adapt to your new situation while still remembering what (or who) was lost.

6. **Re-invest** the energy previously spent mourning into doing something new and different.

Many people turn to their faith in times of grief and loss. Our Catholic Faith reassures us that death is not final. Jesus Christ has conquered death, and through him we have the hope of resurrection and eternal life. Frequent prayer and reception of the Sacraments assist us in remembering this and coping with loss. We can also ask for the prayers of the Church, as we are called by Christ to support one another, especially during difficult times.

## Funerals and Rites

The Christian funeral is a liturgy in the Church that unites the community with the dead. The Order of Christian Funerals includes the vigil, the liturgy, and the Rite of Committal. The order has four principal elements:

- *Greeting of the Community,* where the family and friends of the deceased person are welcomed with consoling words (see CCC, 1987).

- The Greeting and the *Liturgy of the Word* should lead to the "true perspective of faith in the risen Christ." This focus on

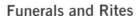

### APPLY

Use Therese Rando's "6 Rs" and apply them to a loss you have experienced. Begin by describing the loss. Recall the words or emotions that reflect each stage of the process.

Christ is important because those attending may include people who have not recently attended any liturgy and people who are not Christians (see CCC, 1688).

- *Eucharistic Sacrifice* is the heart of liturgy. "It is by the Eucharist thus celebrated that the community of the faithful, especially the family of the deceased, learn to live in communion with the one who 'has fallen asleep in the Lord,' by communicating in the Body of Christ of which he is a living member and, then, by praying for him and with him" (CCC, 1689).

- The *Farewell* to the deceased is the last "commendation to God" before the person is buried. We don't see this as a

permanent separation because we believe we will all be together again in Christ (see CCC, 1690).

Death points to the importance of how we live our lives. Jesus told us this in different ways—always with the same point—*God holds us accountable for the way we live the life we have been given.*

## GO TO THE SOURCE

**Read the following passages** and identify the truths that Jesus is pointing to regarding how death should shape our lives.

Read *Matthew 24:45-50, Matthew 25:1-13, Matthew 25:14-30, Matthew 25:31-46.*

# SECTION 2 REVIEW

## QUICK REVIEW

1. **Reevaluate** Look at your responses to the statements found in the attitudinal survey and list at least three that you now have a different response for. Explain why you would change your response.

2a. **List** What is Therese Rando's "6 'R' Process of Mourning"?

 b. **Summarize** Write about your own experience of grieving by writing a brief essay that begins with this sentence: *I have found it to be true that . . .*

3. **Explain** What does the Church teach about each of the following?

 - Care for the dying
 - Burying the dead
 - Autopsies
 - Organ donation
 - Cremation
 - A happy death
 - Death as a result of sin

**Assignment** Interview a family member or friend about their experience of grieving the loss of a loved one. Here are some questions to ask:

○ Which of the emotions discussed in this chapter did they primarily experience? How would they describe their emotions about the loss of their loved one presently?

○ How did belief in God, prayer, and the afterlife console them?

○ What do they think got them through it?

○ What advice could they share with someone who is grieving?

## SELF-ASSESS

Which statement best reflects where you are now?

☐ I'm confident enough about the material in this section to be able to explain it to someone else.

☐ I have a good grasp of the material in this section, but I could use more review.

☐ I'm lost. I need help catching up before moving on.

# Death and Judgment

Germany, Bavaria,
Wieskirche, Frescoes
Depicting Door of Heaven

**eschatology** literally means the study of "last," and refers to the part of theology that studies topics related to the end of time: death, judgment, resurrection of the body, Heaven, Purgatory, and Hell, the coming of Jesus on the last day, etc.

**Particular Judgment** the judgment of each individual at the moment of death by Christ and determines the immediate entrance of the soul into Heaven, Purgatory, or Hell

Because of Jesus Christ, Christian death has positive meaning. When we die, God calls us to himself. For it is through death that we are able to enter into eternal life (see CCC, 1010-1011). God wants all of us to be virtuous because at the end of our life on Earth every one of us will be judged. We can be consoled that God our Savior "desires everyone to be saved and to come to the knowledge of the truth" (1 Timothy 2:4). "The Lord . . . is patient with you, not wanting any to perish, but all to come to repentance" (2 Peter 3:9; CCC, 1037). Recall that the study of these things that happen at the end of life is called **eschatology**.

Death is the end of our earthly life. It was not part of God's original plan for our lives, but exists as a consequence of sin. Death is not the end; rather, it is transformed by Christ. "Jesus, the Son of God, also suffered the death that is part of the human condition. Yet, despite his anguish as he faced death, he accepted it in an act of complete and free submission to his Father's will.[68] The obedience of Jesus has transformed the curse of death into a blessing"[69] (CCC, 1009).

At the very moment of our death, we will each encounter what we have come to call **Particular Judgment**, when Christ will make a judgment on our eternal reward.

## GO TO THE SOURCE

**Our understanding of judgment** comes from Scripture.

Read *Luke 16:19-31*.

○ What does this account teach about death, judgment, Heaven, Hell, and Resurrection?

○ What does the story teach about our actions on Earth, particularly regarding the rich and the poor?

Another passage used to understand the immediate judgment after death is the "Good Thief" passage in Luke.

Read *Luke 23:39-43*.

○ Explain how the story alludes to immediate judgment after death.

The New Testament speaks of judgment primarily in its aspect of the final encounter with Christ in his second coming, but also repeatedly affirms that each will be rewarded immediately after death in accordance with his works and faith.

—CCC, 1021

Since we will die as we have lived, it makes sense to spend each day full of love for others and always deepening our friendship with God.

Either we will enter into the blessedness of **Heaven** (whether immediately or through a process of purification, which we call **Purgatory**) or we will enter "immediate and everlasting damnation"[70] known as **Hell**. (CCC, 1022).

Saint Paul refers to this purification in Scripture when he says:

> the work of each will come to light, for the Day will disclose it. It will be revealed with fire, and the fire (itself) will test the quality of each one's work. If the work stands that someone built upon the foundation, that person will receive a wage. But if someone's work is burned up, that one will suffer loss; the person will be saved, but only as through fire (1 Corinthians 3:11-15).
>
> —Saint Paul

Our Tradition tells us that most souls enter Heaven through Purgatory. That is why we read the following:

> In doing this he acted very well and honorably, taking account of the resurrection. For if he were not expecting that those who have fallen would rise again, it would have been superfluous and foolish to pray for the dead. But if he was looking to the splendid reward that is laid up for those who fall asleep in godliness, it was a holy and pious thought. Therefore he made atonement for the dead, so that they might be delivered from their sin.
>
> —2 Maccabees 12:43-46

In other words, it is good to pray for those who have died as they undergo their final purification, that God may quickly welcome them into Heaven.

"The Last Judgment will reveal that God's justice triumphs over all the injustices committed by his creatures and that God's

## DISCUSS

What do you think about death?

○ Is it something you fear or something you have made peace with?

○ How has the experience of death impacted your life today as a defining moment?

○ How has Catholic teaching on death, judgment and Resurrection given you peace and hope?

love is stronger than death"[71] (CCC, 1040). "At the evening of life, we shall be judged on our love" (CCC, 1022, Saint John of the Cross, *Dichos* 64).

**Describe** What did Jesus' obedience do to the curse of death?

**Explain** Why does God want all of us to be virtuous?

## Experiencing Loss and Saying Goodbye

Teenagers can experience many different kinds of loss. The following interview excerpts describe different situations and student reactions.

"I played this sport all through elementary school. Made the freshmen team here last year. Played all summer with the JV and varsity. We had JV tryouts two weeks ago, and I got cut. All my best friends are on the team. Now we can't hang out cause they have practice and games, and I don't. I feel like a failure. Plus I put in so much time into it. Years

**Heaven** the state of supreme happiness for those who have died in God's grace and friendship; being united forever with God the Father, Son, and Holy Spirit, the Virgin Mary, the angels, and the just after death

**Hell** the state of eternal self-isolation from God after death, through the free choice to reject God's offer of forgiveness and Redemption

**Purgatory** "A state of final purification after death and before entrance into heaven for those who died in God's friendship, but were only imperfectly purified" (CCC, Glossary, p. 896)

## GO TO THE SOURCE 📖

**Following is a list of Scripture passages that refer to death** and judgment from the Old and New Testaments.

Read and summarize at least four of the Scripture passages: *Daniel 7:9-10; Malachi 3:16-4:3; Matthew 3:10-12; Matthew 12:1-3; John 3:17-21; Romans 2:16; 1 Corinthians 4:4-5; Matthew 25:31-32, 40; John 5:27-29; Acts 10:42; 17:30-31; 2 Timothy 3:6; John 3:18.*

○ What role will Christ play in our judgment?

into it. And I loved it more than anything. It was like the best thing in my life. Now it's all over. Gone."

"My dad lost his job five months ago, just before Christmas. He can't find another one. Now it looks like my sister and I will have to leave our school because we can't afford the tuition. We may even move to another state if he gets a job offer. I don't want to go to another school, another state. I like my life here."

"My parents are getting a divorce. They've been separated for a year now. Both of them have found someone else. Both say they are getting married. So what's that do for me and my two brothers? We lose a dad? We get a new mom to replace our real mom? We get a new dad? New family? We just want our real family back. What happened to that?"

"My family came here from Mexico. I was born here so I am a citizen. But my parents are not. I knew something was wrong when my uncle picked us up after school instead of my older sister. My father was picked up by Immigration and deported back to Mexico. None of us ever got to say goodbye. And none of us know if we will ever be together again."

## IDENTIFY

Imagine that you are each of the different students quoted in these descriptions. Once you get into their shoes, try naming the primary and secondary emotion each student might be experiencing as a result of their loss. Remember the importance of accuracy when it comes to naming emotions.

"I put something on my social media page that was completely inappropriate. It caused a lot of embarrassment. I got in trouble for it at school, and my reputation is ruined. It's like I will always be remembered in a bad way for what I did. But the worst part is that I think I broke something between me and my parents. I don't think our relationship will ever be the same. We'll never be as close as we were."

Sometimes we lose a loved one who dies. But more often we lose other things we love in life. Sometimes we lose what is closest to our heart. Sometimes the things we care most about, the things we love the most, end.

When something we love or cherish comes to an end, it's like dealing with a different kind of death. It's like dealing with the death of a favorite piece of our life. Something we really loved is gone.

The end of life or the end of something we love in life forces us to do the same thing: say goodbye. Most of our heartache comes from having to say goodbye to something we don't want to end.

The word *goodbye* originally came from the words, "God be with ye" and was a phrase of faith used to signify that God was present as a relationship ended or a person left for a far away land—maybe never to be seen again.

Every fall we are reminded that we cannot control everything. We watch the colorful leaves fall off the trees. We accept it. We say goodbye. A Paschal Mystery spirituality asks us to accept life's other goodbyes because, as difficult as they are, they are a natural part of living. Just like the seasons of the year, goodbyes are essential if we are to find new life.

In the film *Indiana Jones and the Last Crusade,* the characters set out on a quest to find the Holy Grail—the cup that Jesus used at the Last Supper.

At the end of the film, they find the cup, but it falls on a ledge above a great abyss. Indiana Jones tries to reach the cup, but he slips and his father Henry grabs his hand. Henry has spent his entire life trying to find the Grail, but at that moment he realizes there is more to life than the pursuit of an object. As Jones is reaching for the Grail, his father smiles at him and says gently, "Indiana, let it go." For a moment, Jones is confused, but then he understands. Henry is able to let go of his lifelong pursuit because he realizes that his priorities have changed. His search for the Grail was once the most important thing in his life, but it has been replaced by his concern for his son.

○ When have you realized that someone was more important than something?

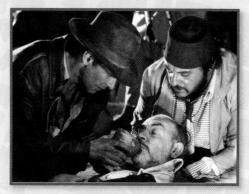

In *Indiana Jones and the Last Crusade,* the Holy Grail is depicted as a simple wooden cup.

# Faith & Culture

↗ Go to the student site at **hs.osvcurriculum.com**

Sometimes we choose a goodbye and sometimes a goodbye chooses us. Some goodbyes are small ones, like giving away games that once were our favorites, ending a hobby, or leaving your favorite middle school teacher or coach. And goodbyes go on throughout life. You might see your parents say goodbye to a home full of memories, a career they loved, or valuable possessions lost or destroyed.

## ANALYZE

○ What is something or someone you have had to say goodbye to?

## Abandonment to Divine Providence

In the eighteenth century, a popular French Catholic writer, Father Jean-Pierre de Caussade wrote a book called *Abandonment to Divine Providence.* In it, he talked about trusting God with the circumstances of our lives. Some people call this idea "letting go and letting God." De Caussade's work inspired Saint Thérèse of Lisieux and countless other people to trust God even when things were difficult.

Letting go is a process made up of a mental and a spiritual act. Praying is at the heart of this process. Letting go means dropping a grudge, knowing when a relationship has ended, not keeping alive painful memories, or reopening our wounds.

Letting go does not mean forgetting how much something or someone means to you. It doesn't mean hardening your heart so that you won't be hurt anymore. And it doesn't mean denying the pain of loss.

Abandonment to divine providence is about acceptance and freedom. We accept the loss of something we love, and it frees us by surrendering these things to God just as Jesus did. Letting go means offering our suffering to God the Father as Jesus did. This offering is celebrated in the Eucharist. Contemplative prayer is also a way of surrendering to God's loving will. Recall in the Garden of Gethsemane, Jesus praying to the Father:

Father, if you are willing, remove this cup from me; yet, not my will but yours be done.

—Luke 22:42

Surrendering to God is hard. Sometimes we are advised to let go as if it were painless. It's not. You have to be deliberate about letting go. You have to intentionally decide to do it. Letting go doesn't always happen all at once, or once and for all.

Praying after a loss can include a lamentation in which you express your emotion to God. Psalm 22 is an example of a lamentation: "My God, my God, why have you forsaken me? Why are you so far from helping me, from the words of my groaning? . . . Yet you are holy, enthroned on the praises of Israel. In you our ancestors trusted; they trusted, and you delivered them" (Psalm 22:1-4).

Praying after a loss can include a prayer of thanksgiving for the experience we were given, for example, "Thank you Lord for all the good times I had during . . ."

Praying after a loss can include a prayer of petition in which you ask God for what you need in letting go: "Dear God, please give me the _____ I need to handle this because I'm feeling pretty _____ right now and I need to let go."

Praying after a loss can include a prayer of blessing on the unknown aspects of the future for yourself or others: "Lord, take care of _____ and _____. Help them/us to do well, stay healthy, and to remember those who care about them/us."

Praying after a loss can include a prayer of praise for God's presence, for example, "I'm confused/hurt/ _____, _____. But I trust you God because I know you love me and will take care of me. You are caring and always there. That's one reason you are so great."

Praying after a loss can include a prayer of intercession, such as, "Lord, this is way bigger than I can prevent or even understand. I/We need your help. Your will be done."

In the Paschal Mystery, Jesus let go in the midst of his suffering. His last words on the Cross were, "Father, into your hands I commend my spirit" (Luke 23:46). This was the ultimate abandonment to divine providence.

While the experience of loss may vary greatly, the actual process of saying goodbye to something you love in life is almost identical to grieving someone's death. But when it comes to dealing with the loss of life and the loss of something you love in life, the difference may be in trusting God. Trusting is taking the risk to live out the lessons from the loss we have experienced, so that we can become more loving and make the world around us better.

When you lose something you love in life, saying goodbye includes prayer. Praying after a loss shouldn't replace all the other dynamics of letting go, but it is the key component of a Paschal Mystery approach to life.

The most beautiful Credo is the one we pronounce in our hour of darkness.

—Padre Pio

## SECTION **3 REVIEW**

### QUICK REVIEW

Instead of a standard review, complete these two section assignments, which focus on the application of the material.

1. **Read** John 14–17, in which Jesus shares his thoughts with his disciples. Make a list of the words in these three chapters that relate to your own experience of loss. Write those words on a sheet of paper. Then write an essay explaining why you chose those words.

2. **Conduct** another interview. This time ask a family member, relative, or friend to describe a loss of something they loved in life (rather than a death of a loved one), particularly their process of saying goodbye.

### SELF-ASSESS

Which statement best reflects where you are now?

☐ I'm confident enough about the material in this section to be able to explain it to someone else.

☐ I have a good grasp of the material in this section, but I could use more review.

☐ I'm lost. I need help catching up before moving on.

# New Life in the Resurrection

Saint Paul knew exactly why he could challenge death with words in the quote below. The Apostles knew, and all the early Christians who were martyred for their faith knew it, too. After death there is new life. This element of the Paschal Mystery, Christ's Resurrection from the dead, signified the new gift God gave to everyone who followed Jesus. This is the Good News.

> Oh death, where is your victory? Where is your sting?
>
> —1 Corinthians 15:55

Because of the Paschal Mystery, our hope lies in the promise of the bodily resurrection of the dead. "Faith in the resurrection rests on faith in God who 'is not God of the dead, but of the living'"[72] (CCC, 993).

Jesus himself shared this Good News. "I am the resurrection and the life. Those who believe in me, even though they die, will live, and everyone who lives and believes in me will never die" (John 11:25-26). At the crucifixion, one of the criminals on the cross next to Jesus asked a favor from him. "'Jesus, remember me when you come into your kingdom.' He replied, 'Truly I tell you today you will be with me in Paradise'" (Luke 23:42-43). Jesus died to benefit every one of us. The Son of God became man, died, and was buried. The Apostles were witnesses to this and to Jesus' Resurrection, when they encountered the Risen Christ.

Our beliefs about life after death distinguish us from other religions. Not all members of Judaism believe in life after death as we do. Hindus and Buddhists believe in reincarnation, we do not. Our death is the end of our time on Earth and of God's grace that helped us in our journey. Human beings die only once (see CCC, 2024).

From the beginning, Christian faith in the resurrection has met with incomprehension and opposition.[73] 'On no point does the Christian faith encounter more opposition than on the resurrection of the body.'[74] It is very commonly accepted that the life of the human person continues in a spiritual fashion after death. But how can we believe that this body, so clearly mortal, could rise to everlasting life?

—CCC, 996

First, we need some clarification on what is meant by "rising." In our death, our immortal soul separates from the mortal body, the human body decays and the soul receives its eternal reward. Our soul awaits its reunion with its *glorified* body at the final judgment. At the Last Judgment, "God, in his almighty power, will definitively grant incorruptible life to our bodies by reuniting them with our souls, through the power of Jesus' Resurrection" (CCC, 997).

Moreover, at this Last Judgment, which will occur on the Last Day at the end of the world, we believe that the resurrection of the body applies to all people. All the dead will rise: those in Heaven will experience the resurrection of life, and those in Hell will experience the resurrection of judgment (see CCC, 998). Just as Christ is raised with his own body, in him, all of us will rise again with our own bodies. "Christ 'will change our lowly body to be like his glorious body,' into a 'spiritual body'"[75] (CCC 999).

How this happens "exceeds our imagination and understanding; it is accessible only to faith" (CCC, 1000). The resurrection of the body and the Final Judgment are closely linked to the **Parousia**, or second coming of Christ. At this time, we will witness "the glorious return and appearance of our Lord and Savior Jesus Christ as judge of the living and the dead, at the end of time" (CCC, Glossary, p. 891).

> For the Lord himself, with a cry of command, with the archangel's call and with the sound of God's trumpet, will descend from heaven, and the dead in Christ will rise first.
>
> —1 Thessalonians 4:16

While Christ will raise us up "on the last day," in a certain way, we have already risen with Christ. The *Catechism* says, "we already belong to the Body of Christ. When we rise on the last day we 'also will appear with him in glory'"[76] (CCC, 1003). Through the Holy Spirit, Christian life on Earth is already a participation in the Death and Resurrection of Christ. In his Letter to the Colossians, Saint Paul explains, "You were buried with him in baptism, you were also raised with him through faith in the power of God, who raised him from the dead. . . . if you have been raised with Christ, seek the things that are above, where Christ is, seated at the right hand of God." (Colossians 2:12; 3:1). For now, we are nourished with Christ's body in the Eucharist. "The Eucharist is the memorial of Christ's Passover, that is, of the work of salvation accomplished by the life, death, and resurrection of Christ, a work made present by the liturgical action" (CCC, 1409).

"Belief in the resurrection of the dead has been an essential element of the Christian faith from its beginnings," (CCC, 991).

> The body is meant not for fornication, but for the Lord, and the Lord for the body. And God raised the Lord and will also raise us by his power. Do you not know that your bodies are members of Christ? . . . For you were bought with a price; therefore glorify God in your body.
>
> —1 Corinthians 6:13-15; 20

## GO TO THE SOURCE

The following scriptural passages talk about the impact of the Resurrection.

Read *Romans 8:11, 1 Corinthians 15:12-22, 1 Corinthians 15: 51-53, 2 Corinthians 4:7-14,* and *1 Thessalonians 4:13-14.*

○ What does each passage say about how the Resurrection affects us.

## Life After Loss

Life after death is the final dimension of Paschal Mystery spirituality. As there is life after death, there is also life after loss.

*The athlete cut from the school team will find something else to pursue—but perhaps not until halfway through college.*

*Students who move to other states or schools will make new friends, even though they will be different friends. These students may later point out how they have grown from the experiences.*

*The children whose parents divorce and remarry will still find that they can count on those parents for love and support when they need it most.*

After the painful process of saying goodbye and letting go, God will bring us a new beginning if we stay open and pray

**Parousia** "The glorious return and appearance of our Lord and Savior Jesus Christ as judge of the living and the dead, at the end of time; the second coming of Christ, when history and all creation will achieve their fulfillment" (CCC, Glossary, p. 891)

for it. Bad things can happen to good people. Yet the spirituality of the Paschal Mystery offers us the knowledge that inner wounds heal. A ruined reputation teaches the importance of a fresh start. Experiences of injustice and oppression can lead a person to work for justice and peace. Great pain can produce great wisdom.

After the Son of God suffered and died, the Apostles thought that was the end of the story. They initially hid in fear, having lost all hope. At the time, they did not fully understand the meaning of the Resurrection.

After the Apostles grieved their loss, they found new strength in the Risen Christ and through the Holy Spirit. Nobody is spared from pain, suffering, and loss. The spirituality of the Paschal Mystery believes that loss becomes the opportunity for Redemption.

## Gaining Resiliency

Pain and suffering, the loss of a loved one, or the loss of something you love can make you bitter or it can make you better. Our calling is to walk the path in faith as a disciple of Christ so that we might become a better friend, a better son or daughter, or a better student.

How can it make you better?

- It can make you more empathetic toward the pain and loss others experience.

- It can make you more careful about the ways you might bring pain to others and to yourself.

- It can make you more convinced about getting through it.

- It can make your trust in God grow.

## DISCUSS

Pick three of the statements above that describe how pain, suffering, and loss can make you better and explain how they are true.

**Resiliency** is the ability to recover from adversity. But the Paschal Mystery of Christ gives resiliency new meaning. By taking away the sins of the world, Christ gives us hope for eternal happiness. Our suffering then connects us to Christ, who, on the Cross, took on the weight of all evil. If we are united to Christ's suffering, our own suffering no longer discourages us, but instead can sustain us with the hope won on the Cross. If Jesus conquered death through the Paschal Mystery, we too can "rise again," even though we have suffered. This kind of resiliency based in hope can be learned. We can each learn how to more readily recover from adversity by connecting with Christ's Death and Resurrection. We can use the pain, suffering, death, and loss we experience to increase our hopeful resiliency. Christ strengthens us to undergo suffering and thereby become more like Christ himself.

> We . . . [know] that suffering produces endurance, and endurance produces character, and character produces hope, and hope does not disappoint us, because God's love has been poured into our hearts through the Holy Spirit that has been given to us.
>
> —Romans 5:3-5

There are false notions of resiliency. For example, the ability to hold back tears has nothing to do with resiliency. Not showing emotion during times of loss has nothing to do with resiliency. It's what you do after a loss that determines resiliency.

Sometimes, people choose to medicate themselves with unprescribed drugs or alcohol. Rather than seeking help, some decide to numb the pain through illegal and irresponsible means. Medicating oneself to bury bad memories, anger, or guilt is a false sign of resiliency. Nurturing a life of prayer, on the other hand, can lead to a deeper trust in God and to a greater resiliency in life. In particular, praying by reflecting on the Paschal Mystery of Christ can bring us God's healing and peace.

**resiliency** the ability to recover readily from adversity

# Holding HOPE

A 2005 study by *Time* magazine showed that nearly fifty percent of thirteen year olds believed that the United States would be a worse place to live by the time they reached their parents' age. Those kids are now adults in college. And you're not thirteen anymore, either. But staying hopeful can be hard, especially when bad things happen to you or your loved ones, the economy tanks, or war and violence increases. Lose hope and you lose heart. That's why "holding hope" is a spiritual practice.

Catholics are a people of hope. Because of the Paschal Mystery, we have every reason to be hopeful, in this life and the next one.

> For surely I know the plans I have for you, says the Lord, plans for your welfare and not for harm, to give you a future with hope.
>
> —Jeremiah 29:11

Even though we know the reasons for our hope, it's often hard to know how to actually hold on to hope. We can ask ourselves questions when a situation makes us feel like we're losing hope. Get in the habit of asking yourself:

- *Is this situation permanent or temporary?*
- *Do I have the power to change what's happening?*
- *Is this typical of what happens to me?*

From a spiritual perspective, the practice of holding hope asks one more question:

- *Have I taken this situation to God?*

**Try it.**
Call to mind something that is causing or has caused you to seriously lose hope.
Answer the four questions.

Remember: Holding Hope is a *spiritual* practice.

What are some examples of things that give you hope?

How is Jesus the ultimate sign of hope?

Likewise, suppressing our feelings may give us the feeling of resiliency, but it won't bring the hope that the Paschal Mystery gives us. People who won't forgive themselves for their part in creating a loss become victims not victors, even if they appear resilient on the surface.

> Let nothing trouble you
> Let nothing frighten you
> Everything passes
> God never changes
> Patience
> Obtains all
> Whoever has God
> Wants for nothing
> God alone is enough
>
> —Saint Teresa of Ávila

Resiliency is about having the inner strength to bounce back. This resiliency comes first and foremost through God's grace and the help we receive from God through the Sacraments. We can also experience resiliency through a combination of three things:

- the support of family and friends that you can depend on.

- a spiritual relationship with God that you can count on.

- prior experience of the getting through tough times.

Throughout this chapter you have been introduced to the spirituality of the Paschal Mystery. This is a Catholic approach to life's pain, suffering, and loss as revealed through Christ and offers us resiliency and hope.

The Paschal Mystery that encompasses the life of Jesus is like no other event in history. Every other moment takes place just once, then joins history. The Paschal Mystery, however, does not remain in the past. The reason is that Christ destroyed death by giving up his own life. Everything that Jesus is, everything that he did, everything that he suffered for us all is part of "the divine eternity" (CCC, 1085). The Paschal Mystery transcends time. It is not limited by time. Christ makes the Paschal Mystery present for all times in the liturgy. Jesus shows us through the whole Paschal Mystery that giving of ourselves is the path to eternal life and happiness and gives us the example of accepting the Father's will even when it involves suffering.

The Paschal Mystery connects us to Christ through his dying and rising. It is a unique event that—unlike every other event in history—does not just exist in the past. Instead it remains for all time because death was destroyed and the Paschal Mystery of Christ transcends time by becoming present in the Eucharist and for eternity (see CCC, 1085). There is the possibility of us joining in the Paschal Mystery. We have been called to the Paschal Mystery because Christ suffered for us (see 1 Peter 2:21).

> He himself bore our sins in his body on the cross, so that, free from sins, we might live for righteousness; by his wounds you have been healed.
>
> —1 Peter 2:24

## What Does the Paschal Mystery Teach Us?

**Here are the main points we have discovered about experiencing the Paschal Mystery.**

Suffering and pain are part of life

Death and loss are unavoidable

Faith doesn't protect you from loss, but it offers an opportunity for conversion

After death there is new life

After loss there is new life

There are healthy and unhealthy ways of dealing with loss

Saying goodbye takes letting go

## QUICK REVIEW

**1a.** **Explain** When it comes to death, what is the Good News?

**b.** **Clarify** What is the difference between the Christian view of death and the Hindu or Buddhist view?

**2a.** **Summarize** How does our belief in life after death apply to our other experiences of loss?

**b.** **List** What are five ways pain can make us better?

**3a.** **Define** What is resiliency?

**b.** **List** What practices in times of difficulty can help someone develop resiliency?

**Listen and Discuss** Read in the New Testament what Mary had to go through as they crucified her Son, Jesus.

○ How did Mary experience abandonment to divine providence?

○ Have you ever experienced your own suffering after considering what Mary went through?

## SELF-ASSESS

Which statement best reflects where you are now?

☐ I'm confident enough about the material in this section to be able to explain it to someone else.

☐ I have a good grasp of the material in this section, but I could use more review.

☐ I'm lost. I need help catching up before moving on.

# PRAYER

**Family Prayer**

Father of life, you have called us to eternal life after our faith journey on
Earth. You want us to have perfect joy after the troubles of this life. We
commend to you those who are seriously ill in our family, among our
friends, and those who have no one to pray or care for them. Help us to
live today with love, compassion, and sympathy for others so that when we
arrive at our own death, our last moments will be filled with those virtues
that make life worth living and death a friend that takes us to glory.
Amen.

**Prayer of Saint Pio of Pietrelcina after Holy Communion**

Stay with me, Lord, for it is necessary to have
You present so that I do not forget You.
You know how easily I abandon You.

Stay with me, Lord, because I am weak
     and I need Your strength,
     that I may not fall so often.

Stay with me, Lord, for You are my life,
     and without You, I am without fervor.

Stay with me, Lord, for You are my light,
     and without You, I am in darkness.

Stay with me, Lord, to show me Your will.

Stay with me, Lord, so that I hear Your voice
     and follow You.

Stay with me, Lord, for I desire to love You
     very much, and always be in Your company.

Stay with me, Lord, if You wish me to be faithful to You.

Stay with me, Lord, for as poor as my soul is,
     I want it to be a place of consolation for You . . .

With a firm love, I will love You with all my heart while on Earth
     and continue to love You perfectly during all eternity.     Amen

## TERMS

Use each of the following terms in a sentence that shows you know what the term means. You may include more than one term in a sentence.

| | |
|---|---|
| sacrifice | Particular Judgment |
| paradise | Heaven |
| paradox | Hell |
| passion | Purgatory |
| compassion | Parousia |
| eschatology | resiliency |

## PEOPLE

Identify why each of these people are significant.

1. Cardinal Bernardin

2. Saint John of the Cross

3. Blessed Mother Teresa

4. Saint Padre Pio

5. Therese Rando

6. Saint Teresa of Ávila

## UNDERSTANDING

Answer each question and complete each exercise.

### SECTION 1

1. **Summarize** Give the paradox of suffering.
2. **List** What are the different kinds of pain mentioned in this section?
3. **Explain** Why do we call the first aspect of Christ's Paschal Mystery his Passion?
4. **Describe** What does the Church teach about God's presence when we are suffering?

### SECTION 2

5. **List** What are some different kinds of responses that we may have to the death of a loved one?
6. **Connect** What kind of merit can suffering have?
7. **Explain** Describe Therese Rando's 6 R's of Mourning.
8. **Explain** What will happen to our bodies at the end of time?

### SECTION 3

9. **Tell** How has Christ transformed death?
10. **Identify** What is Particular Judgment?
11. **Explain** What is involved when we say goodbye and in letting go?
12. **Summarize** What is abandonment to divine providence about?

### SECTION 4

13. **Infer** Make the connection between the Resurrection of Christ and dealing with loss.
14. **Connect** What will God bring after the painful process of saying goodbye and letting go?
15. **Recall** What does Saint Paul advise for us since we have been "raised with Christ"?
16. **Summarize** What have you found to be true about resiliency? What can you do to become more resilient? What role has your faith played in your resiliency so far?

## CONNECTING

**Visual** What does this tree with the sunlight streaming through it symbolize for you?

Choose four symbols that best express something about your experience of the Paschal Mystery. Choose a symbol that reflects a time of suffering, loss, resurrection, and new life in your life.

**Challenge** You and your cousins are standing in the lobby at an elderly relative's wake, one says that they don't understand why that relative had to suffer so much before dying because she or he was such a good person. In your own words, explain Church teaching on the meaning of suffering.

**Question**

Review a current or past situation of suffering or loss in your own life and complete each of the following.

○ What was the situation?

○ Accurately **name** the primary and secondary emotion you felt in that past or current experience.

○ To what extent did you pray or ask for God's help in his situation?

○ What do you want to own or **claim** regarding this situation?

○ How did you, or could you best **tame** the emotions associated with this experience?

○ To what degree did you exercise your **trust** in God uring this time?

○ What about the **trust** you placed in family and friends?

○ Where are you in the process of **Saying Goodbye** to your loss?

○ How would you describe your experience of **letting go**?

○ What have you **found to be** true about experiencing the Paschal Mystery?

**Imagine** First, explain what we mean by the statement "every goodbye is followed by a hello." Then name the basis of our faith that allows us to make that statement.

## SELF-ASSESS

**On Your Own** Make a list of the most important things you learned from this chapter.

Select three things that represent your growth in understanding as you worked through this chapter. Write a paragraph explaining your choices.

**With a Partner** List what you found most helpful or interesting in this chapter as well as any other questions that have surfaced.

# Conversion and the Moral Life

 Go to the student site at
**hs.osvcurriculum.com**

## YOU WILL

- Discover the role of conscience in conversion.

- Practice evaluating moral behavior.

- Chart the three sources of morality in human acts.

- Study the cardinal and theological virtues.

- Write about your hopes and dreams for the future.

- Examine the consequences of the seven deadly sins.

- Memorize the social justice teachings of the Catholic Church.

- Critically examine Church documents on social justice.

## DEFINE

| | |
|---|---|
| *metanoia* | fortitude |
| conversion | temperance |
| conscience | vices |
| correct conscience | gluttony |
| virtue | sloth |
| theological virtues | stewardship |
| cardinal virtues | evangelization |
| prudence | injustice |
| justice | |

# HOW DO YOU RESPOND?

*High school students were asked to describe how their consciences work:*

**My conscience never** seems to help me make decisions. When I face a dilemma, it's like I have no idea what to do. I think I have a conscience, but it needs work. I keep making mistakes.

**As soon as** something happens, I know exactly what to do because my conscience tells me. Sometimes there's a deep feeling in the pit of my stomach that tells me I'm going in the wrong direction. If that feeling disappears, I'm good to go.

**When I face** a decision, my conscience reminds me of the things I know are right and wrong. I follow my conscience, and I feel confident that I have done the right thing.

# WHERE ARE YOU?

**Check the answer that best matches where you are today.**

I know how we form our consciences.
☐ Quite a bit ☐ Somewhat ☐ A little ☐ Not at all

It's easy for me to figure out what's right and wrong.
☐ Quite a bit ☐ Somewhat ☐ A little ☐ Not at all

I understand what virtues contribute to discipleship.
☐ Quite a bit ☐ Somewhat ☐ A little ☐ Not at all

I know the Catholic principles regarding justice.
☐ Quite a bit ☐ Somewhat ☐ A little ☐ Not at all

Discipleship interests me.
☐ Quite a bit ☐ Somewhat ☐ A little ☐ Not at all

# The Process of Conversion

*What actions can we take to live out the Paschal Mystery?*
*How does the Paschal Mystery help us?*
*What can we do about the problems in the world?*

We are not born saints, but we can become saints. Saint Camillus de Lellis of Italy illustrates this fact very well. He was a stubborn and self-centered youth who followed in his father's footsteps as a gambling addict and professional soldier. Whenever he needed money, he hired on with some army that needed men. He never cared about the cause, and he disrupted life wherever he went.

Eventually, Camillus' father became ill confessed his past sins, and received the Sacraments before he died. Camillus decided that he should change his life. It wasn't easy, and an infected wound on his leg made it more difficult. Eventually, he ended up devoting his life to caring for the sick. He was ordained a priest and founded his own order called the Ministers of the Sick, or the Camellians. The group ministered to sick and wounded soldiers on the battlefield. Camillus died in 1607 after being gravely ill for years. He was canonized in 1746 and is the patron saint of hospitals and nurses.

'If any want to become my followers, let them deny themselves and take up their cross and follow me.'

—Mark 8:34

It took a while for Saint Camillus to learn, but the Paschal Mystery—the Passion, Death, Resurrection, and Ascension of Christ—has meaning for each of us in the way we live our daily lives.

As Jesus began his public ministry, he announced, "The time is fulfilled, and the kingdom of God has come near; repent, and believe in the good news" (Mark 1:15). Clearly, Jesus calls us to believe and to repent which leads to conversion.

The Greek word used for "repent" throughout Scripture is **metanoia**, which means repentance. When we refer to people who "convert" to Christianity, we tend to think of it as a one-time decision. However, in truth, **conversion** is a lifelong process of growth in the Holy Spirit.

This endeavor of conversion is not just a human work. It is the movement of a 'contrite heart,' drawn and moved by grace to respond to the merciful love of God who loved us first.[77]

—*Catechism of the Catholic Church*, 1428

**metanoia** Greek word meaning repentance; to change in direction or to turn around

**conversion** the lifelong process of turning away from sin and toward God

**Like Saint Camillus, this religious sister working in Burundi has dedicated her life to serving others.**

183

Jesus calls us to conversion and reconciliation with God. Like the prophets before him, however, Jesus' call to conversion does not aim only at outward actions, "but at the conversion of the heart, interior conversion" (CCC, 1430). This interior conversion is then genuinely expressed outwardly and visibly.

"Interior repentance is a radical reorientation of our whole life, a return, a conversion to God with all our heart, an end of sin, a turning away from evil, with repugnance toward the evil actions we have committed. At the same time it entails the desire and resolution to change one's life, with hope in God's mercy and trust in the help of his grace" (CCC, 1431).

### The Role of Conscience

Interior conversion leads us to action in both our moral decision making as well as our commitment to justice in the world. Moral decision making begins with our conscience, which is basically a "judgment of reason" (CCC, 1796). It is a right guaranteed by the U.S. Constitution and one that the Church has tried to protect in recent years. In a statement on religious liberty, the U.S. Bishops described conscience as our most cherished freedom.

**conscience** "the interior voice of a human being, within those heart the inner law of God is inscribed. Moral conscience is a judgment of practical reason about the moral quality of a human action. It moves a person at the appropriate moment to do good and to avoid evil" (CCC, Glossary, p. 872)

That is our American heritage, our most cherished freedom. It is the first freedom because if we are not free in our conscience and our practice of religion, all other freedoms are fragile. If citizens are not free in their own consciences, how can they be free in relation to others, or to the state? If our obligations and duties to God are impeded, or even worse, contradicted by the government, then we can no longer claim to be a land of the free, and a beacon of hope for the world.

—Our First, Most Cherished Liberty, Ad Hoc Committee for Religious Liberty, U.S. Conference of Catholic Bishops

Referencing the Vatican II document *Gaudium et Spes*, the *Catechism* describes what **conscience** is.

Deep within his conscience man discovers a law which he has not laid upon himself but which he must obey. Its voice, ever calling him to love and to do what is good and to avoid evil, sounds in his heart at the right moment . . . For man has in his heart a law inscribed by God. . . . His conscience is man's most secret core and his sanctuary. There he is alone with God whose voice echoes in his depths.[78]

—CCC, 1776

One metaphor for conscience is a voice speaking from within us, telling us what is right and wrong. "Conscience is a judgment of reason whereby the human person recognizes the moral quality of a concrete act that he is going to perform, is in the process of performing, or has already completed." A person "is obliged to follow faithfully what he knows to be just and right" (CCC, 1778).

Listening to one's conscience is much like discerning the will of God, which is already written on one's heart. When prudent people listen to their conscience, they can hear God speaking (see CCC, 1777).

## Forming and Informing a Healthy Conscience

While one's conscience is internal and personal, it is not just doing whatever you feel like doing. Our conscience must be both formed and informed. We *form* our conscience to be upright and truthful when we intensify our desire to truly be good people. We *inform* our conscience when we seek the wisdom to do the right thing in every situation. Conscience is formed from our own human reason in unison with the goodness given to us by God. We must all make the effort to form and inform our conscience.

Forming a healthy conscience is about increasing our honest desire to be good people. Informing a healthy conscience means seeking the wisdom to do what is right. We have the teachings of the Church, the Old and New Testament teachings, and especially the life of Jesus, to form our conscience. We can also look to our parents and other role models to develop a healthy conscience.

The Word of God has a critical place in developing a healthy conscience and learning right from wrong. The Beatitudes are a good place to start, as are the two greatest commandments:

'You shall love the Lord your God with all your heart, and with all your soul, and with all your mind.' This is the greatest and first commandment. And a second is like it: 'You shall love your neighbor as yourself.'

—Matthew 22:37-39

We are called to practice what we preach. The Letter to the Romans tells us that it is not those who hear the law who are righteous, but those who follow it. "They show that what the law requires is written on their hearts, to which their own conscience also bears witness; and their conflicting thoughts will accuse or perhaps excuse them on the day when, according to my Gospel, God, through Jesus Christ, will judge the secret thoughts of all" (Romans 2:15-16). When we need to make a moral decision, our conscience will either choose the right option through reason and what we know of God's law, or a wrong one that disregards both (see CCC, 1799).

We are also called to forgive others and not to seek revenge. Jesus teaches us in both Word and example to refrain from revenge and to forgive those who hurt or sin against us.

We have an obligation to follow what our conscience judges to be the right decision (see CCC, 1801). We may not be guilty of sin if we make a poor judgment with an uninformed conscience. Still, "such ignorance and errors are not always free of guilt" (CCC, 1801). An example of choosing ignorance would be if we decided not to find out more about a situation, or allowed something to happen because we did not want to be involved.

James 1:22 urges us to be "doers of the word," because those who simply hear it and do nothing else deceive themselves. "Let us love, not in word or speech, but in truth and action" (1 John 3:18).

We need to develop a well-formed conscience—what we may call a **correct conscience**, informed by faith—because our love for God and others proceeds from it. The more this correct conscience guides our life, the more often we will make good moral choices. For example, someone with a correct conscience will be better able to separate the good messages in mass media from the harmful. "They will want to form enlightened and correct consciences the more easily to resist unwholesome influences" (CCC, 2496).

**correct conscience** a good, pure, and well-formed ability to judge what is right and wrong, enlightened by faith, which guides us to make good decisions

## GO TO THE SOURCE

**The following Scripture passages offer good advice** and encourage good actions for Christians.

Read *Tobit 4:14-19; 1 John 4:7-21; 5:1-5; 3 John 1:2-4, 11; 1 Peter 4:1-6, 12-19; 2 Peter 1:3-14; James 1:19-22; 2:1-13, 4:11-12.*

○ Summarize the advice or encouragement offered in each reading.

**A wealthy young man with many possessions approaches Jesus and asks: "Good Teacher, what must I do to inherit eternal life?"** (Mark 10:17). Jesus tells the young man to sell all that he owns, give the money to the poor, and follow him. In a Lenten reflection for young adults, Father Thomas Weinandy talks about what many people today think are "great possessions." In Western society, we learn from an early age that money—and everything that can be bought with it—brings happiness. Father Weinandy, however, says youth itself is a "great possession." "Young people have a flair for living and relishing all the things life holds out to them," he writes. However, sometimes young people view their future selfishly. "It is not seen as an opportunity to live the Gospel, but rather to pursue careers and material successes."

○ What is your greatest possession?

○ What is your attitude about the future?

# Faith & Culture

↗ Go to the student site at **hs.osvcurriculum.com**

As the ultimate role model, Jesus invites us to become his disciples and follow him. He left us his example of prayer and poverty to help us reject the enslavement that possessions can become and to accept and be ready for the persecution and suffering that may come our way (see CCC, 520). And as his disciples, we do not want anything to hold us back from acting on and experiencing the fullness of the Gospel. Our universal call to holiness of life includes living as a disciple of Jesus, adhering to him, and accepting his teachings.

**Recall** How does the *Catechism* describe conscience?

**Infer** Why isn't it enough just to hear the law or the Word of God?

## Examination of a Moral Act
When we speak of one's conscience, we are not only concerned with *what* decision one makes, but also *why* one makes *that* decision. We can discover why we make the decisions we do by performing an examination of conscience. Self-examination is crucial to a healthy spiritual life and spirituality rooted in a relationship with God in and through the Paschal Mystery. Such examination is one way by which conversion takes place (see CCC, 1435).

> It is important for every person to be sufficiently present to himself in order to hear and follow the voice of his conscience. This requirement of *interiority* is all the more necessary as life often distracts us from any reflection, self-examination or introspection: 'Return to your conscience, question it. . . . Turn inward, brethren, and in everything you do, see God as your witness.'[79]
>
> —CCC 1779

When we discuss conscience and whether a given decision is right or wrong, there are actually three sources of morality that are evaluated.

In order for an action to be considered morally good, all three parts—object, intention, and circumstances—must each be good. If one of those three parts is "disordered," then the action is no longer considered morally good.

| The Three Sources of the Morality of Human Acts | |
| --- | --- |
| **1** The goodness of **Object** chosen | The action itself |
| **2** The end or the **Intention** | The motivation for doing that action |
| **3** The **Circumstances** of the action | The conditions under which the decision is made and the actual consequences or outcome |

SOURCE: CCC, 1750-1757

This means that it is never morally permissible to do something evil (object) with the goal of achieving something good (intention). Notice that while the act may seem to be helpful and useful to others (circumstances), it would still not be a decision made in "good conscience." For example, one cannot achieve a good end result like getting into college through an evil means like cheating on an SAT exam. As the saying goes, the end does not justify the means. One must never do evil just so that good may come of it.

We use our conscience to judge the moral quality of an act. The Church teaches that we are obligated to follow what we know to be just and right. In other words, we have a moral obligation to follow our conscience. In fact, the Catechism puts it this way: "A human being must always obey the certain judgment of his conscience" (CCC, 1800). God has given us the gift of reason to apply our conscience to following God's will in our decisions and daily actions. We are called to put Jesus' moral and spiritual teaching into practice.

All decisions of conscience must be made freely. No one should be forced to violate his own conscience. "Nor must he be prevented from acting according to his conscience, especially in religious matters"[80] (CCC, 1782). Keep in mind, however, that this obligation involves following one's formed and informed conscience. Again, this is not a license to do whatever we want. Rather, this is an affirmation of our freedom to genuinely choose to do what we know in the depths of our being to be right.

**Name** What are three sources of the morality of human actions?

**Develop** Give an example of "The end does not justify the means."

## GO TO THE SOURCE

**Jesus warns against** doing something good for the wrong reasons.

Read *Matthew 6:1-4*.
- What is Jesus warning about in this passage?
- How does this apply to something other than giving alms?

## ELABORATE

Evaluate three current events according to the Three Sources of the Morality of Human Acts.

- Choose a newspaper or online article about a current moral problem and evaluate the situation based on the object, intent, and circumstances.
- Expand on the idea that all Three Sources of the Morality of Human Acts must be good in order for the action to be evaluated as good. Imagine a situation in your school or community in which moral decisions determine paths to a resolution.
- Describe the same situation in three ways, once with all good object, intent, and circumstances, then two more times with each of the three aspects being "disordered."

## QUICK REVIEW

**1a. Consider** Why do people choose to do the wrong thing?

**b. Differentiate** How long does it take for true conversion toward God to take place? Why?

**2a. Explain** What obstacles keep people from making right decisions?

**b. Tell** What are Jesus' criteria for being a disciple?

## ACT

Make a list of ways that you can help yourself refine your conscience. Include the following:

○ ways of learning from Scripture.

○ ways of learning from others you see every day.

○ ways you can practice good actions to turn them into habits.

○ ways you can increase your knowledge of the Church's teachings.

**Pray** Compose a short prayer asking Jesus to help you make the right decisions.

## SELF-ASSESS

Which statement best reflects where you are now?

☐ I'm confident enough about the material in this section to be able to explain it to someone else.

☐ I have a good grasp of the material in this section, but I could use more review.

☐ I'm lost. I need help catching up before moving on.

# The Role of Virtues in Our Moral Life

Most of us have habits, which can be good or bad. You can probably think of a half dozen of both types right off the top of your head. How many of us, however, would list virtues among our habits? To truly understand and accept the Paschal Mystery as a real gift in our lives, we must strive to adopt virtuous lifestyles.

The Catechism defines a **virtue** as "a habitual and firm disposition to do good" (CCC, 1833). The Letter to the Philippians urges us to adopt virtuous thoughts:

> Whatever is true, whatever is honorable, whatever is just, whatever is pure, whatever is pleasing, whatever is commendable, if there is any excellence and if there is anything worthy of praise, think about these things.
>
> —Philippians 4:8

Virtues help people to act in good and just ways and to give the best of themselves. Virtuous people lean toward the good and pursue it with concrete actions. "The goal of a virtuous life is to become like God"[81] (CCC, 1803).

There are seven key virtues, divided into two "groups." The **theological virtues** are faith, hope, and charity (or love). The word *theological* means, "concerning God." They are called the theological virtues because they come from God, are directed toward him, and reflect his presence in our lives. The theological virtues are gifts "infused by God (at Baptism) into the souls of the faithful to make them capable of acting as his children and of meriting eternal life" (CCC, 1813).

The **cardinal virtues** are prudence, justice, fortitude, and temperance. The cardinal virtues are also called moral virtues, and

In 2010, people in Chile and around the world, hoped for the safe rescue of thirty three trapped miners.

they are acquired by human effort and grow stronger in cooperation with God's grace.

## The Theological Virtues

Christians are called to participate in the divine nature of God. The theological virtues of faith, hope, and charity or love originate with the Trinity, and they help us live in relationship with our Triune God. Faith, hope, and charity "are the foundation of Christian moral activity" (CCC, 1813).

### Faith

What do we mean when we say we believe in God? Are we saying we believe God exists, or are we saying much more? There is a story about a man who advertises that he is going to walk a tightrope across Niagara Falls, blindfolded and pushing a wheelbarrow. Hundreds turn out to cheer him on. He says to the crowd, "Before I begin, who is going to get into the wheelbarrow?" It is the virtue of prudence that drives our decision not to recklessly get into the wheelbarrow. If we say we believe in God, however, are we willing to get into God's wheelbarrow?

**virtue** a good moral and spiritual habit that help us make good moral decisions, avoid sin, strengthen character, and perform good deeds

**theological virtues** faith, hope, and charity or love

**cardinal virtues** the moral virtues of prudence, justice, fortitude, and temperance

Through the God-given theological virtue of faith we believe in God and in all he revealed to us. We also have faith in what the Church teaches about God. We are created in God's image and likeness, so we are gifted with the light of faith that seeks the truth that is God. Our souls want not only to know God, but to love him with our whole heart. Unfortunately, the hurts and fears we experience in life can hide the light of faith within us. The light that seeks God is still there, but we may try to fill our lives with things and activities. Our only real satisfaction will come when we answer the call of faith. "By faith 'man freely commits his entire self to God.'[82] For this reason the believer seeks to know and do God's will. 'The righteous shall live by faith.' Living faith 'work[s] through charity'"[83] (CCC, 1814).

Faith prompts us to lead a good life and do good things for others. The three theological virtues are united. Without hope and love, faith "does not fully unite the believer to Christ" (CCC, 1815). We can't just hear the Word of God; we must act on it. "You see that a person is justified by works and not by faith alone" (James 2:24).

## DISCUSS

○ What are some ways in which you put your faith into action?

○ What obstacles do you face when it comes to living your faith? How do you overcome them?

The very personal virtue of faith involves an agreement from ourselves to the things that God has revealed to us. We need the Holy Spirit's help to accept and respond to this supernatural gift from God through our own free will. The Church also helps support and nurture our faith because it is necessary for our salvation. As our faith grows, we eventually prefer God above all else.

So to be a disciple of Christ, we not only need to have faith and act on it, but we also must profess our faith and share it. Serving others, including the poor and marginalized, and proclaiming our faith are necessary for salvation. "So every one who acknowledges me before men, I also will acknowledge before my Father who is in heaven; but whoever denies me before men, I also will deny before my Father who is in heaven"[84] (CCC, 1816). Christ gave us the Church so we could be his disciples. As Christ's body, through the Church we fulfill our calling to seek, learn, and act on our faith. We grow in holiness of life in and through the Church.

### Hope

The theological virtue of hope is the one "by which we desire the kingdom of heaven and eternal life as our happiness, placing our trust in Christ's promises and relying not on our own strength, but on the help of the grace of the Holy Spirit" (CCC, 1817). The virtue of hope helps us avoid becoming discouraged. Hope emphasizes the value of our participation in building up the Kingdom of God on earth by discerning God's will for our lives. Hope also counters despair, since we understand that our own efforts can only get us so far. Hope sustains us when we feel lonely. Hope springs from God's love. God has placed an aspiration for happiness in every human heart, and hope is our response to that gift (see CCC, 1818).

Hope opens our hearts to the expectation of eternal happiness. How will we feel, what words will we say, how will we act, and who will we be once we are in Heaven with God for all eternity? The virtue of hope helps us through life by keeping us from becoming discouraged and sustaining us during times when we feel abandoned. The Catechism teaches that for every person: "Buoyed up by hope, he is preserved from selfishness and led to the happiness that flows from charity" (CCC, 1818).

Because they embraced the hope of Heaven, the saints were inspired to prepare themselves and live in a way that reflected the reality of Heaven. They were already living the life of Heaven before they got there. Through our faith we are called to live the heavenly life the best we can before we ever get there.

How is it possible that a timeless God can enter into our time? This is the gift of the Trinity. By the power of the *Holy Spirit*, our heavenly *Father* sends his *Son* to give us the gift of Christian hope, saving us from the devastating effects of our sins. Through hope we are called to experience love and give up the pain of our hate and selfishness, to experience peace and give up the anxiety of our fear and worry, and to experience life's abundance and give up the hunger of our endless wants and desires.

The opposite of hope is despair. Despair is dangerous because it can undermine our faith in God. Bishop Thomas J. Olmsted wrote that we are surrounded by examples of despair. Hope, however, relies not only

### Hope: Past, Present, and Future

**1** Past—trusting in the promises made by God

**2** Present—seeing the value of our actions while maintaining the perspective that the whole world does *not* depend on our efforts alone

**3** Future—eternity with God in Heaven

Hope prevents us from experiencing two negative extremes: on the one hand thinking that *everything* depends upon us, and on the other hand feeling that *nothing* we do matters. Hope reminds us to do what we can, and to trust in God.

on our own efforts, but also on the grace of God. "Persons who hope see the terrible forces of evil in the world, but they maintain their confidence in God," he wrote. He pointed out that hope grows when we cooperate with God's grace. "As we do so, hope strengthens us to bear with hardships in the present. It helps us to repent after we have sinned and to trust in God's mercy to forgive and restore. It helps us, no matter how tough things are in the present, to look to the future with glad expectation."

Hope "affords us joy even under trial" and is "expressed and nourished in prayer, especially in the Our Father, the summary of everything that hope leads us to desire" (CCC, 1820).

### Charity/Love

The theological virtue of charity (love) is the supernatural virtue by which we love God above all things for his own sake and love our neighbor as ourselves for the love of God. "Charity is superior to all the virtues" (CCC, 1826). "And now faith, hope, and love abide, these three; and the greatest of these is love" (1 Corinthians 13:13).

Faith, hope, and charity (love) are tied together. Charity is the virtue and grace that binds these three together. Christ himself is our motivation and model on the virtues of faith, hope, and charity. We cannot truly love as Christ loved unless our faith is a belief that gives us the courage to pick up our cross. Christian hope can compel us to pick up that cross.

### IMAGINE

Think about what you like to do right now in your life, and what you would like to do in the future.

○ What are your hopes and dreams for the future?

○ How important to your hopes and dreams are education and living a Christian life? Are these elements separate from, or part of, your hopes and dreams?

○ How do you see your hopes and dreams fulfilled?

This is the love that we also call charity. Scripture and the accompanying chart call it *agape*. "God's love has been poured into our hearts through the Holy Spirit that has been given to us" (Romans 5:5). It is an unconditional love, not based on a feeling, a special relationship, or an expectation of being loved in return. Agape love is based on the unconditional kind acts that we perform for the well-being of others. It extends to your worst enemy, and includes strangers in need, such as the homeless or people devastated by natural disasters. It can also include loving parents, other family members, and friends, especially when you are not getting along.

To love this way as Christ does brings us again into the Paschal Mystery. "Love is itself the fulfillment of all our works. There is the goal; that is why we run: we run toward it, and once we reach it, in it we shall find rest"[85] (CCC, 1829, Saint Augustine). The beliefs of our faith call us to imitate Christ's Passion each time we become aware of the suffering of others or are confronted with our own suffering. We freely and willingly imitate the Passion of Christ because through the virtue of hope we know God can bring about good from our sacrifice. That good reflects the Kingdom of God, which is promised through Christ's Resurrection and Ascension into Heaven. Followers of Jesus Christ know that suffering can help us move toward Heaven and eternal life.

"By loving one another, the disciples imitate the love of Jesus which they themselves receive" (CCC, 1823). Jesus makes a direct appeal for us to love as he does, even to love our enemies. He asks us to be neighbors of the most foreign stranger and to love children and the poor as he did (see CCC, 1825). "The *fruits* of charity are joy, peace, and mercy" (CCC, 1829). Christ is our example. The Paschal Mystery expresses this love par excellence, for Christ died because of his love for us (see CCC, 1825).

### The Cardinal Virtues

The *Catechism* introduces the cardinal virtues as a pivotal part of the human virtues of "firm attitudes, stable dispositions, habitual perfections of intellect and will" (CCC, 1804). They make leading a morally good life possible and even joyful. "They are the fruit and seed of morally good acts; they dispose all the powers of the human being for communion with divine love" (CCC, 1804). These human virtues are described as "stable dispositions of the intellect and the will that govern our acts, order our passions, and guide our conduct in accordance with reason and faith" (CCC, 1834).

The word cardinal includes the Latin root *cardo*, which means "hinge." The moral virtues are like hinges from which hang all the other human virtues. The notion that the cardinal virtues have a pivotal role in developing all other virtues and moral behavior dates back to the Greek Philosophers in the fourth century B.C.

| Greek Terms for Love |
|---|
| **1** *philia* – friendship love |
| **2** *eros* – passionate, romantic love |
| **3** *agape* – unconditional care and concern for the well-being of another |
| While all forms of love are good, the virtue of love refers to *agape*. This form of love is so selfless and centered on the needs of others that you will often see it being referred to as charity. |

And if anyone loves
   righteousness,
her labors are virtues;
for she teaches self-control and
   prudence,
justice and courage;
nothing in life is more profitable
for mortals than these.

—Wisdom 8:7

As the quotation from the Book of Wisdom shows, all four cardinal virtues are referenced in the Bible. They are also explained in the *Catechism*. **Prudence** "is the virtue that disposes practical reason to discern our true good in every circumstance and to choose the right means of achieving it." **Justice** is the "moral virtue that consists in the constant and firm will to give their due to God and neighbor." **Fortitude** (courage) "is the moral virtue that ensures firmness in difficulties and constancy in the pursuit of the good." **Temperance** (self-control) is "the moral virtue that moderates the attraction of pleasures and provides balance in the use of created goods" (CCC, 1806-1809).

By their definition, human virtues are good habits that we can get better at practicing. "Human virtues acquired by education, by deliberate acts and by a perseverance ever-renewed in repeated efforts are purified and elevated by divine grace. With God's help, they forge character and give facility in the practice of the good" (CCC, 1810).

**Recall** What New Testament passage urges us to adopt virtuous thoughts?

**Elaborate** Why are virtues important to leading a moral life?

## APPLY

- Write an allegorical story turning the virtues into characters. The meaning of the virtues should be expressed through the characters. Vices should also be represented to provide the tension in choosing to do good or evil.

## Seven Capital Sins

Every judgment or action we make as a society reflects our vision of people and their destiny. When Gospel values are absent, society tends to become totalitarian. A healthy society and world is the fruit of people living virtuous lives. Living according to the virtues and the concrete actions flowing from them enables society to bring about a just world. A disordered society is heavily influenced by **vices** or bad habits that lead to the injustice and evil that exist today. Vices are associated with sinful behavior and the seven deadly sins: lust, pride, wrath, greed, **gluttony**, envy, and **sloth**.

In the Catholic Tradition, we refer to these sins as the seven capital sins. Sin is a personal act, but we have a responsibility for the sins of others when we take part in them. That responsibility can come from directly sinning with the other person; by encouraging or approving their sins; by not disclosing them or stopping them; and

**prudence** using practical reasoning to figure out the good in every circumstance and to choose the right way to achieve it

**justice** the constant and firm goal of giving to God and others what is due to them

**fortitude** courage; being firmly committed to pursue good actions no matter what

**temperance** moderating the attraction of pleasurable things to provide balance when using created goods

**vices** habits formed through repeated sins, even venial sins, that violate human morality

**gluttony** "overindulgence in food or drink" (CCC, Glossary, p. 880)

**sloth** having a lack of physical or spiritual effort; laziness

*The Seven Deadly Sins and the Last Four Things*
**by Hieronymus Bosch**

by protecting those who are evil (see CCC, 1868). We offend God when we sin and act contrary to Christ's model of obedience.

The capacity for evil lies in our hearts, but God's grace turns our hearts away from sin. "It initiates them into desire for the Sovereign Good; it instructs them in the desires of the Holy Spirit who satisfies man's heart" (CCC, 2541). When we think about it, sin is contrary to reason. "It wounds man's nature and injures human solidarity" (CCC, 1872). Evil separates us from God, so we must remain fully aware of our ability to sin and the presence of evil.

It is not easy to live a virtuous life, but the Paschal Mystery gives us the grace to persevere in the pursuit and practice of the virtues. "Everyone should always ask for this grace of light and strength, frequent the sacraments, cooperate with the Holy Spirit, and follow his calls to love what is good and shun evil" (CCC, 1811). The sacramental life, the Mass, and the Sacrament of Reconciliation are rich sources of food for the soul that allow our virtues to grow and strengthen as we confront the daily challenges to work toward the Kingdom of God in faith, hope, and charity (love). We need to accept and live the grace of Redemption by practicing the virtues of faith, hope, and love.

**Identify** From where does hope spring?

**Summarize** How do virtues and vices impact society?

## CONNECT

- With a partner, memorize the seven capital sins: pride, anger, envy, wrath, lust, gluttony, and sloth.
- Reflect on how you can ease the hold of these sins on your life.

## SECTION 2 REVIEW

### QUICK REVIEW

**1a. Define** What is a virtue?

**b. Relate** What is the relationship between society and virtues?

**c. List** Tell the two main groups of virtues and list the virtues within each group.

**2a. Describe** What is the role of faith in our lives?

**b. Explain** What does hope prepare us for?

**c. Apply** How do we demonstrate charity?

**Listen and Discuss** Read Saint Paul's advice in Philippians 4:8-9.

- Give an example for each trait listed in Verse 8.
- How can you use this advice in your life?

**Pray** Compose a prayer to God about your awareness of sin and asking for his help in avoiding evil.

### SELF-ASSESS

Which statement best reflects where you are now?

☐ I'm confident enough about the material in this section to be able to explain it to someone else.

☐ I have a good grasp of the material in this section, but I could use more review.

☐ I'm lost. I need help catching up before moving on.

# Living as a Disciple

To be a disciple of Jesus is to live the spiritual and moral teachings of Christ. We can imitate his humility, pray as he so frequently did, and, through the example of his poverty, face the difficulties that will come our way (see CCC, 520). As disciples, we can put into practice what we have already discussed—conversion, the theological and moral virtues, a well-informed conscience, and a willingness to confront the injustices of the world. These aspects of faith challenge us to reach the high standard set by Jesus. All of this we can do because Jesus did it first, and his Father's grace makes it possible.

Christ always obeyed the Father. He was always in communication with the Father through prayer, and Jesus invited those who believe in him to live the same way because the Father knows what we do. Nothing is secret with God. Jesus invites us to "Be perfect . . . as your heavenly Father is perfect" (Matthew 5:48). We can call God "Father" because Jesus revealed him to us.

When we pray to our Father, we are developing the will to become like him.

We may think that striving to be perfect is an unrealistic goal, but consider this: We are already united with Christ through Baptism. Since Jesus became man and retained his divine nature, he has united himself to all of us. You might even say we are partners with God. How is that possible? It is possible in a way known only to God through the Paschal Mystery (see CCC, 618).

Christ did what he did primarily for our Salvation and in accord with his Father's will. Christ's sacrifice is an example for us to follow and gives us courage to take up our own cross. The grace of the Holy Spirit

## DISCUSS

- What is the difference between society's idea of perfection and the Gospel idea of perfection?
- How can you be perfect as God is perfect?
- Do you think Jesus is asking us to do something impossible? Explain your answer.

gives us the help we need to be examples for others, so that the people we meet in life can also know Christ through us. That is our mission, and the mission of the Church. We do not make ourselves perfect, but we can grow in holiness of life in and through the Church. As disciples, we can live in Christ through the power of the Holy Spirit, and Christ, the One who is perfect, lives in us.

Recall the description of discipleship: It is our response to faith in Jesus Christ

- It is a life rooted in Jesus and lived out within the Church

- It means *believing* and *living* a life based upon our belief

- It is about responding to Jesus' call in the many areas of our lives

- It is about what we say, how we act, and with whom we spend time

- It is about our priorities: the place Christ and the Church occupy in our lives

- It is about the choices we make

God has always given his People guidance for living. The ancient Israelites had the Ten Commandments from the covenant agreement between God and Moses. The Law of Moses included many laws for living as the People of God, but Jeremiah spoke of a future covenant. It won't be like the old one, Jeremiah said, when God led the Israelites by the hand out of Egypt. The New Covenant would be written inside the people, on their hearts (see Jeremiah 31:31-34). The New Law, called the Law of the Gospel, is the work of Christ and the Holy Spirit, and it's spelled out in particular in the Beatitudes and the Sermon on the Mount. In fact, the *Catechism* says: "The New Law is the *grace of the Holy Spirit* given to the faithful through faith in Christ" (CCC, 1966).

> The Law of the Gospel 'fulfills,' refines, surpasses, and leads the Old Law to its perfection.[86] In the Beatitudes, the New Law *fulfills the divine promises* by elevating and orienting them toward the 'kingdom of heaven.' It is addressed to those open to accepting the new hope with faith—the poor, the humble, the afflicted, the pure of heart, those persecuted on account of Christ—and so marks out the surprising ways of the Kingdom.
>
> —CCC, 1967

The U.S. Catholic Bishops' Pastoral Letter *Stewardship: A Disciple's Response* (1992) expands our understanding of discipleship and links it to stewardship:

1. Mature disciples make a conscious, firm decision, carried out in action, to be followers of Jesus Christ no matter the cost to themselves.

2. Beginning in conversion this commitment is expressed not in a single action, nor even in a number of actions over a period of time, but in an entire way of life. It means committing one's very self to the Lord.

3. Stewardship is an expression of discipleship, with the power to change how we understand and live out our lives. Disciples who practice stewardship recognize God as the origin of life, the giver of freedom, the source of all they have and are and will be. They are deeply aware of the truth that "The Lord's are the Earth and its

# My Faith

**"THEN JESUS SAID** to the Jews who had believed in him, 'If you continue in my word, you are truly my disciples; and you will know the truth, and the truth will make you free'" (John 8:31-32).

No doubt you've heard this quotation before. It says a lot about the nature of discipleship, without giving a lot of specifics. When we look more closely at the words of Jesus, we see he is explaining to believers what it takes to become a believer and a disciple. These are not exactly the same. You can be a believer but not necessarily a disciple. Second, in John 8:30 Jesus says if we remain in his Word, we will be his disciples and know the truth. Discipleship is conditioned not only on knowing, but also on living out Jesus' words. Living as a disciple of Jesus includes adherence to Jesus and acceptance of his teaching, and putting his moral and spiritual teaching into practice.

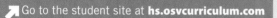
Go to the student site at **hs.osvcurriculum.com**

Consider some private discipleship questions about your faith. As always, take this time to honestly answer them and make yourself some notes.

○ Discipleship includes studying *and* living the words of Jesus. Which of the two are you doing most?

○ Would you describe yourself as a disciple, or as a believer but not yet a disciple? Why?

○ What do you think is the next step for you to take in order to get on—or stay on—the path of discipleship?

○ From what has your faith helped free you?

○ What has your faith helped you do?

○ Would you say you have a *correct conscience* or an *erroneous conscience*? List some reasons for your answer.

You can include some of your responses here as part of the final report you will make at the end of this course.

*Discipleship ... within the Body of Christ ...*
*for the glory of God and the good of the world.*

---

fullness; the world and those who dwell in it" (Psalm 24:1). They know themselves to be recipients and caretakers of God's many gifts. They are grateful for what they have received and eager to cultivate their gifts out of love for God and one another (p. 10).

First, notice that there are three specific characteristics of discipleship: It is a *conscious choice*, carried out in *action*, involving personal *sacrifice*. Second, notice that discipleship is rooted in conversion and is a lifelong process. Third, notice that while discipleship concerns what we do and how we live, **stewardship** refers to how we understand ourselves and our role in relationship to God, who gave us dominion over the resources of the world.

Jesus sometimes describes discipleship in terms of stewardship because being a steward sheds light on the way of discipleship. A "steward" is one to whom the owner of a household turns over responsibility for caring for the property, managing affairs, making resources yield as much as possible, and sharing the resources with others. The position involves trust and accountability." (*Stewardship: A Disciple's Response*, p. 24).

Christians understand that God is the "owner" and we are the "stewards" in this analogy. An important element of living as a disciple of Jesus is fulfilling our responsibility for stewardship.

Catholic teaching on stewardship holds that people have a right to private property as a means of providing for basic needs. This ownership also gives freedom and dignity to people as well as the ability for solidarity to build up among people (see CCC, 2402). That right, however, does not outweigh the fact that God gave the Earth to all of us. The Vatican II document, *Gaudium et Spes*, made this point:

'In his use of things man should regard the external goods he legitimately owns not merely as exclusive to himself but common to others also, in the sense that they can benefit others as well as himself.'[87]

—CCC, 2404

We have to respect the integrity of Creation, including our stewardship of animals. We can use animals for food and clothing as well as for work and leisure. Experimentation must be reasonable and contribute to caring

**stewardship** the responsibility God has given us to care for the resources of the Earth, and to use the time and talent God has given each of us for the good of the Church

**Thousands of Catholic people from the United States and Canada serve as missionaries around the world.**

According to the U.S. Catholic Mission Association, more than 3,350 missionaries were spread out around the world in 2010. About half of them served in North America. The rest brought the Good News to all corners of the world, including South America, Africa, the Middle East, and Oceania. More than 2,200 of the missionaries were religious sisters. The others included diocesan or religious priests, religious brothers, seminarians, and lay people.

**The Missionaries of the Poor care for the handicapped in Jamaica.**

➚ Go to the student site at **hs.osvcurriculum.com**

**evangelization** sharing the Good News of Jesus Christ with others through our words and actions

for or saving lives (see CCC, 2417). "It is contrary to human dignity to cause animals to suffer or die needlessly. It is likewise unworthy to spend money on them that should as a priority go to the relief of human misery" (CCC, 2418).

"In the beginning God entrusted the earth and its resources to the common stewardship of mankind to take care of them, master them by labor, and enjoy their fruits"[88] (CCC,

2402). Stewardship involves our attitude, or how we regard what we have worked for and what we have been given. That includes more than just what we personally have, and it must also determine how we spend our time and use our God-given talents.

## No Matter the Cost

Discipleship means being a follower of Jesus Christ no matter the cost. In the Beatitudes, we hear Jesus recognizing the reality of personal sacrifice with reference to the persecutions of the prophets before him.

> 'Blessed are those who are persecuted for righteousness' sake, for theirs is the kingdom of heaven. Blessed are you when people revile you and persecute you and utter all kinds of evil against you falsely on my account. Rejoice and be glad, for your reward is great in heaven, for in the same way they persecuted the prophets who were before you.'

—Matthew 5:10-12

The particular sacrifices one will make and the persecutions one will face depend a lot on the circumstances of each individual person. Nonetheless, each of us will face societal struggles on our path of discipleship.

One of the aspects of discipleship that may involve sacrifice and persecution is **evangelization**, which is sharing the Gospel of Christ with the world in both word and deed. We fulfill this prophetic mission in the ordinary workings of daily life and when we share love with and for others. But that is not the only time. The true disciple looks "for occasions of announcing Christ by word, either to unbelievers . . . or to the faithful"[89] (CCC, 905). Evangelization is about bringing the Word of God into the world. This is not an easy task, and it is often met with hostility. Jesus Christ predicted that we would suffer for our faith and promised that he would be with us in our suffering. We can rely on the Holy Spirit's gift of fortitude to grow in the virtue of fortitude.

In certain parts of the world, discipleship literally involves risking one's life. In 2006,

## GO TO THE SOURCE 📖

**We often miss the Scripture passages about stewardship.** Although contemporary translations reference the concept, the word "stewardship" is not used.

Read the following two stories and identify how each relates to the concept of stewardship.

○ The Parable of the Faithful Servants in *Luke 12:35-48*

○ The Parable of the Talents in *Matthew 25:14-30*

an Italian priest named Father Andrea Santoro, 61, was shot and killed while praying at the altar of St. Mary Church in the parish he served in Trabzon, Turkey. In December 1980, three religious sisters and a lay worker were kidnapped, raped, and shot to death in El Salvador. Four Salvadoran national guardsmen were convicted in the killings of Maryknoll Sisters Ita Ford and Maura Clarke, lay worker Jean Donovan, and Ursuline Sister Dorothy Kazel.

Few of us will be called to make this kind of sacrifice, but we will certainly encounter everyday incidents that will challenge our commitment to the path of discipleship. Sometimes there are negative social consequences for being a good person who is committed to doing what is right.

> 'Everyone therefore who acknowledges me before others, I also will acknowledge before my Father in heaven; but whoever denies me before others, I also will deny before my Father in heaven.'
>
> —Matthew 10:32-33

What is it that we can share with others? The most important thing we can share is the love of God and our neighbor, taught to us through the example of Jesus and the Paschal Mystery. Part of living as a disciple of Christ is fulfilling the responsibility for the mission of evangelization. It is important that we do not confuse evangelization with charity and other works of service. We are also mandated to serve the poor, but for a different reason. We would do this whether or not people being served were open to Christ.

According to Church teaching, serving the poor can go hand in hand with evangelization and missions, and can sometimes be considered pre-evangelization, but it is not exactly the same as sharing the faith and leading others to Christ. Despite difficulties, a disciple of Jesus will keep his word and know "the truth [that] will make you free"[90] (CCC, 2466).

**Restate** What kinds of sacrifice and persecutions might contemporary discipleship involve?

**Develop** How can we be perfect as God is perfect?

## RECALL

Every generation has its negative nicknames that criticize good people who are committed to doing the right thing.

○ In your experience, what negative name-calling and judgments are passed on people who are essentially on the path of discipleship?

○ Would you consider yourself one of the persecutors or one of the persecuted, and why?

## SECTION 3 REVIEW

### QUICK REVIEW

**1a. Recall** How long must we be formed in Christ's likeness?

**b. Identify** Name one of the three ways the U.S. Bishops link stewardship to our understanding of discipleship.

**2a. Infer** Why must all Church members be ready to profess their faith?

**b. Explain** What did Jesus say would happen to us if we deny him before others?

**3a. Conclude** Why did Jesus tell us to abide in his love?

**b. Connect** How does Jesus light up the darkness?

### ACT

Come up with a plan to bring about reversal of injustices in your community.

### SELF-ASSESS

Which statement best reflects where you are now?

☐ I'm confident enough about the material in this section to be able to explain it to someone else.

☐ I have a good grasp of the material in this section, but I could use more review.

☐ I'm lost. I need help catching up before moving on.

# Catholic Social Teachings

A virtuous life that has developed a good conscience leads to awareness about **injustice** in the world.

Scripture helps us see that struggles against injustices have been pervasive since long before the time of Jesus. The problems of hunger, war, sickness, disease, and poverty have shared similar characteristics over the centuries. These issues make the call for justice and conversion even more urgent.

We hear about injustice all the time, often in the headlines, and the statistics can sometimes numb us to the reality of a given situation. The problems can seem too big to handle, especially when the injustice is connected to human laws or structures in society that promote it.

Statistics can also make injustice seem like a nameless, faceless problem. We know injustice exists in the poverty that stems from a lack of jobs and affordable housing, as well as in war that kills innocent men, women, and children. Yet we can forget that there are real individuals—whole families—affected by these injustices.

Statistics can't give us the whole picture, but they can provide a glimpse of the problem. According to the U.S. Catholic Bishops' 2002 statement, *A Place at the Table*, more than half of the world's population makes less than two dollars a day.

This figure represents international purchasing power expressed in U.S. dollars. The United Nations reported that 1.02 billion people suffered hunger on a regular basis in 2009. The poverty line in the United States is established at an annual income of $22,350 for a family of four, according to the U.S. Census Bureau. Forty-six million Americans live in that situation—one in eight U.S. citizens. The younger you are, the worse it can be, as more than twenty percent of preschool children are considered poor.

In response to injustice, Jesus challenged us to recognize him in the faces of the poor; in those who suffer from hunger; those who are strangers; and those who are imprisoned. In fact, he said that when we help these people, we are helping him. This is not just a measure of how nice we are to people; it is a measure of our faithfulness and what we truly hold in our hearts. It is a call to act with justice. Justice, you will recall, is the constant and firm goal of giving to each person and God what is due to them.

> Action on behalf of justice and participation in the transformation of the world fully appear to us as a constitutive dimension of the preaching of the Gospel, or, in other words, of the Church's mission for the redemption of the human race and its liberation from every oppressive situation.
>
> —*Justice in the World*, World Synod of Bishops, 1971

In *A Place at the Table*, the bishops acknowledged that four distinct groups share the responsibility of serving the poor. Like the four legs of a table, each group has a specific, necessary, and supportive role to play. They are families and individuals, communities and religious institutions, the private sector, and government. Working together, these four groups can

CAREER FAIR

form a safety net for people by respecting dignity and people's rights, helping people overcome obstacles, and contributing to the common good of everyone. By pulling together as a group, we can accomplish those things we couldn't individually.

Social justice is just one part of cooperating with the Kingdom of God, which we have described throughout this course. It is important to remember that the Kingdom of God is his reign in our lives and the world with the final goal of union with him. We are in the "end time," when Christ ushered in the beginning of the Kingdom. Christ has also revealed the Holy Spirit, who has written the New Law of love in our hearts. As Jesus taught us, we pray for the coming of the Kingdom and respond to the Holy Spirit's prompting to spread the Good News.

The Catholic Church speaks of the four last things at the end of time for the individual. They are (1) death, (2) judgment by Christ, and entrance to (3) heaven or (4) hell. For the universe, they are the end of the world, the resurrection of dead, the general judgment, and the completion of all things. The end of time will see the fullness of the Kingdom of God and "the universe itself, which is so closely related to man and which attains its destiny through him, will be perfectly re-established in Christ"[91] (CCC, 1042).

**List** Give some examples of injustice in our world.

**Analyze** Why don't statistics give us a good picture of injustice?

## Seven Key Justice Themes

The social justice teachings of the Church are rooted in the stories and teachings of the prophets and psalms in the Old Testament and the life and teaching of Jesus, his Mother Mary, and his disciples in the New Testament. Modern Catholic Social Teaching has been articulated through a series of Church documents and are summarized on the U.S. Catholic Bishops website. Seven key themes of Catholic Social Justice teaching are passed down from the Church to our current generation.

**GO TO THE SOURCE**

**Sometimes people justify** their inaction by quoting Jesus.

Read *Matthew 26:6-13*.

○ What line is taken out of context to justify inaction?

○ Summarize Jesus' explanation of the consequences for one's response to injustice in Matthew 25:31-46.

○ Given Jesus' teaching in Matthew 25, what do you think Jesus' intention was in saying what he said in Matthew 26?

The **Dignity** of the human person: The Book of Genesis contains this central teaching of the Church, that each person is made in God's image and likeness and is deserving of being treated with respect and dignity. Human life is sacred; the dignity of all human persons must always be respected. Violations of this principle have been mentioned throughout this book: abortion, racism, sexism, anti-Semitism, ecological crises, war, poverty, the death penalty, violence, and other issues.

"What is at stake is the dignity of the human person, whose defense and promotion have been entrusted to us by the Creator, and to whom the men and women at every moment of history are strictly and responsibly in debt"[92] (CCC, 1929, Pope John Paul II).

Call to **Family**, Community and Participation in Society. The Church teaches that a stable family is necessary for the survival of a civilization. "No community is more central than the family: it needs to be supported, not undermined. It is the basic cell of society and the state has an obligation to support the family. A central test of political, legal, and economic institutions is what they do *to* people, what they do *for* people, and how people *participate* in them" (Bright, Thomas. *Basic Themes of Catholic Social Teaching.* 1993)

"Participation begins with education and culture. 'One is entitled to think that the future of humanity is in the hands of those who are capable of providing the generations to come with reasons for life and optimism'"[93] (CCC, 1917).

# Venerable Matt Talbot

## (1856–1925)

Sometimes it's hard to imagine is a saint being anything other than, well, saintly.

Even though we hear more about their virtue than their struggle with vice, saints have always had to pick up their cross and follow Jesus daily. And it is in their willingness to struggle with those vices that they often witness the heroic virtues that give us hope. Even the holiest among us are tempted to do the wrong thing—that's part of being human. However, what sets some people apart is that they work harder to overcome their temptations—one day, one temptation at a time.

One saint-in-making whose struggle was a life-long challenge is Venerable Matt Talbot.

Matt Talbot was the second of twelve children born into a poor family in Dublin, Ireland. His father was a heavy drinker as were most of his uncles. He left school when he was 12 and began working, but spent most of his wages on alcohol. Drinking was his life. One could say that he lived to drink.

After sixteen years of heavy drinking, he found himself outside a pub, hoping a friend would buy him another drink. When no one would, he went home and angrily decided to stop drinking for three months. After three months, he extended it to six and eventually, with the help of a priest, he stopped drinking permanently.

It wasn't easy for him. For the next forty years he suffered with constant temptation. In fact, he wrote to his sister, "Never look down on a man, who cannot give up the drink. It is easier to get out of hell!" As part of his conversion, he repaid all the debts he had racked up.

Despite his inner battle, most people who knew him thought he was just an ordinary laborer. During

his life, Talbot gave most of his money to the poor, lived very simply, and got up every morning at 5 to attend Mass before work. On June 7, 1925, he was on his way to Mass when he collapsed on the street and died of heart failure.

Soon after his death, stories of his holiness began to circulate and Church officials began an investigation of his life. Nearly forty years later, in 1975, Pope Paul VI declared him to be venerable. In a speech to the Calix Society, an organization for Catholic alcoholics, Pope Paul VI said, "It is our hope that his success will encourage countless men and women throughout the world to realize the need for conversion, the possibility of real rehabilitation, the serenity of Christian reconciliation, and the peace and joy of helping others to overcome abuses, disorders and sin."

**Think About It** What temptation do you struggle with the most? Matt Talbot went to daily Mass. What has your experience with daily Mass been like? Matt Talbot went out of his way to make up to those he harmed. How can you let someone you've hurt know that you are sorry? What can you do to help a friend who is dealing with alcohol or drug abuse?

Go to the student site at
**hs.osvcurriculum.com**

Everyday life challenges you to think about right and wrong, to sort out the good from the bad, and to inform and form your conscience. Here's an example. . . .

A high school guidance counselor has a social media page, and several students add her as a friend. Students like after-school advice without an appointment. The counselor also hears details about students' lives. Two parents find out about some dangerous things their children have been doing, and that the counselor knew but didn't tell anyone. The parents are furious.

**"She cared more about being their friend than helping me help my child!"**

*Counselor was helping kids by keeping things confidential.*

Teachers and counselors, by law, have to let parents know, right?

*If the counselor tells, the students will stay away.*

**Parents should focus on their kids.**

The parents have a point.

**What difference does it make? These young people need help.**

**What do you think?**

# Going Moral

In the early 1980s, the Solidarity movement helped change Polish society and improved workers' rights.

The **Rights and Responsibilities** of the human person. Each person is entitled to basic rights and responsibilities. "People have a fundamental right to life and to those things which make life truly human—food, clothing, housing, health care, education, security, social services, and employment. Corresponding to these rights are duties and responsibilities—to one another, to our families and to the larger society, to respect the rights of others, and to work for the common good."

"The common good presupposes *respect for the person* as such. In the name of the common good, public authorities are bound to respect the fundamental and inalienable rights of the human person. Society should permit each of its members to fulfill his vocation. . . . such as 'the right to act according to a sound norm of conscience and to safeguard . . . privacy, and rightful freedom also in matters of religion'"[94] (CCC, 1907, which also quotes *Gaudium et Spes*).

Preferential **Option** for the Poor and Vulnerable. In *Economic Justice for All*, the U.S. Catholic Bishops explain, "As followers of Christ, we are challenged to make a fundamental 'option for the poor'—to speak for the voiceless, to defend the defenseless, to assess life styles, policies, and social institutions in terms of their impact on the poor. This 'option for the poor' does not mean pitting one group against another, but rather, strengthening the whole community by assisting those who are the most vulnerable. As Christians, we are called to respond to the needs of all our brothers and sisters, but those with the greatest needs require the greatest response."

In *Faithful Citizenship: A Catholic Call to Political Responsibility*, the U.S. Catholic Bishops go on to clarify, "Scripture teaches that God has a special concern for the poor and vulnerable. . . . The Church calls on all of us to embrace this preferential option for the poor and vulnerable, to embody it in our lives, and to work to have it shape public policies and priorities. A fundamental measure of our society is how we care for and stand with the poor and vulnerable."

The Dignity of **Work** and the Rights of **Workers**. Catholic teaching insists that work is good—so good, in fact, that there is a dignity that develops from the very process of a job well done. Yet it is not the product of work itself that gives a person the sense of dignity; rather it is the process of using one's gifts and talents in an environment that respects the human dignity of each person. The value of labor is that people take part in the work of Creation.

The U.S. Catholic Bishops explain, "The economy must serve people, not the other way around. Work is more than a way to make a living; it is a form of continuing participation in God's act of creation. If the dignity of work is to be protected, then the basic rights of workers, owners, and others must be respected—the right to productive work, to decent and fair wages, to organize and choose to join a union, to economic initiative, and to ownership and private property. These rights must be exercised in ways that advance the common good."

**Solidarity** The principle of solidarity recognizes that "we are one human family whatever our national, racial, ethnic, economic, and ideological differences. We are our brothers' and sisters' keepers, wherever they may be. Loving our neighbor has global dimensions in a shrinking world.

At the core of the virtue of solidarity is the pursuit of justice and peace. Pope Paul VI taught that 'if you want peace, work for justice.' The Gospel calls us to be peacemakers. Our love for all our sisters and brothers demands that we promote peace in a world surrounded by violence and conflict" (USCCB "Themes of Catholic Social Teaching"). Jesus himself shows solidarity with us by becoming human and enduring the utmost human suffering.

"The principle of solidarity, also articulated in terms of 'friendship' or 'social charity,' is a direct demand of human and Christian brotherhood"[95] (CCC, 1939). "Solidarity is manifested in the first place by the distribution of goods and remuneration for work" (CCC, 1940). "Socioeconomic problems can be resolved only with the help of all the forms of solidarity: solidarity of the poor among themselves, between rich and poor, of workers among themselves, between employers and employees in a business, solidarity among nations and peoples. International solidarity is a requirement of the moral order; world peace depends in part upon this" (CCC, 1941).

**Restate** What are the seven key themes of Catholic Social Justice teaching?

**Summarize** What rights and responsibilities does the Church support?

## SECTION 4 REVIEW

### QUICK REVIEW

**1a. Tell** How many people in the United States live in poverty?

**b. Analyze** How do some people try to justify allowing people to live in poverty by quoting Jesus?

**c. List** Name four groups that the Church explains should help the poor.

**2a. Explain** What is the basis of Catholic Social Justice teaching?

**b. Summarize** List and define the seven principles of Catholic Social Justice teaching.

**c. Categorize** Which social justice principle is the most basic? Explain.

### ACT

Write a journal page reflecting on a principle of social teaching you would like to emphasize in your own life.

○ Write a description of the principle.

○ Tell why it is important to you.

○ List ways that you can promote it.

### SELF-ASSESS

Which statement best reflects where you are now?

☐ I'm confident enough about the material in this section to be able to explain it to someone else.

☐ I have a good grasp of the material in this section, but I could use more review.

☐ I'm lost. I need help catching up before moving on.

# PRAYER

**Immaculate Heart of Mary, help us to conquer the menace of** evil, which so easily takes root in the hearts of the people of today, and whose immeasurable effects already weigh down upon our modern world and seem to block the paths toward the future.

From famine and war, deliver us.

From nuclear war, from incalculable self-destruction, from every kind of war, deliver us.

From sins against human life from its very beginning, deliver us.

From hatred and from the demeaning of the dignity of the children of God, deliver us.

From every kind of injustice in the life of society, both national and international, deliver us.

From readiness to trample on the commandments of God, deliver us.

From attempts to stifle in human hearts the very truth of God, deliver us.

From the loss of awareness of good and evil, deliver us.

From sins against the Holy Spirit, deliver us.

Accept, O Mother of Christ, this cry laden with the sufferings of all individual human beings, laden with the sufferings of whole societies. Help us with the power of the Holy Spirit conquer all sin: individual sin and the "sin of the world," sin in all its manifestations.

Let there be revealed once more in the history of the world the infinite saving power of the redemption: the power of merciful love.

May it put a stop to evil.
May it transform consciences.
May your Immaculate Heart reveal for all the light of hope.

## TERMS

Use each of the following terms in a sentence that shows you know what the term means. You may include more than one term in a sentence.

| | |
|---|---|
| *metanoia* | fortitude |
| conversion | temperance |
| conscience | vices |
| correct conscience | gluttony |
| virtue | sloth |
| theological virtues | stewardship |
| cardinal virtues | evangelization |
| prudence | injustice |
| justice | |

## PEOPLE

Identify why each is important in the context of the chapter.

1. Father Thomas Weinandy
2. Saint Augustine
3. Pope Paul VI
4. Father Andrea Santoro

## UNDERSTANDING

Answer each question and complete each exercise

### SECTION 1

1. **Recall** What is our most cherished and first freedom according to the U.S. Bishops?
2. **Restate** Where does interior conversion lead?
3. **Conclude** The morality of an act depends on what?

### SECTION 2

4. **Explain** What is the purpose of virtues?
5. **Elaborate** Why are the theological virtues given that name?
6. **Apply** What can you do to develop virtues in yourself?

### SECTION 3

7. **Tell** How does Jesus model the concept of reversal?
8. **Connect** What do the Beatitudes say about personal sacrifice?
9. **Explain** What is evangelization?

## SECTION 4

10. **List** According to the U.S. Bishops, what are some solutions to counter poverty?

11. **Infer** How did Matt Talbot demonstrate principles of social justice in his life?

12. **Analyze** Which principle of social justice is most important to you? Explain your answer.

## CONNECTING

**Visual** This is an illustration by Jean Colombe, a French painter and illuminator of manuscripts. The illustration appears in *The Book of Hours of Louis d'Orleans* and is dated 1469. A "book of hours" contained prayers that were said at different times of the day, and wealthy people often commissioned artists to create illustrations for their personal books. This particular illustration is titled "Christ in Majesty."

Which details in the illustration convey the idea of Christ's majesty? Why did the artist put so much open space between the angels and Jesus? What might be the purpose of the designs around the central illustration?

**Challenge** You are walking with a friend near the mall when a disheveled man walks up to you and asks for a handout. Your friend doesn't want to give him any money, and instead insults the man.

○ How do you handle this situation?

○ What if the man said he needed the money for his children? How would that change the situation?

○ What if the man is drinking or on drugs?

**Question** After working through this chapter, what advice would you give someone who wants to know how to fight injustice in the world?

**Imagine** You are the host of a radio show. You would like to construct a show that promotes one of the Catholic Social Justice principles.

○ Select a principle that you want others to know about.

○ Make a list of guests (living or dead) whose lives indicate that they have lived in situations that relate to this issue. What sort of questions would you ask them, and how might they respond?

○ What songs would you use to emphasize the principle you are focusing on?

## SELF-ASSESS

**On Your Own** Make a list of the most important things you learned from this chapter. Select three things that represent your growth in understanding as you worked through this chapter. Write a paragraph explaining your choices.

**With a Partner** List what you found most helpful or interesting in this chapter as well as any other questions that have surfaced.

- ○ What might people pray about in this setting?
- ○ How does prayer connect with the Paschal Mystery?

# Celebrating the Paschal **Mystery**

 Go to the student site at
**hs.osvcurriculum.com**

# WHAT DO YOU SAY?

## How do you **pray?**

A Catholic high school religion class was asked: What's your favorite way to pray? Here are some of the responses:

"Praying the Our Father, laying down."

"In Church when everyone is praying with me."

"Adoration helps."

"By singing in Mass as loud and freely as possible."

"When the lights are off in my room, I am by myself with some music. It makes me real calm and I can really open up."

"When I first wake up, when I go to sleep, and before I play a sport."

"In my room kneeling by my bed."

"Praying before a meal with my family."

"Alone, under an open, starry sky. I imagine that my prayers reach God better that way."

# WHERE ARE YOU?

**Check the answer that best matches where you are today.**

*Prayer is a key part of my life*
☐ Quite a bit  ☐ Somewhat  ☐ A little  ☐ Not at all

*I pray about everything*
☐ Quite a bit  ☐ Somewhat  ☐ A little  ☐ Not at all

*I pray a lot of different ways*
☐ Quite a bit  ☐ Somewhat  ☐ A little  ☐ Not at all

*I pray from my heart*
☐ Quite a bit  ☐ Somewhat  ☐ A little  ☐ Not at all

*I use the Bible when I pray*
☐ Quite a bit  ☐ Somewhat  ☐ A little  ☐ Not at all

*I can explain the Triduum*
☐ Quite a bit  ☐ Somewhat  ☐ A little  ☐ Not at all

# The Power of Prayer

What exactly is prayer and how does it work?
Why doesn't God always grant what we pray for?
How can we pray the Paschal Mystery?

"Prayer and *Christian life* are *inseparable*" (CCC, 2745).

Just as a body without a spirit is dead and faith without works is dead, a Christian life without prayer is also dead. We pray in or with Christ in the Paschal Mystery. These are inseparable is because both concern the love of God given to us through Jesus. This love transforms us through the Holy Spirit, who teaches us in the life of prayer.

When Jesus gave his disciples the commandment to "love one another as I have loved you," he also said "the father will give you whatever you ask him in my name" (John 15:12, 16). This is a bold promise with enormous power. Sometimes God says "no" in response to our prayers. Since it's not what we thought we needed and asked for, we might think God hasn't heard us. But that's not the case. God responds to our prayers in what he knows to be the best for us, even when we don't understand his plan for us.

Prayer is a relationship with God, trusting he knows what is best for us and will give us what we need. We give of ourselves in prayer, and we turn to him for ourselves and for others. In order to truly love one another, we need to pray about what we can give rather than what we can get. Prayer must be connected with Jesus' command to be in communion with one another.

Prayer is a way of engaging with God who constantly calls each of us to him. We can take a deep journey into prayer and discover God's grace in places we may not have seen previously. We will start to see God working throughout the day.

Prayer is the raising of one's mind and heart to God.[96]

—CCC, 2590

The Acts of the Apostles describes prayer as one of the practices of the Christian community. It is through prayer that Christians are able to stay in a relationship with God, who calls all of us to a vital relationship with him experienced through prayer. "They devoted themselves to the apostles' teaching and fellowship, to the breaking of bread and the prayers" (Acts 2:42).

"This sequence is characteristic of the Church's prayer: founded on the apostolic faith; authenticated by charity; nourished in the Eucharist" (CCC, 2624). Therefore

it is important to ask ourselves three questions about our prayer life:

- Is there depth to our prayer life based on the teachings of the Apostles and their successors, which can be found in Sacred Scripture and Church teaching?

- Is our prayer life backed up with our actions that imitate Christ's love for others, including family, friends, strangers, and enemies?

- Is our prayer nourished by the Eucharist, especially during Sunday Mass?

We will conclude this course on the Paschal Mystery by exploring the role prayer plays in our lives as Catholics. We will cover the different forms and expressions of prayer, the tradition of prayer in the Old and New Testaments, and how the **Easter Triduum** celebrates the Paschal Mystery as the defining moment for all Christians. Finally, you will have the opportunity to choose several ways to pray through some of your experiences of the Paschal Mystery.

**Tell** What do "a body without a spirit," "faith without works," and "a Christian life without prayer" have in common?

**Explain** How is prayer a relationship?

**Easter Triduum** three holy days including Easter that commemorate the Paschal Mystery beginning on Holy Thursday and ending with evening prayer on Easter Sunday

## The Heart of the Matter

When we pray, we pray with our whole person, but the source of prayer is the heart. "According to Scripture, it is the *heart* that prays. If our heart is far from God, the words of prayer are in vain" (CCC, 2562). Our prayer can become distracted and not bear much fruit. In fact, the *Catechism* names distraction and lack of energy as the main obstacles to prayer. "The remedy lies in faith, conversion, and vigilance of heart" (CCC, 2754).

> The heart is the dwelling-place where I am, where I live . . . the heart is the place 'to which I withdraw.' The heart is our hidden center, beyond the grasp of reason and of others; only the Spirit of God can fathom the human heart and know it fully. The heart is the place of decision, deeper than our psychic drives. It is the place of truth, where we choose life or death. It is the place of encounter, because as image of God we live in relation: it is the place of covenant.
>
> —CCC, 2563

The heart is the place of decision, deeper than our psychic or emotional drives. It is the place of truth where we choose life or death, as the *Catechism* mentions. This means that the heart is what we mean when we talk about our will. Our hearts are also the way in which we express our deepest desires and longing for God. Saint Augustine asks what many have over the millennia: Why does God want us to pray when he already knows our needs before we ask? Augustine's answer is that God wants us to "exercise our desire" through prayer in order to prepare us for what he will give us:

> His gift is very great indeed, but our capacity is too small and limited to receive it. The deeper our faith, the stronger our hope, the greater our desire [acts of our hearts] the larger will be our capacity to receive.
>
> —Saint Augustine, Liturgy of the Hours, Volume IV, p. 408

## REFLECT

**Research indicates that about eighty percent of Catholic teens pray regularly.**

- How would you describe your prayer?
- Why do you pray?
- What did you ask for and/or who did you pray for?
- Would you say that you pray mostly from your heart, or from your mind? Explain.
- Do you agree that the heart is the place most people fear to go? Explain.
- When do you pray best?
- List what you think are the top four obstacles to prayer.

Prayer for Catholics focuses above all other things on meditating on the mysteries of Christ. The ancient practice of *lectio divina* is one method to do that. It is a way to read Scripture so that it becomes prayer. It is a prayerful conversation. Here are some steps to follow lectio divina:

- lectio—Read a passage from Scripture several times, slowly and attentively.

- meditatio—Focus on a word or phrase from the passage; memorize it and slowly repeat it to yourself.

- oratio—Allow the meditation to lead you to a conversation with God.

- contemplation—Rest in the presence of God.

If the heart plays such an important part as the spiritual center of each person, why is it the place that many people fear to go?

One reason may be that some people believe opening their heart will make them soft or weak, especially since the heart is often associated with emotions. A second reason could be because God's will can be discovered there. Many people fear that God will show them the truth about right and wrong, or the truth about themselves. *Others measure themselves only by what they do rather than being aware of what's in their hearts.*

Another reason that people might avoid looking into their hearts is because there are too many distractions in life. The constant noise of the world around us can distract us and interfere with our relationship with God, especially as we reduce the time and silence needed for prayer.

Prayer is a great tool to allay these fears. We are collaborators with God's will through our prayers. Together with our actions and suffering, we become God's co-workers for his Kingdom (see CCC, 307). Saint Augustine says those who wish to do God's commandments have a good will, but it is weak at first. As we cooperate with God's plan, our will and our love will allow us to do greater actions, such as those of the martyrs. One way to do this is through prayer and meditation. Christian meditation can lead you to a deeper trust in God and to a greater resiliency in life. "Meditation is above all a quest. The mind seeks to understand the why and how of the Christian life, in order to adhere and respond to what the Lord is asking" (CCC, 2705).

Prayer deepens our faith, converts our heart to God's will, and "strengthen[s] our will to follow Christ." Prayer helps us meditate on the mysteries of Christ, but it should go even further: "to the knowledge of the love of the Lord Jesus, to union with him" (CCC, 2708). A perfect way to start is to pray to the Father that our will unites with his Son's. We cannot do this on our own, but we can surrender our will to the Holy Spirit in order to bring about God's plan of salvation for the world. That describes just how important a will to pray and to unite with Christ is. We do this in the Lord's Prayer when we say: "Thy will be done."

**Identify** What is the source of our prayer?

**Summarize** Why do some people fear what's in their heart?

## GO TO THE SOURCE

**Jesus warned us** against becoming too attached to material goods.

Read *Matthew 6:19-21*.
- Explain how this Gospel addresses our consumer culture.
- Do you find this passage affirming or challenging? Why?

# My Faith

**ANSWER EACH QUESTION** in order before you go to the next one. Use the *Catechism* quotation number 2563, on page 214 (the quote that talks about the heart as the place of decision).

- We often describe ourselves and others by the condition of our hearts, like big-hearted, light-hearted, heavy-hearted, good-hearted, hard-hearted, soft-hearted, etc.

- We also use our hearts to describe our emotions and interests, like "heartache," "sweetheart," and "with all my heart." The heart is the part of the body we use most often to describe the things that we cherish or hold dear.

- Sometimes you can tell what your heart holds most sacred by what causes you the most amount of anger. When something we truly cherish is harmed in some way we find our anger comes from deep within.

- How would you describe your heart?

- What does your heart love most? What brings you deepest joy?

- When is your heart filled with the most gratitude?

- What does your heart consider the most important, most sacred—never to be tarnished?

- What have you "learned by heart"? What do you carry with you everywhere you go because your heart has kept it?

- Your heart has a story: What has shaped its past and its present condition? What has helped develop the characteristics you have used to describe it?

- Remember that you can use this as part of the final report you will give at the end of this course.

Go to the student site at **hs.osvcurriculum.com**

*Discipleship ... within the Body of Christ ... for the glory of God and the good of the world.*

### QUICK REVIEW

**1a. Define** What is prayer?

**b. List** What three questions are important to ask ourselves about prayer?

**2a. List** What are four reasons people might fear opening their heart?

**b. Predict** What happens when we try praying when our heart is far from God?

### ACT

With a partner discuss whether there is a wrong way to pray.

**Pray** Compose a prayer that will help strengthen your will to follow Christ.

### SELF-ASSESS

Which statement best reflects where you are now?

☐ I'm confident enough about the material in this section to be able to explain it to someone else.

☐ I have a good grasp of the material in this section, but I could use more review.

☐ I'm lost. I need help catching up before moving on.

# Forms and Expressions of Prayer

We have a rich and diverse tradition of prayer. The forms of prayer include: blessing, adoration, petition, intercession, thanksgiving, and praise. Three major expressions of prayer include: vocal prayer, meditation, and contemplation.

Prayer is primarily addressed to the Father, through Christ, and in the Holy Spirit. "The grace of the Lord Jesus Christ, the love of God, and the communion of the Holy Spirit be with all of you" (2 Corinthians 13:13).

**prayer of blessing** the human response to gifts from God, the source of all blessing; God's gift and our acceptance communicate with each other

The basic movement of prayer is a **prayer of blessing** in which God's gift of grace and human acceptance of this grace are united. This is an encounter between God and us. The prayer of blessing is our response to God's gifts: "because God blesses the human heart, it can in return bless him who is the source of every blessing" (CCC, 2645).

We see the prayer of blessing come together in two fundamental expressions: "our prayer *ascends* in the Holy Spirit through Christ to the Father—we bless him for having blessed us;[97] it implores the grace of the Holy Spirit that *descends* through Christ

**prayer of adoration** prayer that acknowledges the greatness of God

from the Father—he blesses us"[98] (CCC, 2627). Our prayers of blessing are our response to God's gifts for which we praise him and show gratitude. We acknowledge what God has done for us.

This type of prayer can be heard during the Liturgy of the Eucharist, at the preparation of the gifts, over the bread and wine: "Blessed are you, LORD God of all creation, for through your goodness we have received the bread we offer you: fruit of the earth and work of human hands, it will become for us the bread of life. Blessed be God for ever" (*Roman Missal*).

Because the Eucharist is the real body and blood of Jesus, the community gathered is blessed by the supernatural event of being made holy by the sacrifice of Jesus on the Cross. Because Jesus is the "Alpha and the Omega," (Revelation 21:6) the beginning and the end, any blessing that is given or received comes in and through the Paschal Mystery of Jesus.

A **prayer of adoration** honors our Creator, acknowledges that we are his creatures, and exalts the greatness of God. Adoration is traditionally a prayer of respectful silence in which we adore God who made all things. Adoration of the Triune God humbles us and gives us assurance that our prayers will be heard (see CCC, 2628).

Adoration includes a strong desire to be in the present moment in an intimate relationship with God. It is realizing that our past failings and shortcomings do not stop God from loving you right here, right now. It gives you the freedom to ask for forgiveness because you know you are forgiven. From adoration we realize we no longer need possessions to fill our emptiness and restlessness. We realize we are already filled with eternal love through the Paschal Mystery of Jesus and by the power of the

Holy Spirit. The question isn't where we will find love, instead we ask where we can give the love we already have.

> The worship of the one God sets man free from turning in on himself, from the slavery of sin and the idolatry of the world.
>
> —CCC, 2097

A **prayer of praise** is meant to be a joyful song of glory to God recognizing him for his own sake. "O come, let us sing to the Lord; let us make a joyful noise to the rock of our salvation! Let us come into his presence with thanksgiving; let us make a joyful noise to him with songs of praise! . . . O come, let us worship and bow down, let us kneel before the Lord, our Maker!" (Psalm 95:1-2, 6).

We are able to give up our selfishness and out of humility praise God. With our selfishness gone, the natural joy of life can be experienced. "To adore God is to praise and exalt him and to humble oneself, as Mary did in the Magnificat, confessing with gratitude that he has done great things and holy is his name"[99] (CCC, 2097). If there is nothing that we need and all of our losses are insignificant to what we now have, nothing can stop our joy. Choosing to praise God is making the choice to let go of our selfishness and recognize the gifts around us. Like the Magnificat, many prayers come from Scripture or are based on Scriptural passages or events.

> Praise is the form of prayer which recognizes most immediately that God is God. It lauds God for his own sake and gives him glory, quite beyond what he does, but simply because HE IS. . . . Praise embraces the other forms of prayer and carries them toward him who is its source and goal: the 'one God, the Father, from whom are all things and for whom we exist.'[100]
>
> —CCC, 2639

The prayer of praise is an instrument that has to be practiced like any other instrument. We have to choose to pick it up. Anyone can play it and we have an entire Church willing to help us. Praise was a form of prayer used by the Apostles and the early Church in Jerusalem: "Day by day, as they spent much time together in the temple, they broke bread at home and ate their food with glad and generous hearts, praising God and having the goodwill of all the people" (Acts 2:46-47). No one is expecting you to do this on your own. Jesus gave us the Church so that all may come to know the Father, Son, and Holy Spirit.

Notice the rich liturgical language that describes the various types of prayer that take place on any given Sunday in churches around the world: "Let us sing to the Lord, let us make a joyful noise;" "Let us come into his presence with thanksgiving;" "with songs of praise;" "let us worship and bow down, let us kneel before the Lord our Maker" (Psalm 95:1-2,6).

The liturgy of the Church and Word of God are two rich sources for prayer. Being part of the Church gives us all a regular invitation to pray daily prayers, and to pray during the Liturgy of the Hours, Sunday Eucharist, and the feasts of the liturgical year. Scripture is our source and guide for prayer.

**Describe** To whom is prayer directed?

**Connect** Explain the fundamental movement of prayer in a blessing.

**prayer of praise** offering a joyful recognition of God for his own sake that gives him glory

**The Western Wall in the Jerusalem is all that remains of the ancient Hebrew Temple, which was destroyed in the year 70 A.D.**

It is one of the places we can imagine the adolescent Jesus coming to celebrate the great Jewish festivals. Like other Jews, he would have sung the Songs of Ascents (Psalms 120-134) as he approached the Temple. Then each year at Passover, he would have joined others there in the Great Hallel (Psalm 136). Here is the beginning of that Psalm: "O give thanks to the LORD, for he is good, for his steadfast love endures forever. O give thanks to God of gods, for his steadfast love endures forever. O give thanks to the Lord of lords, for his steadfast love endures forever" (Psalm 136:1-3).

○ Read the rest of Psalm 136. What event in your life has had such an effect that you want to praise God?

○ Compose your own psalm about this event or about God in general.

➚ Go to the student site at **hs.osvcurriculum.com**

## Prayers of Petition, Intercession, and Thanksgiving

**prayer of petition** bringing our needs to God and asking God to respond

**supplication** asking for something

A **prayer of petition** expresses our relationship with and our reliance on God. We bring our needs to God, which is also described as **supplication**. "The vocabulary of supplication in the New Testament is rich in shades of meaning: ask, beseech, plead, invoke, entreat, cry out, even 'struggle in prayer'"[101] (CCC, 2629).

A prayer of petition also reflects the hope of the Paschal Mystery. Though we are faced with life's struggles, our hope is in our life with God, no matter the immediate result of our petition. We affirm God as our primary source of life, not because he can fix every problem but because we believe that love is always the final answer. The Good News is that with love Jesus embraced the Cross and in love Jesus rose from the dead.

Given the human tendency to confuse needs with wants, petition is too often reduced to merely asking God for what we want. The *Catechism* reminds us that the first step to petition should be forgiveness. "The first movement of the prayer of petition is *asking forgiveness,* like the tax collector in the parable: 'God be merciful to me a sinner!'"[102] (CCC, 2631). Confession, or acknowledging wrongdoings and imperfections, is a prerequisite for genuine prayer, which is both pure and righteous.

"Christian petition is centered on the desire and search f*or the Kingdom to come,* in keeping with the teaching of Christ"[103] (CCC, 2632). We see a hierarchy for these petitions in the Our Father. First we pray for the Kingdom of God, then for what we need to cooperate with the Kingdom's coming. Through prayer every baptized person works to bring about the Kingdom of God (see CCC, 2632).

## GO TO THE SOURCE 📖

**The following Scripture passages give us insight** about prayer.

Read *Philippians 1:9-10; James 1:5; Romans 8:26-27; Romans 10:1; Philippians 4:6-7; Ephesians 1:16-17; 1 Thessalonians 5:16-18; and Colossians 4:2-3; 1 Timothy 2:5-6; Hebrews 7:24-25.*

Read the following passages and write your own prayer to the Trinity drawing from the Scripture: *1 Timothy 2:5-6; Hebrews 7:24-25; and Romans 8:26-27.*

> But strive first for the kingdom of God and his righteousness, and all these things will be given to you as well.
>
> —Matthew 6:33

# PRIMARY SOURCES

**W**e recite this prayer at every Mass, but how often do we stop to look more closely. The Lord's Prayer came in response to a request from Christ's Apostles: "Lord, teach us to pray just as John taught his disciples." (Luke 11:1). The Apostles asked Jesus about prayer because they were anxious to follow him in every way. They also saw how prayer renewed Jesus himself in body and spirit.

"Run through all the words of the holy prayers [in Scripture]," wrote Saint Augustine, "and I do not think that you will find anything in them that is not contained and included in the *Lord's Prayer*." At right is the Latin form.

Pater noster, qui es in caelis:
sanctificetur nomen tuum;
adveniat regnum tuum;
fiat voluntas tua, sicut in caelo, et in terra.
Panem nostrum quotidianum da nobis hodie;
et dimitte nobis debita nostra,
sicut et nos dimittimus debitoribus nostris;
et ne nos inducas in tentationem;
sed libera nos a malo.
Amen.

## The Seven Petitions of the *Lord's Prayer*

| | Blessing | Adoration | Praise | Petition | Intercession | Thanksgiving |
|---|---|---|---|---|---|---|
| Hallowed be Thy Name | We use God's name with respect. | We adore God because everything about him is holy. | We praise God with our words and deeds. | | | |
| Thy Kingdom come | We bless God since he sent Jesus, our Redeemer and King. | We adore Jesus. He really is the Son of God and our King. | We praise God for his faithfulness; he sent the promised redeemer. | We ask God's help in welcoming the Kingdom. | | We thank God for His Kingdom. It's in our midst and continuing to take root among us. |
| Thy will be done on earth as it is in heaven | Like Jesus, we pray to know and do the Father's will. | We worship God, Our Father. We know that His will is best. | We try to obey God's will; we know this also praises God. | We pray to know and do God's will. | We pray that others see and accept God's sovereignty and will in their lives. | We thank God that we have the Church and Sacraments to help us see and follow his will. |
| Give us this day our daily bread | | | | We ask our Father for the things we need. | We pray for our brothers and sisters who are hungry and in need. | We thank God that it is he who answers our needs. |
| And forgive us our trespasses | | | | We ask for forgiveness for our own sins. | We pray for others who need God's mercy and forgiveness. | Trusting in God's merciful heart, we thank him for welcoming us home. |
| And lead us not into temptation | We bless God, the source of all that is good and holy. | We adore God, our Creator. He created us and knows we are good. | We praise God who will never abandon us. | We ask God and the Church for strength against evil. | We pray for the conversion of others so that they know God's love and mercy. | |
| But deliver us from evil | | | We praise Jesus who delivers us all from evil. | We ask God to save us from sickness and sin. | We pray for the protection of family, friends and people all over the world. | We thank God because Jesus conquered sin and death — for good. |

↗ Go to the student site at
**hs.osvcurriculum.com**

**prayer of intercession** bringing the needs of others to God and asking his help on their behalf

A **prayer of intercession** leads us to pray for others as Jesus did. "Since Abraham, intercession—asking on behalf of another—has been characteristic of a heart attuned to God's mercy. . . . In intercession, he who prays looks 'not only to his own interests, but also to the interests of others,' even to the point of praying for those who do him harm"[104] (CCC, 2635). Our interest in helping others should not stop just because we have done everything physically possible. The power of prayer reaches beyond our physical existence.

**prayer of thanksgiving** identifying those things for which you are grateful and giving thanks to God

Prayers of intercession are often made to Christ. "He is the one intercessor with the Father on behalf of all"[105] (CCC, 2634). Catholics also ask Mary and others in the Communion of Saints to join the one Body of Christ in our prayers of intercession. You can ask Mary and the saints in Heaven to pray just as you can ask your parents, relatives, or best friend to pray for you or someone you love.

Most of the prayers that we offer in the Prayer of the Faithful during Mass are prayers of intercession and petition. These prayers have also been known as General Intercessions. The Third Edition of the *Roman Missal,* which is the text of prayers for Mass, uses the terms Universal Prayer, Prayer of the Faithful, and Bidding Prayers.

A **prayer of thanksgiving** is marked by gratitude and giving thanks to God. Mystics and saints throughout history have spoken of the power of a grateful heart. There is so much to be grateful for, even in times of stress. The Letters of Saint Paul often begin and end with thanksgiving: "Give thanks in all circumstances; for this is the will of God in Christ Jesus for you" (1 Thessalonians 5:18). "Devote yourselves to prayer, keeping alert in it with thanksgiving" (Colossians 4:2).

The Mass contains many of these forms of prayer but thanksgiving is at the core of the Mass in the Eucharist. The Greek word for the Eucharist means "to give thanks." Therefore, at the core of the Paschal Mystery lies thanksgiving because hope is never lost, even at the darkest hour of our Christian faith. While we should never take for granted being thankful for the gifts of our life, being thankful in prayer when things go wrong becomes particularly important. Just as Adam and Eve demonstrated that we have the free will to turn our backs on God, the Paschal Mystery demonstrates that in the midst of great pain and suffering we have the free will to turn to God and give thanks.

**Define** What is a prayer of intercession?

**Distinguish** What is the first movement of the prayer of petition?

**APPLY**

The Prayer of the Faithful, or intercessions, are read every Sunday at Mass. They include specific prayer intentions, such as the healing of the sick, prayers for the dying, and prayers for people caught in terrible tragedies like tornados, hurricanes, and earthquakes. During Mass, they follow a particular order:

    a) for the needs of the Universal and local Church

    b) for public authorities and the salvation of the world

    c) for those oppressed by any need

    d) and for the local community

○ Write your own Prayer of the Faithful for each of these categories.

# Liturgy of the Hours

In a wonderful and timeless way, the *Liturgy of the Hours* incorporates the major forms of prayer throughout the day and week. Also known as the *Divine Office*, it is an official set of daily prayers for the Church and was originally intended for those in major orders—bishops, priests, and deacons as well as for some in religious communities. Those groups were obliged to pray the hours in the morning, evening, and before retiring for the night. The book used for this prayer practice is called the Breviary.

During Vatican II, however, the bishops emphasized the importance of the Liturgy of the Hours for the whole Church. In 1971, the *Divine Office* was published as the Liturgy of the Hours.

The Liturgy of the Hours is rooted in the Jewish tradition of praying at certain times of the day just as Jesus did. For years, monks organized their days around this prayer schedule which included seven canonical hours or times of prayer. They based their schedule on a line from Psalm 119:164: "Seven times a day I praise you for your righteous ordinances."

Today, the Liturgy of the Hours includes readings from the Old and New Testaments, prayers, canticles, hymns, petitions, and psalms. Most Catholics who practice this devotion use these prayer times: morning, mid-day, and evening.

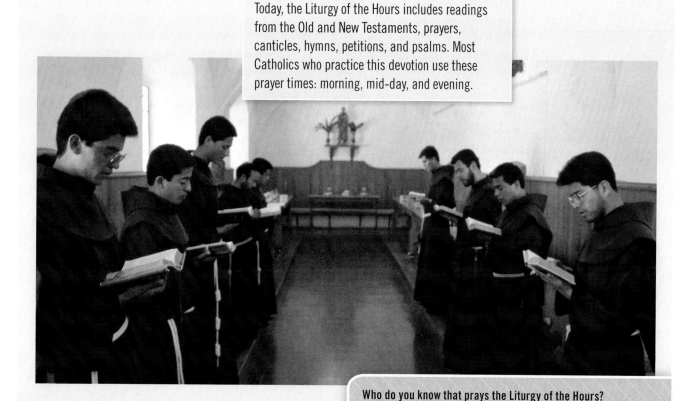

Who do you know that prays the Liturgy of the Hours?

How could you fit this prayer into your life?

What impact could this have on the Church's and the individual's relationships with God?

| Prayers of Virtue | |
|---|---|
| The prayers discussed each develop a different virtue within you. Indicate which virtue(s) each type of prayer cultivates for you. Some forms of prayer may cultivate more than one virtue. | |
| **Type of Prayer** | **Virtues:** humility, gratitude, wonder (or awe), trust, hope, compassion |
| blessing | |
| adoration | |
| praise | |
| petition | |
| intercession | |
| thanksgiving | |
| What type of prayer do you engage in most often? What type of prayer would you like to use more often? Which virtues would you like to cultivate within yourself? | |

> First of all, then, I urge that supplications, prayers, intercessions, and thanksgivings be made for everyone, for kings and all who are in high positions, so that we may lead a quiet and peaceable life in all godliness and dignity.
>
> —1 Timothy 2:1-2

The task when praying through your experience of the Paschal Mystery is to be intentional and sincere as you deliberately engage in prayer. Here's an example from Romans 12:15: "Bless those who persecute you; bless and do not curse them."

## Expressions of Prayer

When we reflect on the ways in which we pray, we find that there are three different expressions of prayer: vocal prayer, meditation, and contemplation. These three methods of prayer have one trait in common: "composure of heart," meaning they help us keep control of our heart's desires and focus on our true longing to love and serve God (see CCC, 2699). The Lord's Prayer forms the basis for the Church's understanding of the value of prayer.

> Vocal prayer is an essential element of the Christian life. To his disciples, drawn by their Master's silent prayer, Jesus teaches a vocal prayer, the Our Father. He not only prayed aloud the liturgical prayers of the synagogue but, as the Gospels show, he raised his voice to express his personal prayer, from exultant blessing of the Father to the agony of Gesthemani.[106]
>
> —CCC, 2701

### GO TO THE SOURCE

**Many of Jesus' parables referenced nature** such as the Parable of the Sower.

Read *Mark 4:1-20*.

- What are the different kinds of soil and how are they similar to the kinds of people one encounters?
- Explain which kind of soil is most analogous to you, and why.

Vocal prayer is raising our voice to pray. The longest vocal prayer, expressed by Jesus, is found in John 17:1-26. In this prayer, called the "priestly" prayer of Jesus, he "fulfills, from within, the great petitions of the Lord's Prayer: concern for the Father's name;[107] passionate zeal for his kingdom (glory);[108] the accomplishment of the will of the Father, of his plan of salvation;[109] and deliverance from evil"[110] (CCC, 2750).

Vocal prayer is the form most used by groups, but even prayer from within an individual uses a voice. "Prayer is internalized to the extent that we become aware of him 'to whom we speak.'[111] Thus vocal prayer becomes an initial form of contemplative prayer" (CCC, 2704). We join with others in verbal prayer during Mass and various prayer experiences. And some of us grew up in families where everyone was expected to offer a vocal prayer occasionally—like speaking a blessing over a meal.

Many people find quiet meditation to be their favorite expression of prayer. Meditation is a form of prayer in which you are engaged—using your intellect, imagination, and emotions.

The Church reminds us that, "There are as many and varied methods of meditation as there are spiritual masters. Christians owe it to themselves to develop the desire to meditate regularly, lest they come to resemble the first three kinds of soil in the parable of the sower.[112] But a method is only a guide; the important thing is to advance, with the Holy Spirit, along the one way of prayer: Christ Jesus" (CCC, 2707). The Church's living tradition of prayer includes various ways or schools of Christian spirituality. All of these are "precious guides for the spiritual life" (CCC, 2693).

Christian meditation is different from other forms of meditation, such as those found in eastern or "New Age" religions. In contrast to "Transcendental Meditation," Christian meditation is not about focusing within or emptying the mind, but rather focusing the mind on God and his word (for more information, see Letter To The Bishops Of

The Catholic Church On Some Aspects Of Christian Meditation from the Congregation for the Doctrine of the Faith). In Christian meditation "The mind seeks to understand the why and how of the Christian life, in order to adhere and respond to what the Lord is asking" Christian meditation takes some discipline because "The required attentiveness is difficult to sustain. We are usually helped by books . . ." (CCC, 2705).

Contemplative prayer is a form of solitude in which we let go of all of our images, thoughts, and emotions. We empty ourselves and take no action, allowing God to fill us. We sit and rest in the presence of Jesus.

Regardless of form, developing intimacy and communion with Jesus through prayer is an essential aspect in the life of a believer or disciple.

Saint Teresa of Avila describes contemplative prayer as "nothing else than a close sharing between friends; it means taking time frequently to be alone with him who we know loves us"[113] (CCC, 2709).

Besides the definition by Saint Teresa, the *Catechism* describes contemplative prayer as:

• the prayer of the child of God

• the prayer of the forgiven sinner who agrees to welcome God's love and wants to respond to it by loving even more

• a humble surrender to God's will

## GO TO THE SOURCE

**Let's look at the account of Martha and Mary.**

Read the story of Martha and Mary in *Luke 10:38-42*.

○ Who was praised for simply sitting in the presence of Jesus?

○ What was the focus of the other sister?

○ Which sister are you more like? Offer an example of this behavior.

# EUCHARISTIC Adoration

The Eucharist is a priceless treasure: by not only celebrating it but also praying before it outside of Mass we are able to make contact with the very wellspring of grace.

—Blessed Pope John Paul II

The presence of Christ in the Eucharist begins at the moment of consecration during Mass and lasts as long as the Blessed Sacrament exists. Christ is completely present in every part of the Eucharist (see CCC, 1377). The Church has always offered the Eucharist for adoration during Mass, but also outside of it. For adoration outside of Mass, the Eucharist is exposed with great care for the veneration of the faithful and often for carrying it in procession (see CCC, 1378).

Eucharistic adoration is a Catholic expression of faith that takes place in the presence of Christ in the Blessed Sacrament. Worship of the Eucharist outside of Mass begins with Exposition. Eucharistic Exposition provides us with the opportunity to worship the Lord in the Blessed Sacrament exposed in either a ciborium or monstrance, which are vessels that hold the Eucharist.

Exposition of the Blessed Sacrament begins after Mass and ends with Benediction. The priest approaches the altar where the Blessed Sacrament is exposed. When the Eucharist is exposed for worship, it is often placed in a luna, a circular gold container with glass sides. The luna containing the Blessed Sacrament is placed in the center of a large gold monstrance for our worship.

The priest genuflects and kneels, then incenses the Blessed Sacrament from the kneeling position. He stands and faces the Blessed Sacrament while praying the closing prayer. Then wearing the humeral veil, a scarf-like garment that covers his hands, the priest steps up and genuflects. He blesses the people using the monstrance or ciborium. The Blessed Sacrament is then placed into the tabernacle to end exposition.

There are some parishes that have perpetual adoration—the Exposition of the Blessed Sacrament twenty-four hours per day.

- a communion in which the Holy Trinity helps conform us "to his likeness"

- an intense time of prayer

- a gaze of faith fixed on Jesus

- hearing the Word of God

- silent love (see CCC, 2712-2717)

One of the biggest challenges to contemplative prayer is finding the time and place to enter into it. Once again, the duration of prayer will come from the heart. "One does not undertake contemplative prayer only when one has the time: one makes time for the Lord, with the firm determination not to give up, no matter what trials and dryness one may encounter. One cannot always meditate, but one can always enter into inner prayer, independently of the conditions of health, work, or emotional state. The heart is the place of this quest and encounter, in poverty and in faith" (CCC, 2710).

**Identify** How does Saint Teresa of Avila describe contemplative prayer?

**Conclude** Why is vocal prayer essential to Christian life?

## SECTION 2 REVIEW

### QUICK REVIEW

**1a.** **Recall** What kind of example did Jesus give us involving vocal prayer?

**b.** **Explain** What makes for a proper prayer of petition?

**2a.** **List** During Liturgy, our intercessions in the Prayer of The Faithful focus on what four groups (in proper order)?

**b.** **Summarize** What does the Church say about Christian meditation and the way it describes contemplative prayer?

**c.** **Connect** Describe some aspect of your past and present prayer life that was affirmed or challenged by something contained in this section.

**Pray and Act** Take at least ten minutes today to meditate on the Paschal Mystery.

### SELF-ASSESS

Which statement best reflects where you are now?

☐ I'm confident enough about the material in this section to be able to explain it to someone else.

☐ I have a good grasp of the material in this section, but I could use more review.

☐ I'm lost. I need help catching up before moving on.

# Prayer in Salvation History

The *Catechism* describes prayer as a two-way call between God and people. God always makes the initial call to "this mysterious encounter with Himself" (CCC, 2591). Thus there are two universal truths when it comes to prayer: *"Man is in search of God"* (CCC, 2566) and *"God calls man first"* (CCC, 2567).

As God gradually reveals himself to humankind, we see in Scripture prayer appearing as a reciprocal call and response in the stages of the covenant. "Through words and actions, this drama engages the heart. It unfolds throughout the whole history of salvation" (CCC, 2567). Scripture is a guide, in that it gives us models of praying in biblical figures and teaches us about prayer.

Prayer is found in the stories of Genesis through Abel's offering of the first-born of his flock and Noah's offering after the ark makes landfall. "In his indefectible covenant with every living creature,[114] God has always called people to prayer. But it is above all beginning with our father Abraham that prayer is revealed in the Old Testament" (CCC, 2569).

Abraham's prayer is expressed first by deeds. He is a man of silence who constructs an altar to the Lord at each stage of his journey. Only later does Abraham's prayer appear in words for the first time. This prayer includes Abraham's complaint to God. Abraham reminds God that he once promised him countless descendants, but he has no offspring. "Thus one aspect of the drama of prayer appears from the beginning: the test of faith in the fidelity of God" (CCC, 2570).

In the life of Moses, we find in particular two forms of prayer: contemplative and intercessory. "Moses' prayer is characteristic of contemplative prayer by which God's servant remains faithful to his mission. Moses converses with God often and at length, climbing the mountain to hear him and coming down to the people to repeat the words of his God for their guidance" (CCC, 2576). God made himself known to the Old Testament prophets in visions and dreams, but it was different with Moses. "He is entrusted with all my house. With him I speak face to face—clearly, not in riddles; and he beholds the form of the LORD" (Numbers 12:6-8).

'From this intimacy with the faithful God, slow to anger and abounding in steadfast love,[115] Moses drew strength and determination for his intercession. He does not pray for himself, but for the people whom God made his own.'

—CCC, 2577

The prayer life of King David formed the way in which Jesus prayed and, ultimately, the way in which we pray. One of the reasons David was considered such a great king is that he was truly "after God's own heart."

## GO TO THE SOURCE

**Read the following stories,** which illustrate how Moses and God interacted: *Exodus 17:8-13, Exodus 32:1-34, Numbers 12:1-15, and Numbers 21: 1-9.*

○ Summarize each of the stories and describe the way Moses intercedes on behalf of the people of Israel.

○ What do the stories teach us about prayer?

David offered praise along with repentance, and became a model for the prayer of the people.

> "His prayer, the prayer of God's Anointed, is a faithful adherence to the divine promise and expresses a loving and joyful trust in God, the only King and Lord.[116] In the Psalms David, inspired by the Holy Spirit, is the first prophet of Jewish and Christian prayer. The prayer of Christ, the true Messiah and Son of David, will reveal and fulfill the meaning of this prayer" (CCC, 2579).

**Describe** When we pray, what is always offered first?

**Contrast** Compare the prayer of Abraham and Moses.

## Elijah, the Prophets, and Conversion of the Heart

Remember that David's son Solomon built God a Temple. This had a major impact on the prayer life of the Israelites who, from the days of Moses, worshipped a God who had no permanent earthly home, other than the Ark of the Covenant. "For the People of God, the Temple was to be the place of their education in prayer: pilgrimages, feasts and sacrifices, the evening offering, the incense, and the bread of the Presence ('shewbread')—all these signs of the holiness and glory of God Most High and Most Near were appeals to and ways of prayer" (CCC, 2581).

However, having a home for God, which located their prayer in a specific place also had some unintended negative consequences. All of the ritual practices "often encouraged an excessively external worship. The people needed education in faith and conversion of heart; this was the mission of the prophets, both before and after the Exile" (CCC, 2581). Going through the motions of worship without acting with justice was empty faith. Elijah and the prophets called on the Israelites to repent and change their ways when some began worshipping the pagan god Baal.

## GO TO THE SOURCE

**Read the following stories about the prophets** who are called by God to intercede on behalf of the people of Israel: *Amos 7:1-6; Isaiah 6:5,8; Jeremiah 1:4-10.*

○ Summarize each one.

○ What does God relent from doing in Amos?

○ How do Isaiah and Jeremiah respond to God's call?

○ What do these passages reveal about prayer, the nature of God, and our relationship with God?

Elijah then came near to all the people, and said, 'How long will you go limping with two different opinions? If the Lord is God, follow him; but if Baal, then follow him.'

—1 Kings 18:21

The prophets expand our understanding of prayer by modeling a way to encounter God. "In their 'one to one' encounters with God, the prophets draw light and strength for their mission. Their prayer is not [a] flight from this unfaithful world, but rather attentiveness to The Word of God. At times their prayer is an argument or a complaint, but it is always an intercession that awaits and prepares for the intervention of the Savior God, the Lord of history"[117] (CCC, 2584).

# Blessed Pier Giorgio Frassati

**(1901–1925)**

In the thirteenth century, Saint Dominic surprised people when he said that speaking formal words was not the only acceptable form of prayer. He described multiple ways people could pray, including bowing before the altar, genuflecting, reading the Gospels, and making the Sign of the Cross while walking. It's likely that making the Sign of the Cross while walking might have been a favorite of Blessed Pier Giorgio Frassati.

Pier was born in 1901 into a wealthy Italian family. He was an energetic young man who loved the outdoors and belonged to many student groups. In addition, he was deeply involved in works of charity. He was known for giving his train money to the poor and then having to run home in time for dinner, or literally giving the coat off his back to a beggar. After his death, his family learned that among other charities, he supported an elderly woman, an invalid, and a widow with three children out of his own funds.

Pier loved mountain climbing and skiing. He often found God in the kind of physical prayer that Saint Dominic described. He wrote, "I left my heart on the mountain peaks and I hope to retrieve it this summer when I climb Mt. Blanc. If my studies permitted, I would spend whole days on the mountains admiring in that pure atmosphere the magnificence of God." Like Dominic, Pier understood that sometimes we engage our souls the most deeply in prayer when we engage our bodies in physical activity.

But Pier also appreciated the value of spoken prayers. He recited the rosary every day and always remained for a long time in prayer after receiving Communion. Some evenings he would spend the entire night on his knees lost in prayer before the Blessed Sacrament.

He contracted polio, but kept his illness hidden because his family was focused on attending to his dying grandmother. When his condition was finally revealed, it was too late. He died on July 4, 1925.

At his funeral, the streets were lined with thousands of poor and needy people that Pier had helped. On the poor's part, they were surprised to learn that the young man they had known as "Fra Girolamo" actually belonged to a very wealthy family. In the end, it was the poor, not Pier's family

or friends, who asked the Archbishop of Turin to start his cause for sainthood.

At his beatification Mass, Blessed Pope John Paul II said that Pier's life, "testifies that holiness is possible for everyone, and that only the revolution of charity can enkindle the hope of a better future in the hearts of people."

**Think About It** Blessed Pier lived the life of a typical student. How can someone become a saint by living such an ordinary life? In what ways have you encountered God in nature? What good things do you do that your friends and family might not be aware of?

Go to the student site at
**hs.osvcurriculum.com**

## The Psalms

The Psalms were used by the Israelites during their feasts in Jerusalem and on the Sabbath. Among all the Bible's prayers, the Psalms are unique. "Their prayer is inseparably personal and communal; it concerns both those who are praying and all men. . . . Their prayer recalls the saving events of the past, yet extends into the future, even to the end of history; it commemorates the promises God has already kept, and awaits the Messiah who will fulfill them definitively" (CCC, 2586). The Psalms were major sources of prayer for the first followers of Christianity because their faith grew out of Judaism. Today, we have the Liturgy of the Hours, which grew out of the Psalm prayer traditions of the early Church.

The Catechism reminds us that many expressions of prayer are found in the ancient Psalms. Saint Ambrose quotes David in asking "What is more pleasing than a psalm? . . . 'Praise the Lord, for a psalm is good: let there be praise of our God with gladness and grace!' Yes, a psalm is a blessing on the lips of the people, praise of God, the assembly's homage, a general acclamation, a word that speaks for all, the voice of the Church, a confession of faith in song"[118] (CCC, 2589).

**Recall** Where was God's first permanent earthly home?

**Infer** What is unique about the prayers we know as the Psalms?

SECTION **3 REVIEW**

**QUICK REVIEW**

**1a. Name** What are two universal truths about humanity and how are they connected to our understanding of what prayer is?

**b. Describe** How did David pray during his lifetime?

**2a. Recall** What did Elijah and the prophets call on the People of God to pray for?

**b. Connect** What do the Catechism and Saint Ambrose say about the ancient Psalms?

**ACT**

Compare and contrast the prayer of each of the following and point out how they were different.

○ Abraham and Moses

○ Elijah and the Prophets

**SELF-ASSESS**

Which statement best reflects where you are now?

☐ I'm confident enough about the material in this section to be able to explain it to someone else.

☐ I have a good grasp of the material in this section, but I could use more review.

☐ I'm lost. I need help catching up before moving on.

# The Defining Liturgical Moment

When we pray during liturgy, we proclaim the mystery of salvation in our hearts. Our prayer in liturgy is sometimes quiet and personal while remaining the public worship of the Church. It can also be spoken aloud with the whole community, through a confession of faith, a remembrance of the Paschal Mystery, or a confession of sinfulness. We pray prayers of blessing, petition, intercession, thanksgiving, and praise.

> Prayer internalizes and assimilates the liturgy during and after its celebration. Even when it is lived out 'in secret,'[119] prayer is always prayer of the Church; it is a communion with the Holy Trinity.[120]
>
> —CCC, 2655

Our liturgy remembers and proclaims the Paschal Mystery, from the Passion and Death to Jesus' Resurrection and Ascension. There is no better example of liturgy that communicates the mystery of salvation than the Easter Triduum, or three holiest days of the year:

- Day one is from sunset on **Holy Thursday** to sunset on Good Friday—the day of Jesus' Death

- Day two lasts from sunset on **Good Friday** to sunset on Holy Saturday and is the Paschal Sabbath, the day of rest

- Day three is from sunset on **Holy Saturday** until evening prayer on **Easter Sunday**. This includes the holiest night of the year, the vigil of Easter.

Holy Thursday's liturgy is known as the Mass of the Lord's Supper. This service commemorates the institution of the Sacrament of the Eucharist and includes the washing of feet. Good Friday's service is known as The Celebration of the Lord's Passion and includes the veneration of the Cross. The Easter liturgies are the Easter Vigil on Saturday evening and Easter Sunday services.

The Triduum begins on Holy Thursday evening with the **Mass of the Lord's Supper**. We trace our spiritual roots at this Mass, recalling how the blood of the Passover lamb saved the Israelites from death and freed them from slavery. On this night, we remember how Jesus told the Apostles that he was the new Passover lamb and that his blood would save us from death and free us to enjoy eternal life. We celebrate and recall the Last Supper, when Jesus changed bread and wine into his own body and blood and instituted the Eucharist. At this Mass, a foot washing is conducted as a sign of our willingness to serve others as

**Holy Thursday** beginning of the Triduum that celebrates Jesus as the new Passover Lamb on the Thursday before Easter

**Good Friday** recalls Jesus' Passion and Death on the Friday before Easter

**Holy Saturday** on the Saturday before Easter Sunday, this day symbolizes Jesus' time in the tomb after his Death

**Easter Sunday** the final day of the Triduum commemorating the Resurrection of Jesus Christ

**Mass of the Lord's Supper** the Mass celebrated on Holy Thursday evening remembering the Last Supper and the institution of the Sacrament of the Eucharist

Jesus did. After Mass, the Holy Eucharist is transferred to another location, an altar of repose, keeping in mind the Lord's final meal with his followers and anticipating his Death.

Good Friday is the one day of the year on which we do not actually celebrate Mass. We are asked to fast and pray during the day. We gather to read the Gospel account of Jesus' suffering, Passion, and Death. We venerate the Cross by bowing before it or praying before it. We may also receive Communion with the hosts consecrated at the Mass of the Lord's Supper on Holy Thursday. Afterward, the congregation leaves in silence and the altar is stripped, leaving the Cross and candles.

Sunset on Holy Saturday begins the third day of the Triduum. We commemorate the day Jesus spent in the tomb. The Church and the altar are bare.

On Easter Sunday, we celebrate the Resurrection with bright colors, songs of joy, and many lights. The Easter celebration begins on Holy Saturday night at the Easter Vigil. At this time, new catechumens and candidates are received into the Church through the Sacraments of Initiation.

**List** What are three holy days that are celebrated immediately before Easter?

**Analyze** What happens at the Mass of the Lord's Supper?

### Persevering in Prayer

We began this chapter with reasons why people fear going to their heart for prayer. It is fitting that we end with the Christian calling to persevere in prayer. Prayer requires effort and commitment, but the rewards are rich and infinite.

Our Catholic tradition is to begin and end each prayer with the Sign of the Cross. This one gesture summarizes our belief that full prayer is Trinitarian. We pray to God the Father, through the Son, and in the presence of the Holy Spirit.

Saint Paul captured it with these words: "Pray constantly . . . always and for everything giving thanks in the name of the Lord Jesus Christ to God the Father"[121] (CCC, 2742). In Paul's Letter to the Ephesians, he says, "Pray in the Spirit at all times in every prayer and supplication. To that end keep alert and always persevered in supplication for all the saints" (Ephesians 6:18).

We pray using the Scriptures and we pray asking for the help of Mary and the saints (see CCC 2679). The Church encourages us to learn about Jesus Christ through regular reading of the Scriptures. "Let them remember, however, that prayer should accompany the reading of Sacred Scripture, so that a dialogue takes place between God and man. For 'we speak to him when we pray; we listen to him when we read the divine oracles'"[122] (CCC, 2653). "Seek in reading and you will find in meditating; knock in mental prayer and it will be opened to you by contemplation"[123] (CCC, 2654).

We have learned to pray at set times, such as at Mass, but prayer can occur any time and any place. Jesus taught us that time is in his Father's hands. "It is in the present that we encounter him, not yesterday nor tomorrow, but today: 'O that today you would hearken to his voice! Harden not your hearts'"[124] (CCC, 2659).

The Lord's Prayer is a summary of the whole Gospel and the most perfect, or quintessential, prayer. Jesus taught his disciples to pray "Give us each day our daily bread" (Luke 11:3). He taught his disciples to be mindful of the present moment, the eternal now: "So do not worry about tomorrow, for tomorrow will bring worries of its own. Today's trouble is enough for today" (Matthew 6:34).

### IDENTIFY

○ Find out how Catholics of other cultures celebrate the Paschal Mystery with additional forms of prayer, adoration, meals, and devotions during the Easter Triduum.

# The Discipline of FASTING

When Jesus gave us these instructions about fasting properly, he didn't say *if* you fast, but *when* you fast. That's because fasting has always been a common form of prayer, and something spiritually serious people have done throughout history.

> When you fast, put oil on your head and wash your face, so that your fasting may be seen not by others but by your Father who is in secret; and your Father who sees in secret will reward you.
>
> —Matthew 6:17-18

For Catholics, fasting is one of the spiritual disciplines of Lent along with prayer and helping the poor. These work as a three-fold conversion practice as we prepare for Easter. Fasting adds a serious edge to your prayer life. It is a prayer practice that involves denying yourself something in order to increase your spiritual awareness, strengthen a commitment, or petition God for something you or another person really needs.

Fasting also is about detachment—separating yourself from something that you have become overly attached to. It's a way of reclaiming your spiritual strength and regaining some balance. Practicing some denial of our urges in small ways can help us grow in self-discipline and the ability to put off momentary comfort for a larger, more important goal.

See if you can identify the primary purpose of each of the following fasts:

- A wife and mother of three, whose husband has lost his job, silently decides to attend the 7:15 Mass on her way to work every morning instead of stopping at a coffee shop for her regular mocha latte and her fifteen minutes with the morning paper.
- Jesus, before starting his public ministry, goes to the desert and fasts for forty days.
- During the summer, a college sophomore decides to go unplugged for two weeks, staying off all things electric and electronic, and keeps a ten-day prayer journal.
- Three protesters in an Eastern European country go on a public hunger strike "until better working conditions are given to our people."
- A mother asks her eighth-grade son why he has stopped eating desserts. The son replies, "I wanna wait till dad gets home." His father is a soldier deployed in a war overseas.

Fasting should not be misused to gain praise or sympathy, to manipulate, or to harmfully affect the body. Done correctly, it can be a spiritual practice that can take your prayer to a new and different level.

**What has been your experience with fasting?**

**How might the Spirit be inviting you to fast now?**

**For what reason(s)?**

In the Lord's Prayer, we can call God our "Father" because Jesus, his Son, revealed him to us. The prayer brings us into unity with the Father and his Son because we develop the will to be like God. The Lord's Prayer ought to foster in us "a humble and trusting heart" (CCC, 2800).

Prayer is primarily about love. We pray because we know of God's love, and we pray so that we and others can live with love. "This love opens our hearts to three enlightening and life-giving facts about prayer . . . *It is always possible to pray . . . Prayer is a vital necessity . . . [and] Prayer and Christian life are inseparable*" (CCC, 2742-2745).

Persevering in prayer happens when we pray anywhere, anytime, everywhere, every time. "It is possible to offer fervent prayer even when walking in public or strolling alone, or seated in your shop . . . while buying or selling, . . . or even while cooking"[125] (CCC, 2743).

**Recall** According to Catholic tradition when do we make the Sign of the Cross?

**Elaborate** What is the meaning of "Give us this day our daily bread?"

## Praying your Paschal Mystery

This course now sets aside time for you to engage in prayer concerning some of your personal experiences of the Paschal Mystery. Select a few of the following experiences that you can relate to and engage in the prayers as they are described. Each one uses a thought designed to help us listen to God. They also include symbols, Scripture, and spiritual questions. Prayer begins with a focus on God first, then ourselves. These Paschal experience prayers are set up for you to do in class: seriously, silently, and/or entirely on your own.

### Broken hearted

Lord, *when have you felt broken-hearted?*

- Begin your prayer time by taking an index card and tearing it into pieces. Then place it on your desk or on the floor and study it for a minute. Calmly and slowly think about what has caused you to feel broken.

- Try to name your strongest emotion. Pick up a piece of the torn card and write your emotion on it.

- Get a Bible, slowly read Psalm 131. Imitate the psalmist by telling God what your heart is like right now. What are your eyes like these days? What have you been seeing? And how have you treated your soul?

- Slowly read Psalm 143:4-10. What do you remember about God's "deeds in the days of old?"

- When you are ready, stretch open your hands as described in verse 6 of the psalm and bow you head. Wait for God to place something in your hands: perhaps words of comfort, specific direction, wisdom, or new insights.

- When you have finished, go back to the torn piece of paper on which you named your strongest emotions. Turn it over and write down what God brought to you in this prayer.

- Hold onto the torn piece of paper, and return to it from time to time, read both sides of it, until you can tell that God has helped heal your brokenness.

## Emptiness

Lord, *help me understand how you emptied yourself on the Cross.*

- Begin your prayer time by getting an empty cup and holding it with both hands.

- As you look at the empty space inside the cup and the sight of your two hands holding it, take a few minutes "going inward" and name the emptiness that you are holding on to these days: Exactly what kind of emptiness do you feel? Can you name it? What did you once have plenty of? What have you lost, or run out of?

- When you have thought about it enough and have named it, turn the cup upside down and place it on the desk.

- Slowly Read Matthew 5:1-10.

- Think: Which line best describes you? The first Beatitude mentions the poor in spirit? Is that you? Or can you relate better to any of the other ones that Jesus mentions?

- Write it down on the bottom of the cup, and stand the cup right side up when you are finished.

- Slowly read and reflect on these two passages: Philippians 2:5-11 and Philippians 4:4-9. The first one describes how Jesus lived the Paschal Mystery. The second passage describes what you can do to get through your experience of the Paschal Mystery.

- Hold the empty cup in the palm of one hand and rest your hand on the desk or on your knee. Read *Philippians 4:8* again and follow Saint Paul's instructions. He lists eight specific things to identify and think about. Stop at each of the eight and try to call to mind something that resembles that trait. Once you do, imagine putting it in the cup. See if you can do this with all eight.

- When you are finished, write or draw something on the inside wall of the cup based on an insight you gained or a resolution you want make regarding your emptiness. Keep the cup to remind you of this insight or resolution, and remember that the source of your emptiness is listed on the other side of the cup's bottom.

## Vulnerability

Lord, *help me to recall the stormy times in your time among us.*

- Begin your prayer time by opening a small packet of salt and tasting a few grains. Let the taste stay in your mouth as a reminder of the ocean's saltwater.

- Slowly read and reflect on Psalm 107:23-32 and Psalm 55:1-9. Recall the stormy conditions of your life. Is there anything making your life stormy these days? If not, what caused it to be stormy in the past? What caused the rough weather? And how "seasick" are you feeling these days?

- Read Psalm 107:26-28 again. Why do you think they "cried out to the Lord in their distress"? What do you want to cry out to the Lord about your own distress or vulnerability? Close your eyes so you can do this in your mind's eye. When you are finished, keep your eyes closed in stillness for a few moments.

- Read Matthew 8:23-27 and Job 12:8-10. Pick out two or three words that stand out for you in this story. Take several minutes to think: What do these words say to you right now about your stormy journey? What do they say about Jesus and you? What do they say about getting through it?

- When you have finished, make the Sign of the Cross and take a few moments to examine your heart. In your own words ask God to calm the rough waters of your life. Spend a few moments being open to the Holy Spirit. When you are ready, use the Sign of the Cross as a way of closing your prayer and symbolizing your faith in God's help.

| Thanksgiving Prayer | | |
| --- | --- | --- |
| **Column A** | **Column B** | **Column C** |
| *"You O Lord"* | *"I"* | *"I"* |
| saved | know | thank |
| restored | believe | praise |
| gave | see | love |
| protected | understand | offer |
| helped | accept | proclaim |
| showed | trust | will remember |

**Thanksgiving**

Lord, *thank you for the good times and the hard times in my life.*

- Begin your prayer time by getting an index card and a pen.

- Recall your experience of God's goodness and grace. Take a few quiet moments to revisit the specific fears, challenges, needs, and emotions you were dealing with. Take a few minutes to review the way you sensed the Holy Spirit's help.

- Pick three or four excerpts from the following Psalms and slowly read about someone else's experience. Think about how you would capture your experience in words and give thanks: Psalms 30:12-14, 34:1-7, 92:1-5, 103:1-10, 116:1-9, 121, 136:1-9, 138:1-3.

Use the index card to write your own prayer of thanksgiving. Choose one word from each column and build a prayer that tells your story and expresses your feelings.

Go in any order you like, but use one word from each of the three columns.

- Make sure that your prayer reflects your past situation and expresses your thanks. Make as many verses as you like. Write the first draft on one side of the card and then a final draft on the other side.

- Psalms were sung or proclaimed to the people. You won't have to do that. But as a sign of your true gratitude, your teacher will ask you to either turn it in or post it somewhere. It is not necessary to put your name on it.

**Lost, stuck, or going the wrong way**

Lord, *help me to see the narrow path to you.*

- Begin your prayer time by getting a piece of string or twine and tying your shoes to each other while they are still on your feet.

- Quietly turn your legs to the side so you can study your shoes. Try to recall all the places they have been since you have owned them. Spend a few minutes silently letting the memories come back to you . . . places, events, people, laughter, struggles, etc.

- Then move your legs back under your seat so that your shoes are under you again. Focus on the frustrations you feel about the direction you are heading in them. What has happened now or in the past to cause you to feel lost, stuck in a rut, or heading in the wrong direction? Is it the result of some bad decisions or of too much indecision?

- To catch a quick review of the right path, read and reflect on Matthew 7:13,

Romans 12:2 and 9-18, and Galatians 5:7-26.

- Think: How would you describe the road you're on or the place you're at these days? What can you do to renew your mind? Who might you need to start traveling with? What can you do to travel the path of the Holy Spirit as described in Galatians?

- Come up with only one letter or two that represent a word to remind you of how to stay on the right road or get unstuck.

- Write the letter(s) on or inside your shoe. You now have a reminder every time you put those shoes.

## Fear, anxiety, stress

God, *how can I depend more on you?*

- Begin your prayer time by getting a rubber band.

- Let the rubber band symbolize something that you are fearful, anxious, or stressed about now, or maybe there is something that happened to you in the past where you had these emotions. Name the situation. The rubber band now represents that situation.

- Then stretch the rubber band in a length that resembles how much fear, anxiety, and stress you are feeling or had experienced as a result of the situation. When you think you've stretched it to accurately reflect your own degree of anxiety, hold it there for three seconds. Feel the tension in your hands. Feel the emotions inside you. Don't let the rubber band break.

- Relax the rubber band and put it on your left wrist.

- Slowly read and reflect on Matthew 6:25-34. Come up with one word that summarizes the truth Jesus is pointing out in this passage. Write the first letter of that word on the rubber band with a pen.

- Slowly read and reflect on Psalm 139:1-16. What emotion does the psalm suggest?

Write that word or the first letter of that word on your rubber band. Put the rubber band around your left wrist.

- Now find Romans 8:28-39. After you read it once stop for a moment and note the part that speaks out most clearly to you.

- Then go back and read only the first and last lines. (verse 28 and verses 38 and 39).

- If you share the beliefs written in these Scriptures, change the rubber band from your left wrist to your right, symbolizing your willingness to let God's grace help you move past your fear, anxiety, or stress.

- Read and re-read the words from the prophet Isaiah as often as you need to hear them: "For I, the Lord your God, hold your right hand; it is I who say to you, 'Do not fear, I will help you.'" (Isaiah 41:13).

### Reconciliation

Lord, *help me to let go of my resistance to forgive and reconcile with others.*

- Begin your prayer time by getting an adhesive bandage.

- Recall a situation or friendship that you need to reconcile or patch up. Consider your grudges as well as the pain and mistakes involved in that situation or friendship.

- When you are ready, slowly read and reflect on the whole chapter of 1 Corinthians 13.

- Which characteristic of love described in this passage challenges you to reconcile this situation or friendship?

- Unwrap the bandage as a sign of your openness to reconciliation.

- Slowly read and reflect on Matthew 6:14-15 and Luke 6:36-38. What verb describes the way you have approached this situation or friendship? What is to be gained by forgiving someone?

- Sit with the words of God that you just read about love, judgment, condemning, and forgiveness. Consider the hurt feelings and "cuts" that have been part of this situation or friendship.

- Let the bandage remind you of God's desire for you to move on and maybe even "patch things up." Do something symbolic with the bandage: Tape it inside your locker, put it in a pocket of your backpack so that you see it from time to time, or use it as a book mark.

- When the day comes and your pain has been healed or you have patched things up, throw away the bandage.

## SECTION 4 REVIEW

### QUICK REVIEW

**1. Define** What are the three days of the Easter Triduum and the focus of each day?

**2a. Explain** What does the Sign of The Cross symbolize?

**b. Clarify** How is prayer really about love?

### ACT

With a partner, explain one way this section has helped you with your prayer life.

### SELF-ASSESS

Which statement best reflects where you are now?

☐ I'm confident enough about the material in this section to be able to explain it to someone else.

☐ I have a good grasp of the material in this section, but I could use more review.

☐ I'm lost. I need help catching up before moving on.

# PRAYER

**Thanks Be to You, My Lord Jesus Christ**

Thanks be to you,
my Lord Jesus Christ,
for all the benefits and blessings
which you have given to me,
for all the pains and insults
you have borne for me.

O most merciful Friend,
Brother and Redeemer,
may I know you more clearly,
love you more dearly,
and follow you more nearly,
day by day, day by day.
Amen.

**Saint Richard of Chichester**
**Bishop of Chichester, England 1197–1253**

## TERMS

Use each of the following terms in a sentence that shows you know what the term means. You may include more than one term in a sentence.

Easter Triduum

prayer of blessing

prayer of adoration

prayer of praise

prayer of petition

supplication

prayer of intercession

prayer of thanksgiving

Holy Thursday

Good Friday

Holy Saturday

Easter Sunday

Mass of the Lord's Supper

## PEOPLE

Use information from the chapter to tell how each person modeled a different approach to prayer.

1. Abraham

2. Moses

3. David

4. Solomon

5. Elijah and The Prophets

## UNDERSTANDING

Answer each question and complete each exercise

### SECTION 1

1. **Recall** How are Christians able to stay in relationship with the living God?

2. **Imagine** How would prayer be different if it came only from the head instead of the heart?

3. **Select** Which do you think people fear the most and why: that the heart is too emotional or that their heart holds the truth about themselves?

4. **Evaluate** Of the reasons people avoid looking to their hearts for prayer, where does life's distractions rank?

### SECTION 2

5. **Recall** What is prayer of adoration?

6. **Identify** What is the form of prayer that faithfully recognizes God for his own sake and that gives him glory?

7. **Name** What is the highest form of petition?

8. **Elaborate** What is the best use of time in contemplative prayer?

### SECTION 3

9. **Explain** How was the way God revealed himself to Moses different from how he revealed himself to the prophets?

10. **Identify** Where did the ancient Israelites get their education in prayer at pilgrimages, feasts, and sacrifices?

11. **Recall** What did the ritual worship of the Israelites often lead to and how was this fixed?

12. **Summarize** How do the Psalms recall the past and extend into the future?

13. **Develop** How is the mystery of salvation communicated?

14. **Connect** When during the Easter Triduum is the sanctuary of the church bare and what aspect of the Paschal Mystery does it correspond to?

15. **Describe** What does the Sign of the Cross summarize?

16. **Elaborate** What does persevering in prayer mean?

## CONNECTING

**Visual** This photo shows a rosary hanging from a rearview mirror of a car.

What does this say about the prayer life of this person? What might other drivers think when they look over and see this car with the rosary on the mirror?

**Challenge** Your younger cousin says to you: "I believe in God, that he created everything, is in heaven, and is watching out for us and all that. But I don't see why people have to pray and go to Mass. All God wants is for people to be good to each other."

○ Based on what you have studied or experienced in this chapter, write a few sentences that support this sentence from the beginning of the chapter: "Prayer and *Christian life* are *inseparable*" (CCC, 2745).

**Imagine** What word, symbol, or image would you use to represent living the Paschal Mystery?

## SELF-ASSESS

**On Your Own** Make a list of the most important things you learned from this chapter. Select three things that represent your growth in understanding as you worked through this chapter. Write a paragraph explaining your choices.

**With a Partner** List what you found most helpful or interesting in this chapter as well as any other questions that have surfaced.

# THE BODY OF CHRIST

*And I tell you, you are Peter, and on this rock I will build my church, and the gates of Hades will not prevail against it. I will give you the keys of the kingdom of heaven, and whatever you bind on earth will be bound in heaven, and whatever you loose on earth will be loosed in heaven.*

—Jesus in Matthew 16:18-19

**As Catholics, we travel the journey** that Jesus asked his disciples to follow. We do it as a community of believers. Jesus made it clear that discipleship was not something to be lived on one's own in a "me and Jesus" relationship. He established the Church based on the rock of Saint Peter and the Apostles, and entrusted to them the Good News of salvation, his mission, and saving work. In every generation, through their successors, the Pope and bishops in union with him, continue to lead the Church and uphold her in the truth. Inspired by the Holy Spirit, the Pope and bishops hand on the faith of the Apostles until Christ returns in glory.

With Peter as their first universal leader, the Bible says the disciples "devoted themselves to the Apostles' teaching and fellowship, the breaking of the bread and to the prayers" (Acts 2:42). The "breaking of the bread" and "the prayers" refers to the celebration of the Eucharist. In so doing, the Apostles and disciples followed Jesus' command to "do this in memory of me." Catholicism traces its roots to Peter and the Apostles. It is a historical fact.

The Catholic Church preserves the special gifts given to Peter, the Apostles, and the disciples. These make us who we are and are at the center of our Catholic identity. However, we know that many expressions of holiness and truth exist outside the Church. Catholics base their faith and beliefs on Jesus' revelation of the Trinity, his founding of the Church, the Sacraments, Scripture and Tradition, and other gifts listed below. We root our Catholic belief in the Paschal Mystery—Jesus' Passion, death, Resurrection, and Ascension.

The gifts, given by Jesus to the Church, are described here in terms of "special characteristics." Taken together, they form the core of Catholic belief and practice. In a sense, they make us Catholic. These characteristics are consistent in Catholic Tradition from the time of the Apostles. They have not and will not change, no matter what's happening in society and the world. In every generation the Church passes them on to the next and teaches why they are important to understanding ourselves and our calling in life.

As we mature in faith, we better understand our Catholic identity; that is, what it means to be Catholic. Our faith is a way of life that is meant to permeate everything we do. In religion courses over the next several years, we'll study in detail these characteristics of Catholicism. We'll probe into the Church's teachings about them, and experience firsthand how each one enriches our faith.

## Characteristics of Catholicism

**1. The Church is Trinitarian.**

The great mystery of the Trinity—God the Father, God the Son, and God the Holy Spirit—permeates every aspect of Catholic belief, practice, and worship. Our understanding of Trinity is part of everything Catholics believe and do, including how we worship and pray. The Trinity is a unity of three equal, yet distinct, Persons, possessing the same divine nature. The Trinity is a divine community, from which all loving human communities take their origin. The communal nature of the Catholic Church is based in the Trinity.

The Trinity is the central mystery of our faith. Trinitarian belief roots who Catholics are, what we believe, how we pray, and what we teach. The Church administers the Sacraments using the Trinitarian formula. In the Rite of Baptism, for example, the bishop, priest, or deacon baptizes in the name of the Father, and of the Son, and of the Holy Spirit. The priest invokes the Trinity in the Eucharistic Liturgy, the Sacraments, and the Divine Office. Catholics begin and end their prayers with the Sign of the Cross, a reminder of our Baptism and the Trinity.

Every time the Church celebrates the Eucharist, we remember the reality of Trinitarian love, witnessed in Jesus' eternal sacrifice, which he offered to the Father through the Holy Spirit. In the Eucharist, we receive Jesus, really present, Body and Blood, soul and divinity. Church members are united to Christ and one another. Together we form the Mystical Body of Christ.

## Characteristics of Catholicism

**2. The Church is Christ-centered.**

The Catholic faith centers on Jesus Christ " …the eternal Son of God made man" (*Catechism of the Catholic Church*, 423). Jesus is the Alpha and the Omega, the beginning and end of all things. Jesus is the heart and center of the Catholic faith. He is the way, the truth, and the life. He reveals deep mysteries of the Triune God, heads the Church, shows us the moral path to salvation, and gives us the Sacraments as means to salvation. He teaches us about his Father and sends the Holy Spirit to be with us always.

Because of his great love, Jesus died on the cross for our sins and rose from the dead. He left us a perpetual reminder of his sacrifice in the Mass, when he is present among us, Body and Blood, soul and divinity. Jesus invites us into an intimate relationship of friendship with him, encourages us to praise the Triune God, and tells us to ask God for help in our needs. He promises eternal life to his faithful followers.

**3. The Church is a community.**

Jesus gifted us with the love that the three Persons in the Trinity share with each other. He founded his Church on the divine love that the Trinity has for humankind. United in the Holy Spirit, this Pilgrim People lives in the world, as Jesus did, but aspires for a more fulfilling happiness than this world provides. The Church anticipates Jesus' coming again and our eternal reward in Heaven.

The Trinity, a communion of love, shares divine grace through the Church, which is the Sacrament of the Trinity's unity with the People of God. The Church gives us the age-old teachings and practices that keep us on the right path. These are Jesus' gifts to us. Indeed, Catholicism is lived out in community, following Jesus' way and inspired by the Holy Spirit that praises and honors the Father in appreciation for what we received.

Catholics on Earth are united in faith and love with the saints in Heaven and the souls in Purgatory. We call this the "Communion of Saints." Every Sunday at Mass, we pray in the Creed: "I believe in the communion of saints." After Mass, some Catholics remain and pray the Rosary or before a statue of a saint. Our grandparent, aunt, or uncle may have a prayer table at home with a picture of a deceased loved one and a candle. Because we on Earth are united with the saints in Heaven and the souls in Purgatory, we ask all our friends to pray for us—those living on Earth, those being purified in Purgatory, and those rejoicing forever in Heaven.

**4. The Church is sacramental.**

Jesus is the fundamental Sacrament and most fully reveals God to us. The Catholic Church is a sacramental people. She carries on Christ's work on Earth and communicates his message and way of life through her teaching, social ministries, and liturgy. The seven Sacraments of the Catholic Church continue to celebrate Jesus' Paschal Mystery, each one celebrating a special aspect of this Mystery. The Sacraments are holy signs of God's desire to be one with us. For example, Baptism gives us the new life of grace, as we are reborn as sons and daughters of God. Matrimony reflects God's desire to share his love in the love that a husband and wife have for each other. Every Sacrament celebrates God's love and invites us into a special relationship with Jesus through the Sacrament celebrated.

Sacramental belief is fundamental to who we are and what we do as Catholics. The Sacraments help us fulfill our spiritual needs and draw us into relationship with Christ and one another. Instituted by Christ to give us grace, the seven Sacraments are outward signs of this grace. They use rituals and symbols reflecting the holy presence of the divine.

As concrete actions rooted in the things that we use daily (water, bread, wine), Sacraments do two things: they point beyond themselves to something else—a sacred reality—and they bring about what they signify by making that reality present—new life, healing, forgiveness, membership, and so on. We know that Sacraments point to something else, but often we forget that they bring about or effect what they signify. For example, the Anointing of the Sick brings about spiritual and sometimes physical healing.

Catholic sacramentality goes beyond the seven Sacraments. Rooted in them, we celebrate other sacred signs of God's love, called sacramentals. They bear a certain resemblance to the Sacraments, but are given to us by the Church, not Christ. Catholics walk into a Catholic Church, dip their hand into holy water, and make the Sign of the Cross. We genuflect or bow to Jesus, present in the tabernacle, before entering the pew and kneeling down. Some Catholics focus on the life-sized crucifix hanging above the altar. During Advent, we see a wreath with four candles at the front of the church. During Easter, we see a large, white Paschal candle near the altar. If we attend a Baptism, we see oils and water. Catholics use colors, symbols, and actions that speak to us in ways that don't require words.

**5. The Church is Eucharistic.**

The root meaning of Eucharist in Greek means "thanksgiving." Our thanksgiving rests in the great sacrifice that Jesus offered for us on the cross, which we celebrate in the Eucharist.

As a sacramental community, Catholics root everything in the Eucharist. All the other Sacraments lead to it and flow from it. The Eucharist is the source and summit of our lives. Catholics also call the celebration of the Eucharist "Mass." The Eucharist is not simply a symbolic reminder of Jesus' sacrifice. Christ is present in this celebration in special ways. He is present in the community gathered together, in the Word proclaimed, in the person of the priest-celebrant, and most especially in the consecrated Eucharistic species, Jesus' Body and Blood.

By "Real Presence" we mean that the Eucharist is the real presence of Christ, whole and entire, under the appearances of bread and wine. While a memorial of Jesus' sacrifice on the cross, the Eucharist is more than just that. It is Christ's real presence.

In a wide sense, Catholics realize that we can be "eucharist" to each other when we share God's love with others. Since God dwells within us, we give thanks for the blessings we received by sharing our gifts with our brothers and sisters.

**6. The Church is biblically based.**

The *Catechism* says, ". . . the Church has always venerated the Scriptures as she venerates the Lord's Body . . . . In Sacred Scripture, the Church constantly finds her nourishment and her strength, for she welcomes it not as a human word, 'but as what it really is, the word of God'" (CCC, 103–104). These words indicate the importance of Scripture for Catholics.

The early Church saw the Old Testament as containing the revelation of God's plan of salvation for humankind. They recognized the unity of this plan in the Old and New Testaments, studied the prophecies of a coming messiah, and showed how Jesus fulfilled them. New Testament writers wrote down faithfully the teachings of Jesus and interpreted the Old Testament in light of his death and Resurrection (see CCC, 129).

New Testament writers, under the inspiration of the Holy Spirit, testified to the faith of the early Christian community. The New Testament must be interpreted in light of this faith, passed down to us in the Church's Tradition. Scripture and Sacred Tradition are bound closely together, as two distinct modes of transmitting God's Revelation.

Catholics cherish the Scripture, read it, and use it in their prayers. The Church's Liturgy of the Hours and the Sacraments, and especially the Mass, contain readings from both New and Old Testaments. The Church encourages Catholics to read and study the Scriptures as key sources of spiritual nourishment and growth.

**7. The Church is one.**

There are four marks of the Church, that is, essential identifying characteristics by which she is known—one, holy, catholic, and apostolic. The descriptions that follow, like all the summaries in this section, are overviews to give the general sense of each.

"*The Church is one because of her source*: 'the highest exemplar and source of this mystery is the unity, in the Trinity of Persons, of one God, the Father and the Son in the Holy Spirit'" (CCC, 813).

"*The Church is one because of her 'soul'*: 'It is the Holy Spirit, dwelling in those who believe and pervading and ruling over the entire Church, who brings about that wonderful communion of the faithful and joins them together so intimately in Christ that he is the principle of the Church's unity'" (CCC, 813).

The Church is one Body in Christ, in faith, in the Sacraments, and in hope (see CCC, 866). The Church is formed and united through the work of the Holy Spirit and under the leadership of the bishops united with the bishop of Rome, the Pope.

**8. The Church is holy.**

"The Church . . . is . . . holy. This is because Christ, the Son of God, who with the Father and the Spirit is hailed as 'alone holy,' loved the Church as his Bride, giving himself up for her so as to sanctify her . . . . The Church, then, is 'the holy People of God . . . .'" (CCC, 823)

The Church is made holy because of her union with Christ; in turn, she makes others holy. She disseminates through her ministries the graces won by Jesus on the cross that make us holy. The Church, then, is holy in her members.

**9. The Church is catholic (universal).**

The Church is catholic in two ways. "First, the Church is catholic because Christ is present in her . . . . Secondly, the Church is catholic because she has been sent out by Christ on a mission to the whole of the human race" (CCC, 830-831).

Jesus dwells in the Catholic Church. Through his Holy Spirit he energized the Church to live and act in his name. The Church is for all people, everywhere. We are called to share the Good News by what we say and how we act. The Church's missionary work continues today, as the Holy Spirit guides her to go "to the ends of the earth" (Acts 1:8) to preach, baptize, and minister in Jesus' name.

**9. The Church is catholic (universal).** *continued*

Wherever we go, Catholics profess the same beliefs and celebrate the same Sacraments, under the leadership of the Pope and bishops. When at Mass, no matter where we are, we can recognize it as the same Mass as the one in our parish. Its style, language, or music may differ, but it is the same Mass, because Jesus himself again offers his eternal sacrifice to the Father, through the ministry of the priest.

Catholicism accepts people from every place and walk of life. If we want to attend Mass every day, welcome to the Catholic Church. If we want to pray the Rosary, this is a great Catholic blessing. If we want to study the Bible, the Church encourages it on all levels. If we want to serve the poor, this is a prime commitment of the Catholic Church. The Church unites diverse spiritual traditions, interests, devotions, and practices under the essential teachings of our faith.

**10. The Church is apostolic.**

The Church is founded and built on Peter and the twelve Apostles. After his Ascension, Jesus led the Church through Peter and the other Apostles. When they died, his leadership continued through their successors, namely the Pope and the bishops acting in union with him. Pope Benedict XVI succeeded Blessed Pope John Paul II, who succeeded Pope John Paul I, who succeeded Pope Paul VI, who succeeded Pope John XXIII. This line of Popes can be traced historically all the way back to Saint Peter, the first Pope.

The Catholic community is apostolic because we can trace our roots back to Peter and the Apostles and those who came after them. We are the sole Church led and united by the Pope and bishops, and ministered to by the ordained ministry of bishops, priests, and deacons. We profess in the Creed that the Church is one, holy, catholic, and apostolic.

Consecrated brothers and sisters and the laity exercise other important kinds of leadership. Lay ministry today has a big impact on the Catholic Church in the United States. There are lay and consecrated religious diocesan chancellors, canon lawyers, pastoral administrators, pastoral team members, liturgists, musicians, catechists, servers, readers, and others.

National Catholic organizations, social agencies, hospitals, diocesan staffs, pastoral councils, finance councils, youth organizations, and more help to bring Jesus' message to all people. Catholicism has a clear leadership and organizational structure to which many different Church ministries contribute and share in the Church mission.

**11. The Church advocates justice for all.**

Many Catholic organizations serve those in need. Catholic Charities provides direct aid to people in need as a result of various circumstances or natural disasters. Catholic Relief Services works around the world as an advocate for change, empowering people to overcome such things as poverty and armed conflict. Bishops lead national discussions about stopping the nuclear arms race and opposing abortion and euthanasia. They speak out on matters of social justice. The Church encourages her members to perform works of mercy by reaching out to the needy in our midst. She also advocates acts of social justice that challenge unjust social structures that keep people impoverished.

The Catholic Church emphasizes seven principles of social justice. They are: 1) life and dignity of the human person; 2) the rights and responsibilities of humans; 3) call to family, community, and participation; 4) option for the poor and vulnerable; 5) dignity of work and the rights of workers; 6) solidarity of the human family; and 7) care for God's creation.

**12. The Church has a positive view of creation, the world, and human nature.**

The Original Sin of Adam and Eve wounded creation. We are born into a flawed and imperfect world. Catholics believe that this world is not totally corrupt. God is very much present, and we recognize his presence in creation's beauty, truth, and love. We are made in the image of God and enter life with both goodness and imperfection.

To be saved, we need God's grace won by Jesus' death on the cross. As we reflect on our true meaning on Earth, we rely on our faith and reason to know more about God and our eternal destiny. Through faith and reason we probe more deeply into the world and human nature. In so doing, we discover how the Spirit is leading us.

For Catholics, faith and reason are partners. Catholicism fully accepts the Bible as God's word and welcomes ongoing biblical study and discussion. Often new insights come by using our reason to probe into the mysteries revealed in Scripture.

Catholics have always affirmed the importance of both faith and reason. Both are central to us and interconnected. Although we can come to certain knowledge of God's existence through reason alone, knowledge of the divine mysteries requires both faith and reason.

# HOW TO READ THE BIBLE

**The Catholic Church teaches** that the Bible is the inspired Word of God, that *"God is the author of Sacred Scripture."* Through the Holy Spirit, various people were called to use their talents to write down "whatever he wanted written, and no more" (CCC, 105-106; *DV*, 11).

Saint Paul called the Church the "pillar and foundation of the truth" (1 Timothy 3:15). Let's look at what the Church teaches about interpreting and applying Scripture:

### Take into account the time period, culture, and kind of writing.

While the meaning of Sacred Scripture is timeless, each book of the Bible was written in a particular time, place, and style (see CCC, 110). For example, some parts of the Bible are letters from one person to another, or to groups of people, others are written accounts of events that occurred in the lives of God's People, still other portions of Scripture are poems and songs. All of these were written down by people who lived in a particular period and cultural context, but all of the writers of the Bible were inspired by the Holy Spirit in order to guarantee that what was written would teach us the lessons God willed for us to learn through Scripture.

### Read parts of Scripture in the context of the whole message.

The Bible is made up of parts that vary in literary style and tone, but it is also unified because the parts all point toward God's Divine Plan for salvation, with Jesus Christ as the center and heart (see CCC, 112).

### "Read the Scripture within 'the living Tradition of the whole Church'" (CCC, 113).

It is important to remember that as Catholics, we base our faith not on a book, but on the living Word of God, which is present in both Scripture and Sacred Tradition (see 2 Thessalonians 2:15). We understand God's words not only through Scripture but also through the many people who taught Scripture through the generations.

### Pay special attention to the truths of faith expressed in Scripture.

Great truths are always consistent with one another. For example, both the Old and New Testaments present love for God and love for one's neighbor as guiding principles of God's Law.

### Know the senses of Scripture.

To truly understand Scripture, we should pay attention to both the literal and the spiritual meanings (see CCC, 115). There are three categories of the spiritual sense (117):

> *The allegorical sense:* An allegory uses characters or events to symbolize an idea or principle. The *Catechism* speaks of the crossing of the Red Sea as an allegory of Baptism. The Israelites crossed the Red Sea to freedom from captivity in Egypt. We enter into the waters of Baptism and are freed from the captivity of sin.

> *The moral sense:* The moral sense of Scripture is the way in which Scriptures teach us lessons about right and wrong.

> *The anagogical sense:* This gives us signs of eternal things. The *Catechism* points out that the Church on Earth is a sign of God's eternal Kingdom in Heaven.

Knowing how to read and interpret Scripture helps us to hear God's truth.

# CATHOLIC PRAYERS AND PRACTICES

*Prayer and Christian life are inseparable, for they concern the same love and the same renunciation, proceeding from love; the same filial and loving conformity with the Father's plan of love; the same transforming union in the Holy Spirit who conforms us more and more to Christ Jesus; the same love for all men, the love with which Jesus has loved us.*

—Catechism of the Catholic Church, 2745

**The following prayers and practices** are based in Sacred Scripture and have evolved through Church Tradition. Some wording in these creeds changed when the Third Edition of the *Roman Missal* was introduced in November 2011.

## Apostles' Creed

*The Apostles' Creed contains a summary of the faith of the Apostles. It was developed from an early baptismal creed, and has existed since the second century. It was modified by early Church councils.*

I believe in God,
   the Father almighty,
   Creator of heaven and earth,
   and in Jesus Christ, his only Son, our Lord,

*At the words that follow, up to and including
the Virgin Mary, all bow.*

   who was conceived by the Holy Spirit,
   born of the Virgin Mary,
   suffered under Pontius Pilate,
   was crucified, died and was buried;
   he descended into hell;
   on the third day he rose again from the dead;
   he ascended into heaven,
   and is seated at the right hand of God the Father almighty;
   from there he will come to judge the living and the dead.
I believe in the Holy Spirit,
   the holy catholic Church,
   the communion of saints,
   the forgiveness of sins,
   the resurrection of the body,
   and life everlasting. Amen.

## Nicene Creed

*The Nicene Creed was formed as a response to the Arian heresy, which denied the divinity of Christ. It takes its name from the city of Nicea, site of the First Council of Nicea in A.D. 325. The original creed underwent modifications at ecumenical councils in Constantinople in A.D. 381 and Chalcedon in A.D. 451.*

I believe in one God,
   the Father almighty,
   maker of heaven and earth,
   of all things visible and invisible.
I believe in one Lord Jesus Christ,
   the Only Begotten Son of God,
   born of the Father before all ages.
   God from God, Light from Light,
   true God from true God,
   begotten, not made, consubstantial with the Father;
   through him all things were made.
For us men and for our salvation
   he came down from heaven,

*At the words that follow up to and including
and became man, all bow.*

   and by the Holy Spirit was incarnate of the Virgin Mary,
   and became man.
For our sake he was crucified under Pontius Pilate,
   he suffered death and was buried,
   and rose again on the third day
   in accordance with the Scriptures.
He ascended into heaven
   and is seated at the right hand of the Father.
He will come again in glory
   to judge the living and the dead
   and his kingdom will have no end.
I believe in the Holy Spirit, the Lord, the giver of life,
   who proceeds from the Father and the Son,
   who with the Father and the Son is adored and glorified,
   who has spoken through the prophets.
I believe in one, holy, catholic and apostolic Church.
I confess one Baptism for the forgiveness of sins
   and I look forward to the resurrection of the dead
   and the life of the world to come. Amen.

## Glory to the Father

Glory to the Father,
and to the Son,
and to the Holy Spirit,
as it was in the beginning
is now, and ever shall be
world without end.
Amen.

## Gloria Patri

Glória Patri,
et Fílio
et Spíritui Sancto,
Sicut erat in princípio,
et nunc et semper
et in sáecula saeculórum.
Amen.

## Prayer to the Holy Spirit

Come, Holy Spirit, fill the hearts of your faithful.
And kindle in them the fire of your love.
Send forth your Spirit and they shall be created.
And you shall renew the face of the earth.
Let us pray:
Lord, by the light of the Holy Spirit
you have taught the hearts of your faithful.
In the same Spirit, help us to choose what is right
and always rejoice in your consolation.
We ask this through Christ our Lord.
Amen.

Veni, Sancte Spiritus, reple tuorum corda fidelium,
et tui amoris in eis ignem accende.
Emitte Spiritum tuum et creabuntur;
Et renovabis faciem terrae.
Oremus:
Deus, qui corda fidelium Sancti Spiritus illustratione
    docuisti.
Da nobis in eodem Spiritu recta sapere,
et de eius semper consolatione gaudere.
Per Christum Dominum nostrum.
Amen.

## The Hail Mary

*Beginning with Mary's unique cooperation with the working of the Holy Spirit, the Churches developed their prayer to the holy Mother of God, centering it on the person of Christ manifested in his mysteries. In countless hymns and antiphons expressing this prayer, two movements usually alternate with one another: the first "magnifies" the Lord for the "great things" he did for his lowly servant and through her for all human beings;[126] the second entrusts the supplications and praises of the children of God to the Mother of Jesus, because she now knows the humanity which, in her, the Son of God espoused. This twofold movement of prayer to Mary has found a privileged expression in the Ave Maria (CCC, 2675–2676).*

Hail, Mary, full of grace,
The Lord is with thee.
Blessed art thou among women
and blessed is the fruit of thy womb, Jesus.
Holy Mary, Mother of God,
pray for us sinners,
now and at the hour of our death.
Amen.

## Act of Contrition (traditional)

O my God, I am heartily sorry for
having offended you, and I detest
all my sins, because of your just
punishments, but most of all
because they offend you, my God,
who are all good and deserving of
all my love. I firmly resolve, with
the help of your grace, to sin no
more and to avoid the near
occasion of sin.

## Act of Contrition (contemporary)

My God, I am sorry for my sins with
all my heart. In choosing to do
wrong and failing to do good, I have
sinned against you whom I should
love above all things. I firmly intend,
with your help, to do penance, to sin
no more, and to avoid whatever
leads me to sin. Our Savior Jesus
Christ suffered and died for us. In his
name, my God, have mercy.

## The Rosary

*The Rosary is called the* Psalter of Mary *because all fifteen of its mysteries, with their 150* Aves, *correspond to the number of Psalms. Saint Dominic popularized the fifteen-decade Rosary. He is so connected with this form of the Rosary that often it is referred to as the Dominican Rosary. Pope John Paul added five luminous mysteries to the previous fifteen glorious, joyful, and sorrowful mysteries.*

*The Rosary is the most well-known and used form of chaplet (a devotion using beads; from a French word meaning "crown" or "wreath"). There are other chaplets, including Saint Bridget's Chaplet and the Chaplet of the Immaculate Conception.*

1. Sign of the Cross and Apostles' Creed
2. Lord's Prayer
3. Three Hail Marys
4. Glory to the Father
5. Announce mystery
6. Lord's Prayer
7. Ten Hail Marys
8. Glory to the Father

*Repeat last four steps, meditating on the other mysteries of the rosary.*

## The Mysteries of the Rosary and Recommended Scriptural Meditations

### Joyful Mysteries
(Mondays and Saturdays)
1. The Annunciation (humility)
   Isaiah 7:10-14; Luke 1:26-38
2. Visitation (charity)
   Isaiah 40:1-11; Luke 1:39-45; John 1:19-23
3. The Nativity (poverty)
   Micah 5:1-4; Matthew 2:1-12; Luke 2:1-20; Galatians 4:4
4. The Presentation (obedience)
   Luke 2:22-35; Hebrews 9:6-14
5. The Finding of Jesus in the Temple (piety)
   Luke 2:41-52; John 12:44-50; 1 Corinthians 2:6-16

### Sorrowful Mysteries
(Tuesdays and Fridays)
1. The Agony in the Garden (repentance)
   Matthew 26:36-46; Mark 14:26-42; Luke 22:39-53; John 18:1-12
2. The Scourging at the Pillar (purity)
   Isaiah 50:5-9; Matthew 27:15-26; Mark 15:1-15
3. The Crowning with Thorns (courage)
   Isaiah 52:13–53:10; Matthew 16:24-28, 27:27-31; Mark 15:16-19; Luke 23:6-11; John 19:1-7
4. The Carrying of the Cross (patience)
   Mark 8:31-38; Matthew 16:20-25; Luke 23:26-32; John 19:17-22; Philippians 2:6-11
5. The Crucifixion (self-renunciation)
   Mark 15:33-39; Luke 23:33-46; John 19:23-37; Acts 22:22-24; Hebrews 9:11-14

### Glorious Mysteries
(Sundays and Wednesdays)
1. The Resurrection (faith)
   Matthew 28:1-10; Mark 16:1-18; Luke 24:1-12; John 20:1-10; Romans 6:1-14; 1 Corinthians 15:1-11
2. The Ascension (hope)
   Matthew 28:16-20; Luke 24:44-53; Acts 1:1-11; Ephesians 2:4-7
3. The Descent of the Holy Spirit Upon the Apostles (love)
   John 14:15-21; Acts 2:1-11; 4:23-31; 11:15-18
4. The Assumption (eternal happiness)
   John 11:17-27; 1 Corinthians 15:20-28, 42-57; Revelation 21:1-6
5. The Coronation of Mary (Marian devotion)
   Matthew 5:1-12; 2 Peter 3:10; Revelation 7:1-4, 9-12; 21:1-6

### Luminous Mysteries
(Thursdays)
1. Baptism in the Jordan (commitment)
   Matthew 3:13-17; Mark 1:9-11; Luke 3:21-22; John 1:29-34
2. The Wedding at Cana (fidelity)
   John 2:3-5, 7-10; John 13:14-15; Luke 6:27-28, 37; Luke 9:23; John 15:12
3. Proclamation of the Kingdom of God (conversion)
   Mark 1:14-15; Luke 4:18-19, 21; Matthew 5:38-39, 43-44; Matthew 6:19-21; Matthew 7:12; Matthew 10:8
4. The Transfiguration (promise)
   Matthew 5:14, 16; Matthew 17:1-2, 5, 7-8; Luke 9:30-33; John 1:4-5, 18; 2 Corinthians 3:18
5. Institution of the Eucharist (grace)
   John 13:1; Matthew 26:18; Luke 22:15-16, 19-20; Matthew 5:14, 19-20; 1 Corinthians 11:26; John 17:20-21; 1 Corinthians 12:13, 26-27

# GLOSSARY

## A

**agape** describes selfless love that is concerned for the well-being of another, an unconditional gift of oneself, serving others, or making a sacrifice for others (p. 13)

**anthropomorphic** described as attributing human characteristics to an object or a being who is not human (p. 46)

**Ascension** the ascent of Christ into Heaven forty days after his Resurrection (p. 140)

**Assumption** the teaching affirming that at the end of her life, Mary was taken up, body and soul, into Heaven (p. 143)

## C

**cardinal virtues** the moral virtues of prudence, justice, fortitude, and temperance (p. 189)

**compassion** a feeling of empathy for another who is suffering that results in solidarity or a "suffering with" the other (p. 159)

**conscience** "the interior voice of a human being, within those heart the inner law of God is inscribed. Moral conscience is a judgment of practical reason about the moral quality of a human action. It moves a person at the appropriate moment to do good and to avoid evil" (CCC, Glossary, p. 872) (p. 184)

**consecrated** declared sacred or set aside for special purposes to serve God (p. 84)

**conversion** the lifelong process of turning away from sin and toward God (p. 183)

**conviction** a firmly held belief in something that we are sure is real and worth doing or believing (p. 21)

**correct conscience** a good, pure, and well-formed ability to judge what is right and wrong, enlightened by faith, which guides us to make good decisions (p. 185)

**covenant** a sacred agreement or treaty between two parties before God, or between God and persons or a people, such as Israel, that involves agreed-upon commitments and guarantees on both parties (p. 56)

## E

**Easter Sunday** The final day of the Triduum commemorating the Resurrection of Jesus Christ (p. 233)

**Easter Triduum** three holy days including Easter that commemorate the Paschal Mystery beginning on Holy Thursday and ending with evening prayer on Easter Sunday (p. 214)

**Emmanuel** name given to the Messiah by the prophet Isaiah meaning God with us (p. 103)

**eros** describes romantic, passionate love (p. 13)

**eschatology** literally means the study of "last," and refers to the part of theology that studies topics related to the end of time: death, judgment, resurrection of the body, Heaven, Purgatory, and Hell, the coming of Jesus on the last day, etc. (p. 166)

**evangelization** sharing the Good News of Jesus Christ with others through our words and actions (p. 198)

## F

**Feast of the Epiphany** name for the feast day that commemorates the Magi or Wise Men visiting the infant Jesus (p. 106)

**filial** describes the love of a child for a parent (p. 126)

**fortitude** courage; being firmly committed to pursue good actions no matter what (p. 193)

## G

**genealogy** ancestry traced continuously in a direct line (p. 72)

**gluttony** "overindulgence in food or drink" (CCC, Glossary, p. 880) (p. 193)

**Good Friday** recalls Jesus' Passion and Death on the Friday before Easter (p. 233)

**grace** undeserved gift from God that helps us respond to our calling in life to become his children, to take part in his divine nature, to do good and avoid evil (see CCC 1996) (p. 145)

## H

**Heaven** the state of supreme happiness for those who have died in God's grace and friendship; being united forever with God the Father, Son, and Holy Spirit, the Virgin Mary, the angels, and the just after death (p. 167)

**Hell** the state of eternal self-isolation from God after death, through the free choice to reject God's offer of forgiveness and Redemption (p. 167)

**holiness** "A state of goodness in which a person—with the help of God's grace, the action of the Holy Spirit, and a life of prayer—is freed from sin and evil" (*United States Catholic Catechism for Adults*, Glossary, p. 514) (p. 10)

**Holy Saturday** on the Saturday before Easter Sunday, this day symbolizes Jesus' time in the tomb after his Death (p. 233)

**Holy Thursday** beginning of the Triduum that celebrates Jesus as the new Passover Lamb on the Thursday before Easter (p. 233)

**hope** theological virtue through which we desire God's Kingdom and eternal life by putting our trust in Jesus' promises with the grace of the Holy Spirit (p. 144)

## I

**immanent** existing or operating within the human realm and human history (p. 102)

**injustice** qualities or acts that are wrong or unfair, particularly since they violate another's rights (p. 200)

## J

**justice** the constant and firm goal of giving to God and each person what is due to them (p. 193)

**justification** God's gracious action that frees humans from sin and bestows his righteousness through their belief in Jesus Christ (p. 145)

## K

**kenosis** the self-emptying of the Son of God (p. 98)

**Kyrios** a Greek word meaning Lord, that is the translation of the Hebrew name for God (p. 111)

## L

**liturgical year** the cycle of liturgical seasons and feasts which comprise the annual Church calendar (p. 105)

## M

**Magisterium** the official teaching office of the Church, entrusted to the bishops in communion with the Pope, whose task it is to interpret Sacred Scripture and Sacred Tradition and ensure faithfulness to the teachings of the Apostles, and who Christ gave the charism of infallibility when it comes to faith and morals (p. 68)

**Mass of the Lord's Supper** the Mass celebrated on Holy Thursday evening remembering the Last Supper and the institution of the Sacrament of the Eucharist (p. 233)

**Messiah** literally means "the anointed one," and was the person who would bring peace and justice to the world (p. 84)

**Messianic Secret** Jesus' request for people not to tell anyone that he was the Messiah until it was time to reveal it (p. 110)

**metanoia** Greek word meaning repentance; to change in direction or to turn around (p. 183)

**monotheistic** believing in one God (p. 46)

## N

**New Covenant** "the new 'dispensation,' order or covenant, established by God in Jesus Christ, to succeed and perfect the Old Covenant" (CCC, Glossary, p. 893) (p. 67)

## O

**omnipotence** characteristic of being all-powerful, which is attributed to God (p. 126)

## P

**paradise** a perfect place; a state of friendship with God and of original holiness and justice enjoyed by our first parents (p. 158)

**paradox** something that seems contradictory, yet is true (p. 159)

**Parousia** "The glorious return and appearance of our Lord and Savior Jesus Christ as judge of the living and the dead, at the end of time; the second coming of Christ, when history and all creation will achieve their fulfillment" (CCC, Glossary, p. 891) (p. 172)

**Particular Judgment** the judgment of each individual at the moment of death by Christ and determines the immediate entrance of the soul into Heaven, Purgatory, or Hell (p. 166)

**Paschal Mystery** the work of Redemption brought about by Christ's Passion, Death, Resurrection, and glorious Ascension; We celebrate the Paschal Mystery in the liturgy of the Church, during which Christ's saving work is made present and communicated, most especially in the Sacrament of the Eucharist (p. 5)

**passion** from a Latin word which means "to suffer' and also to love (p. 159)

**Passion Narratives** the scriptural accounts of the suffering and Death of Jesus (p. 6)

**patriarch** the title given to the "fathers" of the Israelite People, including Abraham, Isaac, and Jacob (p. 74)

**philia** describes love between friends (p. 13)

**polytheistic** believing in many gods (p. 46)

**prayer of adoration** prayer that acknowledges the greatness of God (p. 218)

**prayer of blessing** the human response to gifts from God, the source of all blessing; God's gift and our acceptance communicate with each other (p. 218)

**prayer of intercession** bringing the needs of others to God and asking his help on their behalf (p. 222)

**prayer of petition** bringing our needs to God and asking God to respond. (p. 220)

**prayer of praise** offering a joyful recognition of God for his own sake that gives him glory (p. 219)

**prayer of thanksgiving** identifying those things for which you are grateful and giving thanks to God (p. 222)

**prefiguration** early indication of something, in biblical usage the coming of Jesus Christ as the Messiah (p. 68)

**protoevangelium** refers to the passage in Genesis describing God's words to the serpent and woman and literally means first Gospel (p. 49)

**prudence** using practical reasoning to figure out the good in every circumstance and to choose the right way to achieve it (p. 193)

**Purgatory** "A state of final purification after death and before entrance into Heaven for those who died in God's friendship, but were only imperfectly purified." (CCC, Glossary, p. 896) (p. 167)

## R

**Redemption** the action of being saved from sin, or God's plan made possible through the life, Death, and Resurrection of Jesus, by which our sins are forgiven and we are reconciled to God (p. 97)

**religious truth** the truth that comes from what God has revealed in divine and natural ways (p. 37)

**repent** to feel or communicate sincere remorse for one's sin (p. 103)

**resiliency** the ability to recover readily from adversity (p. 173)

**Resurrection Narratives** the scriptural accounts of Jesus' bodily rising from the dead three days after his Crucifixion and burial (p. 6)

**Roman Missal** the ritual book for the celebration of the Mass; it includes the presider's prayers, the responses and acclamations of the people, special prayers for each liturgical season, including feasts day of saints (p. 125)

## S

**sacramental grace** "the grace of the Holy Spirit, given by Christ and proper to each sacrament" (CCC, 1129) (p. 145)

**sacrifice** surrendering one thing for the sake of something else; literal Latin meaning is "to make holy". (p. 158)

**Seven Sacraments** effective signs of grace, instituted by Christ and entrusted to the Church, by which divine life is shared with us through the work of the Holy Spirit (p. 145)

**shalom** Hebrew greeting meaning peace (p. 84)

**Sheol** in ancient Hebrew cosmology this was the underworld, the dwelling place of the dead (p. 39)

**sloth** having a lack of physical or spiritual effort; laziness (p. 193)

**Spiritual Exercises** Saint Ignatius' month-long program of prayers, meditations, and practices that help Catholics live their everyday life (p. 26)

**spiritual poverty** refers to an absence of God in our lives (p. 24)

**stewardship** the responsibility God has given us to care for the resources of the Earth, and to use the time and talent God has given each of us for the good of the Church (p. 197)

**supplication** asking for something (p. 220)

## T

**temperance** moderating the attraction of pleasurable things to provide balance when using created goods (p. 193)

**temptation** an attraction from within or from outside that is contrary to right reason and to God's Commandments (p. 125)

## Ten Commandments

**Ten Commandments** the fundamental moral laws given by God to his people to help them live by the covenant. They are also called the Decalogue, meaning "ten words." (p. 81)

**theological virtues** faith, hope, and charity or love (p. 189)

**theology** the study of God or of religious faith and practice based on Divine Revelation to help better understand who God is (p. 35)

**theophany** God revealing himself to humans through nature, or a visible appearance of God (p. 44)

**transcendent** above, beyond, and outside the realm of normal human lives (p. 102)

**Transfiguration** the culmination moment in the public life of Jesus in which his appearance changed in the presence of the Apostles, and Elijah and Moses appeared beside him to reveal him as the true Messiah (p. 128)

**triptych** picture or carving on three panels often connected side by side with the middle panel often larger than the other two (p. 5)

**typology** the study and interpretation of types and symbols that from a theological perspective views Old Testament people and stories as foreshadowing New Testament events (p. 68)

## V

**vices** habits formed through repeated sins, even venial sins, that violate human morality (p. 193)

**virtue** a good moral and spiritual habits that help us make good moral decisions, avoid sin, strengthen character, and perform good deeds (p. 189)

# INDEX

# ENDNOTES

## Chapter 1

1. *GS* 14 § 2.
2. *GS* 16.
3. *GS* 15 § 2.
4. *SC* 24.
5. *GCD* 43.
6. *GCD* 47.
7. St. Augustine, *In ep Jo.* 8, 9: PL 35, 2041.

## Chapter 2

8. Cf. Council of Vienne (1312): DS 902.
9. *LG* 42.
10. St. Irenaeus, *Adv. haeres* 2, 30, 9; 4, 20, 1: PG 7/1, 822, 1032.
11. Cf. CDF, *Donum vitae I*, 1.
12. Cf. *Pss* 33:6; 104:30; *Gen* 1:2; 2:7; *Eccl* 3:20-21; *Ezek* 37:10.
13. St. Maximus the Confessor, *Ambigua*: PG 91, 1156C; cf. *Gen* 3:5.
14. Cf. *Rom* 6:17.
15. Cf. Pius XII, *Humani Generis*: DS 3891; *Lk* 20:36; *Dan* 10:9-12.
16. 1 *Jn* 3:8.
17. Cf. *GS* 13 § 1.
18. Cf. Council of Trent: DS 1513; Pius XII: DS 3897; Paul VI: AAS 58 (1966), 654.
19. Cf. *Gen* 3:9, 15.
20. St. Thomas Aquinas, *STh* III, 1, 3, *ad* 3; cf. *Rom* 5:20.
21. Cf. *Lk* 11:21-22; *Jn* 16:11; 1 *Jn* 3:8.

## Chapter 3

22. *DV* 3; cf. Gen 3:15; Rom 2:6-7.
23. 1 *Cor* 15:28.
24. *DV* 15.
25. Cf. *Zeph* 2:3; Lk 1:38.
26. Cf. *Mt* 2:2; 9:27; 12:23; 15:22; 20:30; 21:9, 15.
27. St. Irenaeus, *Adv. haeres.* 3, 19, 1: PG 7/1, 939.
28. Cf. *Jn* 4:25–26; 6:15; 11:27; *Mt* 22:41–46; *Lk* 24:21.

## Chapter 4

29. St. Gregory of Nyssa, *Orat. catech.* 15: PG 45, 48B.
30. *Jn* 13:3.
31. *Jn* 3:13; 6:33.
32. 1 *Jn* 4:2.
33. *Jn* 1:14, 16.
34. Cf. *Mt* 1:18–25; *Lk* 1:26–38.
35. *Mt* 1:20.
36. *Isa* 7:14 in the LXX, quoted in *Mt* 1:23 (Gk.).
37. *Phil* 2:9–10; cf. *Jn* 12:28.
38. Cf. *2 Cor* 8:9.
39. Cf. *Lk* 2:51.
40. Cf. *Jn* 15:3.
41. *Mt* 8:17; cf. *Isa* 53:4.
42. Cf. *Rom* 4:25.
43. Cf. *Eph* 1:7; *Col* 1:13-14; *1 Pet* 1:18-19.

44. Cf. *Jn* 13:15; *Lk* 11:1; *Mt* 5:11-12.

## Chapter 5

45. *Mt* 3:13–17.
46. *Lk* 15:7; cf. 7:11–32.
47. Cf. *Mt* 13:44–45; 22:1–14.
48. Cf. *Mt* 21:28–32.
49. 266 *Mt* 13:11.
50. Cf. *Jn* 2:11; *Mk* 14:25.
51. St. Thomas Aquinas, *STh* III, 45, 4, *ad* 2.
52. *Acts* 14:22.
53. *Heb* 9:26.
54. *AG* 1; cf. *1 Cor* 11:26.
55. Cf. *Lk* 24:13-35.
56. Cf. St. Augustine, *De libero arbitrio* 1, 1, 2: PL 32, 1223; St. Thomas Aquinas, *STh* I-II, 79, 1.
57. St. Augustine, *Enchiridion* 3, 11: PL 40, 236.
58. Cf. *Lk* 12:50; 22:15; *Mt* 16:21-23.
59. *Mt* 16:24.
60. 455 1 *Pet* 2:21.
61. *Mk* 16:1; *Lk* 24:1; *Jn* 19:31, 42.
62. Cf. *Lk* 24:9-10; *Mt* 28:9-10; *Jn* 20:11-18.
63. Cf. *Jn* 16:28.
64. *Jn* 3:13; cf. *Eph* 4:8-10.
65. *LG* 59; cf. Pius XII, *Munificentissimus Deus* (1950): DS 3903; cf. *Rev* 19:16.

## Chapter 6

66. *Heb* 12:1-2.
67. 1 *Pet* 2:21.
68. Cf. *Mk* 14:33-34; *Heb* 5:7-8.
69. Cf. *Rom* 5:19-21.
70. Cf. Benedict XII, *Benedictus Deus* (1336): DS 1002.
71. 628 Cf. *Song* 8:6.
72. *Mk* 12:27.
73. Cf. *Acts* 17:32; *1 Cor* 15:12-13.
74. St. Augustine, *En. in Ps.* 88, 5: PL 37, 1134.
75. Lateran Council IV (1215): DS 801; *Phil* 3:21; *1 Cor* 15:44.
76. *Col* 3:4.

## Chapter 7

77. *Ps* 51:17; cf. *Jn* 6:44; 12:32; *1 Jn* 4:10.
78. *GS* 16.
79. St. Augustine, *In ep Jo.* 8, 9: PL 35, 2041.
80. *DH* 3 § 2.
81. St. Gregory of Nyssa, *De beatitudinibus*, 1: PG 44, 1200D.
82. *DV* 5.
83. *Rom* 1:17; *Gal* 5:6.
84. *Mt* 10:32-33.
85. St. Augustine, *In ep. Jo.* 10, 4: PL 35, 2057.
86. Cf. *Mt* 5:17-19.
87. *GS* 69 § 1.

88. Cf. *Gen* 1:26-29.
89. *AA* 6 § 3; cf. *AG* 15.
90. *Jn* 8:32; cf. 17:17.
91. *LG* 48; cf. *Acts* 3:21; *Eph* 1:10; *Col* 1:20; 2 *Pet* 3:10-13.
92. John Paul II, *SRS* 47.
93. *GS* 31 § 3.
94. *GS* 26 § 2.
95. Cf. John Paul II, *SRS* 38-40; *CA* 10.

## Chapter 8

96. St. John Damascene, *De fide orth.* 3, 24: PG 94, 1089C
97. Cf. *Eph* 1:3-14; *2 Cor* 1:3-7; *1 Pet* 1:3-9.
98. Cf. *2 Cor* 13:14; *Rom* 15:5-6, 13; *Eph* 6:23-24.
99. Cf. *Lk* 1:46-49.
100. 122 1 *Cor* 8:6.
101. Cf. *Rom* 15:30; *Col* 4:12.
102. *Lk* 18:13.
103. Cf. *Mt* 6:10, 33; *Lk* 11:2, 13.
104. *Phil* 2:4; cf. *Acts* 7:60; *Lk* 23:28, 34.
105. Cf. *Rom* 8:34; *1 Jn* 2:1; *1 Tim* 2:5-8.
106. Cf. *Mt* 11:25-26; *Mk* 14:36.
107. Cf. *Jn* 17:6, 11, 12, 26.
108. Cf. *Jn* 17:1, 5, 10, 22, 23-26.
109. Cf. *Jn* 17:2, 4, 6, 9, 11, 12, 24.
110. Cf. *Jn* 17:15.
111. St. Teresa of Jesus, *The Way of Perfection* 26, 9 in *The Collected Works of St. Teresa of Avila*, tr. K. Kavanaugh, OCD, and O. Rodriguez, OCD (Washington DC: Institute of Carmelite Studies, 1980), II, 136.
112. Cf. *Mk* 4:4-7, 15-19.
113. St. Teresa of Jesus, *The Book of Her Life*, 8, 5 in *The Collected Works of St. Teresa of Avila*, tr. K.Kavanaugh, OCD, and O. Rodriguez, OCD (Washington DC: Institute of Carmelite Studies, 1976), I, 67.
114. *Gen* 9:8-16.s
115. Cf. *Ex* 34:6.
116. Cf. *2 Sam* 7:18-29.
117. Cf. *Am* 7:2, 5; *Isa* 6:5, 8, 11; *Jer* 1:6; 15:15-18; 20:7-18.
118. St. Ambrose, *In psalmum 1 enarratio*, 1, 9: PL 14, 924; *LH*, Saturday, wk 10, OR.
119. Cf. *Mt* 6:6.
120. GILH 9.
121. 1 *Thess* 5:17; *Eph* 5:20.
122. *DV* 25; cf. *Phil* 3:8; St. Ambrose, *De officiis ministrorum* 1, 20, 88: PL 16, 50.
123. Guigo the Carthusian, *Scala Paradisi*: PL 40, 998.
124. *Ps* 95:7–8.
125. St. John Chrysostom, *Ecloga de oratione* 2: PG 63, 585.

## Reference Section

126. Cf. *Lk* 1:46–55.